Buddhist Culture in Korea

Korean Culture Series 3

Buddhist Culture in Korea

CHUN SHIN-YONG
General Editor

International Cultural Foundation
Seoul, Korea

Preface

This series will continue to present articles, in both English and Korean, which, the editors believe, is the most effective way for promoting understanding — one outstanding characteristics of the series worth maintaining. Each volume will certainly continue to present well-chosen articles both by competent Korean writers and distinguished foreigners whose understanding of Korean culture is well recognized. Needless to mention, the Foundation will see that the

We have seen since the Sixties an increasing interest in Korea and Korean culture, both at home and abroad. Koreans themselves wanted to find out the nature of the culture achieved over centuries and bequeathed to them by their ancestors. They renewed their searches into the root of their own culture, the embodiment of the wisdom of yesterday, which engenders pride for today's generation and promises glory for the future. On the other hand, to those foreign friends of Korea to whom this pearl of the Orient with its history, its reality and its potential for tomorrow was of keen interest, the culture of this country has emerged as an object of renewed curiosity. They are especially eager to find in today's Korea a reflection of the nation's ancient culture — to see how the nation means to use their cultural legacy for future development.

It is with this demand that this International Cultural Foundation has programmed the *Korean Culture Series*. *Humour in Korean Litarature* was the first volume of the series which this Foundation published in 1970 to coincide with the PEN International Conference of that year held in Seoul. The Foundation aims to introduce Korean culture to the world and contribute to international cultural exchanges. In order to achieve these objectives, the Foundation will present Korean culture in a series, aspect by aspect, under a consistent editorial policy. The editors intend to set a particular theme in each instance and publish a book of substantial articles, dealing in depth with related aspects of the theme.

Each volume of the series will cover the patterns of Korean culture, Korean mode of thinking, balance and harmony between tradition and reality, and Korean national effort to discover their own identity. The end in view of each and every volume of the series will be the 'Understanding of Korea'. Efforts will be made to make the themes of the series comprehend many of the aspects of Korean culture. However, extreme academism is to be shunned in favour of a format and style which is accessible to educated Koreans on the one hand, and helpful to foreigners seeking to understand Korea, on the other.

This series will continue to present articles, in both English and Korean, which, the editors believe, is the most effective way for promoting understanding—one of the outstanding characteristics of the series worth maintaining. Each volume will certainly continue to present well-chosen articles both by competent Korean writers and distinguished foreigners whose understinding of Korean culture is well recognized. Needless to mention, the Foundation will see that the editorial board consists of competent scholars and specialists in the related fields. The Foundation hopes that its effort will bear worthy fruit in concert with the national goal of constructing a new nation in the Seventies.

Chun Shin-Yong
Chairman, Board of Directors
International Cultural Foundation
Seoul, Korea

Contents

INTRODUCTION

Chun Shin-yong

The International Cultural Foundation, seeing that currently there are widespread and active discussions on the methods of re-evaluating and applying Korea's traditional culture, is publishing the "Korean Culture Series," of which the present *Buddhist Culture in Korea* is the third volume. It follows the first and the second volumes, *Humour in Korean Literature* and *Upper-class Culture in Yi-dynasty Korea.*

Buddhism, which was first introduced to Koguryo toward the end of the fourth century of the Christian era, soon spread to Paekje and Silla. It was a period of transition and unrest in the Korean peninsula, with frequent wars as three nations tried to subdue the tribes and clans, which themselves were struggling to fortify of the power of a central government. In such an era the Buddhist faith, with its profound theology, provided the few members of royal families and elite aristocrats with a new unifying faith needed for the formation of a unified country. Buddhism presented itself as a superior substitute for the tribal myths and primitive religions then already in the process of deterioration. Moreover, the Buddhism which, in the course of its transmission from its native India through China, had taken on a densely nationalistic character, was welcomed by the ruling class of the three countries. It was inevitable that Buddhism, as it was not directly transmitted to Korea from its native India, but had come by way of continental of China, should undergo some degree of transformation. On the other hand, the Buddhist spirit of mercy was a glad tiding of comfort and salvation for the populace which was suffering from the social instability. Buddhism, which suggested a new way to salvation to the masses that had lost faith in the simple tribal myths with the distintegration of tribal nations, attracted great numbers of followers. There arose a great interest and piety among the plain people of faith in Amita Buddha and Maitreya for invocation of blessings. The realistic, grace-soliciting form of Buddhist faith, which was the outcome of the Chinese influence on it, was more readily accepted by the populace than the nihilistic form of Indian Buddhism. Buddhism, in the process of its reception in the Three Kingdoms, had little conflict with native re-ligions—the result of which was the martyrdom of Yi Cha-don in Silla— and on the whole was readily accepted and internalized, thereby forming a climate on which a new culture could be built.

In the course of some 1,600 years of history since its first introduc-tion, Buddhism has provided a variety of cultural blossoms in diverse areas of Korean lives. It not only influenced the nation's philosophy and literature, but inspired the creation of a unique beauty in the arts. Especially, the great Korean talent in plastic arts, inspired by this faith, produced great many art items of incomparable grace and exquisite beauty that occupy the major portion of national cultural treasures and are the pride of the nation before the whole world. We have included in this book a number of photo plates of the representative plastic art products of the Silla period, which marks the peak of Buddhist art in Korea. The fountainhead of the tradition of sculpture and other stoneworks can be found in the Buddhist cultures of the three countries, and especially in the Silla art items. Both in quantity and artistic value the Silla products are representative of the three countries, being definitely superior to those of Koguryo and Paekje, so we have focused our attention mainly on the Silla stonework items.

Buddhism was transmitted from India to China, from China to three Korean kingdoms and from there immediately to Japan. The first Japanese temples and frescoes were made by naturalized Koreans. For this reason, when discussing ancient Japanese culture one must begin with a treatment of the culture and influence of the Three King-doms. Therefore, we have included in this volume an article on the cultural exchanges between ancient Korea and Japan. In accordance with our policy of including an article by a foreigner who can make detached, critical observations on Korean culture, a Japanese scholar of ancient history was requested to write this article.

There is one figure that appears in our minds at the mention of Silla Buddhism. This is the man who set out on a journey to T'ang China in quest of the eternal truth, but who (through accidentally drinking water from a skull on the way) was awakened to the tenet that everything is the creation of the mind and came back to Silla. He was the monk Wonhyo, the foremost priest of Silla Buddhism, whose personality was as peculiar as it was daring. As strange as his own personality was, the fact that his son Solchong, whom he begot by Princess Yosok, became one of the greatest Confucian scholars of the Silla period, is even more intriguing. Wonhyo was also a great scholar who had done a tremendous amount of writing. He not only had realized the profound truth of Buddhism but also actually lived according to the dictates of the truths in his faith. Therefore, we are presenting in this book a translation of one of his writings.

Buddhism was respected as the national religion during the Koryo Dynasty period, and the monks were accorded a social status approximately the same as aristocrats. It was the golden time of Buddhism when a great many Buddhist sects engaged in theological debates and sought competitive growth. Many eminent monks emerged during this period, including the Highest Eminence Daegak, who was originally a prince. Such Buddhist rituals as the lantern ceremony were held annually throughout the peninsula. Buddhism had followers not only among the aristocrats, but penetrated deeply into the total population. One thing that can never be omitted in any discussion of Koryo Buddhism is the printing of the *Tripitaka Koreana* which consists of more than 80,000 wooden printing blocks. It is true that the national undertaking was motivated by the wish for invocation of the power of Buddha for protection of the country in crisis. Nevertheless, the fact that the great volume of Buddhist scriptures scattered all over the country were completely collected and compiled in the thirteenth century, can stand in comparison with the achievements of the encyclopedists of eighteenth century Europe. Also, the accuracy and the intricacy of the *Tripitaka Koreana* is unparalleled by any other such effort and bears testimony to the superior techniques of Korean printing.

The five hundred years of Yi Dynasty was the period of ordeal for Korean Buddhism. The Confucian scholars, who maintained a totally antithetical philosophical stance from Buddhism, did not permit freedom of faith to Buddhists. Moreover, as the Confucian scholars made up the ruling class, the suppression of Buddhism was carried on unilaterally. Some powerful Confucian scholars brandished the sword of oppression on Buddhism and regarded it as a wicked heresy. Many Buddhist monks were forced to lead gloomy existences in the shadows, totally alienated from the society. But when the country fell into danger of total disintegration around the turn of the century amid the tempest of modernization struggles of the period, there appeared a radical monk who asserted that "destruction is the mother of construction" and who attempted to revitalize Korean Buddhism which had fallen into utter despondence and inertia. His name was Hahn Yong-woon. He had struggled against the Japanese government-general rule to the end of his life and refused to the last to register his children at the district office of Japanese administration. With indefatigable willpower inspired by his faith, he kept on fighting against injustice. In addition to his burning patriotism and fervent piety, he had a unique literary genius. His poems, represented by *The Silence of My Beloved,* were the most advanced pioneers in modern poetry of his time. We have printed in this volume an article on his literary and patriotic activities.

At the end of the book we have included a dialogue between a historian and a scholar of Buddhism on the overall view of the history of Korea's Buddhist culture. The exchange is intended to serve as a background that can provide a perspective to the stages on which such great men as Wonhyo and Manhae acted. We hope that the last article will present to the readers an overall view of the Buddhist culture in Korea and thereby help them understand Buddhist culture better.

Lastly, I would like to express my deep felt gratitude to all those who have helped to bring out this book and also hope that our readers will look forward to the future projects of the Korean Culture Series.

HONG JUNG-SHIK was born in Kongju, Chungchung-Namdo Province in 1918. He was graduated from Chungang Buddhism College in 1940, and at present teaches at Buddhism College of Tongguk University in Seoul. Himself a devout Buddhist, Professor Hong has long been the Director of the Buddhist Cultural Institute of the University, President of the Korean Buddhism Academy and Chairman of the Federation of University Student Buddhist Societies.

Professor Hong has published *Introduction to Buddhism*, Korean translations of *Saddharmapundarika-sutra* and *Bodhisattva-sutra,* and several articles including "Political Thought of Buddhism".

The Thought and Life of Wonhyo

Hong Jung-shik

1. The Nature of Early Buddhism of Silla

It was in 527 (the 14th year during the reign of King Pophung,the 23rd monarch) that Buddhism was recognized officially in Silla, about 150 years after its official recognition in Koguryo (in 372) and in Paekche 150 years after its official recognition in Koguryo (in 372) and in Paekche (in 384).That Silla officially recognized Buddhism so belatedly was, however, not due to its late introduction to that kingdom. There are four different explanations on the introduction of Buddhism into Silla. The most convincing one is that a Chinese priest by the name of Mukhoja (Ado) started to propagate Buddhism at the house of Morye in Ilson County during the reign of King Nulcho (417-458), the 19th monarch. The king's reign was not far apart from the date when Buddhism was introduced into Koguryo or Paekche.

The fact that Buddhism was formally sanctioned quite late in Silla, in spite of its early introduction, indicates that the Silla society was very conservative and exclusive. To explain it more concretely, the kingdom of Silla, geographically far from the influence of the continental civilization, still remained on the foundation of clan society.

King Pophung, who gave official recognition to Buddhism in the face of vehement opposition from his courtiers, promulgated the initial law in the seventh year of his reign and strengthened his centralized regal authority. Ich'adon, who died a martyr to enable the monarch to recognize Buddhism officially, was not a priest but the king's nephew. There facts suggest that the king thought that Buddhism would be conducive to strengthening the centralized regal power and in promoting a civilization based on government by law. It can be interpreted that the courtiers who opposed the formal recognition of Buddhism represented the conservative clan force which took a restrained attitude toward the expanding regal authority. King Pophung explained his decision to endorse the propagation of Buddhism as an intention to

15

"give the masses opportunities to enjoy happiness and repent for their sin." Ich'adon, who sacrificed his life for his religious faith, explained that "When people believe in this truth, the country will be able to enjoy peace and this will also contribute to economy." The official recognition of Buddhism in Silla was aimed at accelerating national development and promoting popular welfare. This notion, in fact, characterized the entire nature of Silla's early Buddhism.

King Chinhung, the 24th monarch, promoted Buddhism to a greater extent by following the example set by King Pophung. He completed Hungnyun-sa Temple whose construction was undertaken by King Pophung. Besides this, the monarch also built such imposing temples as Chowon-sa, Silche-sa, and Hwangnyong-sa, and created the priesthood by permitting people to enter it, placing it under the government control. Due to his measures of promoting Buddhism, the religion flooded the conservative Silla society.

It should be remembered that King Chinhung encouraged Buddhism to so great an extent solely for the purpose of insuring national development and prosperity. One outstanding example can be found in the Hwarangdo "Junkerkorps" which the monarch founded to train young men coming from nobility. The corps consisted of one *Kukson*, serveral *hwarang*, and a *nangdo*. The *Kukson* who led the youth corps was revered as a Maitreya. The faith in the Maitreya, the Buddhist messiah, was utilized for the training of young men who would shoulder the future of the nation.

In the Buddhist teaching, the world of Yonghwa on which the Maitreya would descend is a utopia ruled by the sacred king of Chollyun. In other words, the faith in the Maitreya is closely linked to that in the sacred king. King Chinhung called his two sons "Tongnyun" and "Kumnyun," both the alter-ego of the sacred king of Chollyun This fact again shows that King Chinhung promoted Buddhsm for the purpose of of realizing the national ideals of Silla through the faith in that religion. Furthermore, patterning after the wise government of King Asoka of India, King Chinhung made a hunting trip to all parts of the country, an excursion that resembled the former's religious pilgrimage.

Succeeding King Chinhung and King Chinji (Kumnyun), King Chinp'yong and Queens Sondok and Chindok made efforts to further propagate Buddhism, taking a pride in their social status which they called the clan of Sakya. The early Buddhism of Silla prospered mainly

among members of the royal family, being strongly conscious of the
nation concept. High priests of the time, too, were influenced by the
idea of the nation in their Buddhist thought. Assuming the highest post
(Kukt'ong) in the priesthood, Hyeryang, who was active during the reign
of King Chinhung, initiated the *In-wang-baek-ko-jwa* and *P'al-kwan-hoe*
rituals in 551. Both Buddhist masses were aimed at praying for national protection. Returning home from studies in China during the reign
of King Chinp'yong, Won'gwang advocated five precepts for secular
life. As a priest (though he was forced by the king) he composed a letter
asking Sui China for military assistance to destroy Koguryo, Returning from China in the 12th year of Queen Sondok's reign after seven
years of study, Chajang erected a nine-stroy pagoda in the Hwangnyong-sa Temple ground in 645, with the edifice intended for prayer for
national safety and prosperity. Ascending to the position of *Kukt'ong,*
he restored order in the discipline among those in priesthood, and
proposed that the government adopt the T'ang system in ceremonies. In
addition, he emphasized that Silla was a land most deeply related to Buddhism by pointing out that the most ideal abode for the Bodhisattva
of wisdom and intellect was Mount Odae in Kangwon Province.

That the Buddhism of the Three Kingdoms period was so heavily
nationalistic can be fairly well understood in view of the fact that the
three states were engaged in death-or-life struggle. Not only the Buddhism of Silla, but that of Koguryo and Paekche was also nationalistic.
This trend became more pronounced as the hostility and antagonism
among the Three Kingdoms grew in ferocity.

Can the nationalistic trait of Buddhism claim its validity from the
purely religious standpoint? According to Mahayana Buddhism, our
secular reality springs from the illusion of trying to discern being from
non-being, oneness from variousness, and contamination from purity.
It is, therefore, considered the ultimate religious aim in Mahayana
Buddhism to get rid of the attempts to discern, and to return to the
clear and tranquil world of *tathata*. The attempt to discriminate being
from non-being, oneness from variousness, and contamination from
purity is called *samvrti-satya,* while the state of being free from such
discernment is regarded as *paramartha-satya*. It is needless to say that
the latter, rather than the former, has the religious value. Viewed in this
sense, an intention to destroy other countries in order to safeguard the
survival of one's country cannot be considered desirable as a true

Buddhist. This realization may have deepended as the understanding of Buddhism matured.

A gap naturally emerged between secular purposes of the state and the Buddhist view of value; and the gap gradually grew wide. It is noteworthy that Kang Su, who made with the pen as great a contribution to Silla's unification of the Three Kingdoms as any soldiers, said that "I will study Confucianism because Buddhism is an alien religion which is aloof from the secular world." His viewpoint may have stemmed from his failure to grasp the true intention of Buddhism. This must have been a serious problem which required an explanation from the depth of doctrine, for without this the gulf between the secular purposes of the Silla kingdom and the Buddhist view of value would have grown to such an extent that it would have jeopardized own existence.

2. Examination of Wonhyo's *Kishinnon Haedong So*

A great Buddhist thinker who was most needed came into being at that time. Wonhyo (617–686) resolved this problem by developing his remarkable theory of "One Mind and Two Doors" in *Kishinnon* (*Awakening of Faith*).

Wonhyo authored many works on Kishinnon, most noted among which are *Taesung Kishinnon So* (two volumes, extant), *Taesung Kishinnon Chongyo* (one volume), *Taesung Kishinnon Sogwamun* (one volume), *Taesung Kishinnon Yogan* (one volume), *Taesung Kishinnon Pyolki* (one volume, extant), *Taesung Kishinnon Sagi* (one volume), and *Taesung Kishinnon Taegi* (one volume)—seven in all. This illustrates how profound his studies on Kishinnon truly were.

Of these, only two works are extant—*Taesung Kishinnon So* (*Treatise on the Awakening of Faith*) and *Taesung Kishinnon Pyolki* (*Special Commentary on Taesung Kishinnon*). While the former contains his main theories on Kishinnon, the latter presents his revised annotations. Therefore, the two works are inseparable. The two works are combined into one under the heading, *Kishinnon Haedong Sogi*.

In annotating *Kishinnon*, Wonhyo follows the order: 1. Outlook, 2. Subjects, and 3. Interpretation. In the first paragraph in the book, he explains Mahayana:

The essence of Mahayana seems tranquil as if solitary and occult as if clear. As it is so occult and occult that it never presents itself above the surface of all things. As it is so tranquil and tranquil that it only resides in men's words. As it does not appear to the surface, it cannot be seen even with the Five Eyes. As it resides in words, its shape cannot be described even with the Four Explanations. You may say it is large, but it can enter into an indescribably small thing. You may say it is small, but it can embrace what has no outer limit. You may say it does exist, but something which is like one envelops and empties it. You may say it does not exist; but all things derive their existence from it. We do not know how to call it. Mahayana might be a world close to it.

In short, he says that Mayhayana Buddhism cannot be penetrated even with Buddha's Five Eyes and Four Explanations. It is even more difficult for poor souls to say something about Mahayana because the subject defies Buddha's glimpse and explanation. It is possible to see Bhddism as a religion teaching nihility and Nirvana. But it is also apt to think that Buddhism and a state do not help each other. Wonhyo may have intended to criticism such notions.

However, it would be an exaggeration or fantasy to brand Mahayana as mysterious without trying to delve into its essence. In an excerpt from *Pyolki* Wonhyo attempts the following explanation:

Its essence is as expansive as the empty sky and devoid of partiality. It is as boundless as the great ocean and extremely impartial. As it is extremely impartial, movement and stillness arise in order. As there is no partiality, contamination and purity accommodate with each other. As contamination and purity accommodate with each other, what is true and what is secular become equalized. As movement and stillness ensue one after the other, there is difference between ascending and descending As there is difference between ascent and descent, the way is cleared to response. As what is true and what is secular become equal, they way to contemplation is blocked. As the way to contemplation is blocked, those who grasp this truth can ride the shadow and echo and are not pointed. As the way to response is cleared, those who pray for it can transcend color and shape and return. The shadow and echo one rides are not forms and words, and, moreover, they transcend color and shape. Where do they return? This is the profound principle though it seems to have no principle. This may seem to be otherwise, but it is truly so.

Some may complain that these excerpts are filled with strange terms and that theorizing becomes tangled, hard to understand. The first paragraph of *Kishinnon So* consists of 122 Chinese characters and the excerpt from *Pyolki* of 128 characters (250 total) all in really short sentences. In these short sentences Wonhyo crystallized the conclusion of his studies on Kinshinnon. Therefore, in order to understand the gem-like writing which conveys the nucleus in Wonhyo's thought, it is necessary to make a deep study on the whole parts of his *Kishinnon So* and *Pyolki*. Below I shall introduce main points of his thought briefly, hoping that you will read the original texts yourselves.

There are two philosophical systems in Mahayana Buddhism. One is *Madhamika* developed by Nagarjuna (150–250) and Aryadeba (170–270) and the other is *Vijnaptimatrata* developed by Maitreyanatha (270–350), Asanga (310–390), and Vasubandhu (320–400). In Kishinnon the former is called *Chinyomun* and the latter *Saengmyolmun*.

According to Chinyomun, all things are free from creation and extinction, and exist from the beginning in tranquility. Only illusion sees being and non-being, oneness and variousness, contamination and purity, movement and stillness. Therefore, the theory goes, to think that all men once resided in Nirvana and can return there after getting themselves free from wordly desires is a mistaken notion. In other words, life or death is nothing different from Nirvana. On the contrary, it is taught in *Saengmyolmun* that all things derive their existence from Contaminated Mind, and therefore, there is difference between life or death and Nirvana.

Wonhyo saw that the conflicting views in the two systems are largely due to the following four points: First, they are squarely opposite to each other in the realm of doctrine; that is to say, while *Chinyomun* is based on the substance or trueness of things, *Saengmyolmun* belongs to the phenomenon or secularity of things. Second, whereas *Chinyomun* sees life or death (secularity) and Nirvana (trueness) as equal, *Saengmyolmun* recognizes disparity between the two. Third, while there is in *Saengmyolmun* the ability of becoming, there is no such ability in *Chinyomun*. Fourth, the two differ from each other in applying terms. Their basic difference in the doctrine brought about opposition. Because of this, heated arguments arose in India and China between the school of *Madhamika* and that of *Vijnaptimatrata*.

In spite of the opposing standpoints in doctrine, both belong to Mahayana Buddhism. Both are the same in aiming at making the best use of the mind of all men which they regard as the essence of their system. This is the very point of which *Kishinnon* took note. On the viewpoint that "both *Chinyomun* and *Saengmyolmun* claim their validity due to One Mind," Wonhyo did his best to eliminate elements which prevent harmony between the two.

Due to efforts made by Wonhyo in his *Kishinnon, Chinyomun* and *Saengmyolmun* achieved a considerable reconcilization. When *Saengmyolmun* destroys Contaminated Mind and returns to the original source of One Mind, its essence now devoid of all contaminated aspects, all contaminations can assume the aspect of trueness of the *Chinyomun*. Here *Chinyomun* and *Saengmyolmun* unite with each other to form the substance of the mysterious Mahayana branch of Buddhism.

What phenomenon will arise after the union of *Chinyomun* and *Saengmyolmun* in One Mind? The function of *Chinyomun*, seeing purity and contamination as equal, will work on *Saengmyolmun* and help it see trueness and secularity as equal. Then the peculiar function of becoming of *Saengmyolmun* will be freed from the restraint which distinguishes trueness from secularity. At the same time *Chinyomun* will come to secularity from trueness.

As *Chinyomun* comes to secularity from trueness, the function of *Saengmyolmun* to distinguish movement from stillness is strengthened, for this is an area belonging to *Saengmyolmun*. Working on *Chinyomun*, this function enables it to know the difference between ascent and descent. And *Chinyomun*, which is obstinately denying explanation, becomes communicable and descends down from its original position. At the same time *Saengmyolmun* enters into trueness after parting from secularity.

Entering into trueness, *Saengmyolmun* finds the function of *Chinyomun* growing strong, and thus returns to secularity. At this stage, *Chinyomun* finds the function of *Saengmyolmun* growing strong, and thereby returns to trueness. In the essence of Mahayana Buddhism, in which the two doors of *Chinyomun* and *Saengmyolmun* are harmonized with each other, trueness moves to secularity and secularity to trueness in smooth, facile communication.

The communication between trueness and secularity is not given a clear theoretical explanation in *Kishinnon*. What is preached is merely that the religious aims (*artha*) of Mahayana Buddhism are Body (Essence), Aspect (phenomenon) and Use (funtion). That part of *Pyolki* which contains an annotation to Outlook of *Kishinnon So* employs the method of starting a new sentence with the ending word of the preceding sentence, so that it is very hard to comprehend the content. However, we may find two main streams in the essence of Mahayana Buddhism:

(I) a. (Its essence) is as expansive as the empty sky and devoid of partiality. b. Contamination and purity accommodate with each other. c. What is true and what is secular become equalized. d. The way to contemplation is blocked. e. Those who grasp this truth can ride the shadow and echo and are not pointed.

(II) a. (Its essence) is as boundless as the great ocean and extremely impartial. b. Movement and stillness arise in order. c. There is difference between ascending and descending. d. The way is cleared to response. e. Those who pray for it can transcend color and shape and return.

In the two main streams which constitute the essence of Mahayana Bhddhism, the passage "...is as expansive as the empty sky and there is nothing which is partial" (I-a) corresponds to *Chinyomun,* while the passage "...is as boundless as the great ocean and extremely impartial" (II-a) corresponds to *Saengmyolmun.* The above can be easily found out by anybody who reads Wonhyo's *Kishinnon So,* for *Chinyomun* is likened chiefly to the empty sky and *Saengmyolmun* to the great ocean. The two form the predicate for the subject "the essence of Mahayana Buddhism," suggesting that the two gates—*Chinyomun* and *Saengmyolmun*—are harmonized with One Mind in the center.

The passages b, c, d, and e in I indicate the logical process of *Chinyomun's* coming to secularity from trueness, while the corresponding passages in II show the logical process of *Saengmyolmun's* entering into trueness after parting from secularity.

We must take special note of the fact that in passage I-a, *Chinyomun* is explained as "devoid of partiality," while *Saengmyolmun* is called "extremely impartial" in the passage II-a. When the two gates are combined into one, being devoid of partiality and being exremely impartial, they form a direct link between themselves, giving birth to a strong will and to participation in reality by "serving the public without considering one's private interests." We are also called on to give a special attention to the passages II-d and II-e which say: "The way is cleared to response. Those who pray for it can transcend color and shape and return." It is taught here that Buddhism does have the religious power to help its believers and government leaders should convert to the religion with a pure heart which transcends color and shape.

Based on this theoretical foundation expounded in *Pyolki,* the main text explains the mysterious nature of the essence of Mahayana Buddhism: "The essence of Mahayana seems tranquil as if solitary and occult as if clear." Being "tranquil as if solitary" indicates *Chinyomun,* while being "occult as if clear" relates to *Saengmyolmun.* As *Chinyomun* parts from verbalism, it is tranquil. As *Saengmyolmun* gives birth to creation and destruction, despite that it is awakened to no creation and no destruction, it is occult.

The passage, "What is occult is truly occult and so it never emerges to the surface of all things," explains that the essence of Mahayana is extremely true in addition to being "occult as if clear." Even with the Five Eyes of Buddha, therefore, it cannot be seen. The passage, "What is tranquil is truly tranquil and so it rather resides in man's mind," explains that the essence of Mahayana is extremely true in addition to being "tranquil as if solitary" and rather emerges to enter secularity. Therefore, it cannot be described sufficiently even with the Four Explanations of Buddha.

The truth cannot be called Mahayana, because it is small enough to to able to enter that which is so small that it has no substance. At the same time, it is as large as being able to embrace that which is so large that it has no limit. Should we call it being? But we find that something dissipates and empties it. Should we call it non-being? But we find that all things ride on it to emerge. What would be a right word to describe it? At best we call it Mahayana.

Both the passages which open Wonhyo's *Kishinnon So* and *Pyolki* summarize the religious state attained by Mahayana Buddhism. The state finds no obstacles in its movement from trueness to secularity (and vice versa) and the theoretical process leading to the stage. Here the confrontation between Chunggwan and Yusik and all arguments melt into one, and all problems concerning the Buddhist views on trueness and secularity are resolved basically. There is the dynamic stage reached by Mahayana Buddhism. Who would dare call Buddhism a religion that only teaches the way to nihility and Nirvana?

3. Wonhyo's Writing and Practice of 'No Obstacle'

Through writing and living, Wonhyo displayed his thought to the fullest extent. Not only in Korea but in all Buddhist countries, Wonhyo can be considered one of the most prolific writers. Works authored by him and recorded in historical literature number more than 100 kinds, consisting of more than 240 volumes. There are 20 works in 25 volumes now in existence. They are:

Pophwangyong Chongyo (1 volume); *Taehyedogyong Chongyo* (1 volume); *Yolpan'gyong Chongyo* (1 volume); *Muryangsugyong Chongyo* (1 volume); *Miruksangsaenggyong Chongyo* (1 volume); *Amidagyong So* (1 volume); *Kumgang Sammaegyong Non* (3 volumes); *Aengnakponopkyong So* (the last of the 2 volumes); *Posal Kyebon Chibom Yogi* (1 volume); *Posal Kyebon Sagi* (the first of the 2 volumes); *Kishinnon So* (2 volumes); *Kishinnon Pyolki* (1 volume); *Chungbyon Punbyol Nonso* (2 volumes); *Ijangui* (1 volume); *Yusim Allakto* (1 volume); *Taesung Yulchong Ch'amhoebop* (1 volume); *Palsimmun;* *Hwaomgyong So* (5 volumes); *Simmun Hwajong Non* (fragments); *Panbiryangnon* (excerpts); and *Haesimmilkyong So Somun* (fragments).

Most of these works reflect his standpoint based on the harmony between trueness and secularity without obstacles. It is presumed that Wonhyo committed the thought to writing after he secured it on a firm foundation with a view to propagating it widely. One form of writing he was fond of was *Chongyo*, which summarized the essentials of sutras and his treatises. This means that he was more interested in grasping the living thought of sutras and treatises than in word-by-word annotations.

It is *Simmun Hwajong Non,* among Wonhyo's works extant, that most attracts the attention of present-day scholars. This work classifies all scriptural arguments arising from the confrontation between Chunggwan and Yusik into 10 categories and harmonizes them. Based on his theory that trueness and secularity cannot be harmonized with each other without obstacles, this work delves into only that aspect which harmonizes the two—trueness and secularity—by overcoming their opposition. It is truly regrettable, however, that only several chapters of this work now remain.

Kumgang Sammaegyong So (3 volumes) can perhaps be considered as a work which causes the greatest sensation among Wonhyo's works. This work contains his sermons delivered at the Hwangnyong-sa Temple prayer hall, before the king, ranking court officials, monks, and laymen, displaying his profound learning. This work was introduced to China, where it was printed again and where it won the reputation of a truly great treatise.

It goes without saying that the treatise also reflects Wonhyo's theory of harmony between trueness and secularity. Also, it has an especially close connection with his *Kishinnon So*. If *Kishinnon So* and *Pyolki* can be regarded as works which awakened people to faith by clarifying the great religious state Mahayana Buddhism reached, *Kumgang Sammaegyong So* is a work which preaches the principle of practice in order to attain such a state of faith, namely, the state of *Kumgang Sammae*. We may safely assert that the two works are the two pillars which support the greatness of Wonhyo's Buddhist thought.

Extant among Wonhyo's works concerning the thought of 'Pure Land' are *Muryangsugyong Chongyo* (1 volume), *Amidagyong So* (1 volume), and *Yusim Allakto* (1 volume). The three works are threaded with passages similar to those appearing in the opening part of *Kishinnon So*, summarizing the gist. From the theoretical basis, manifest in the opeing paragraphs, Wonhyo preaches that, "all that move and are standstill are but dreams; it becomes clear to all who are initiated into truth that this world and the world yonder are the same, the befouled land and the pure land all spring from One Mind, and life or death and Nirvana are not two." Therefore, his idea of the Pure Land can be regarded as a sermon to promote faith among laymen by explaining his thought on the harmony between trueness and secularity without obstacles.

Through writing, as we have seen, Wonhyo systematized and preached his thought. For him, however, writing was not an end in itself. He showed his thought brilliantly in his life. As important materials which convey reports on his activities, we may cite *Sung Biography of Eminent Priests, Samguk Yusa* (*Memorabilia of the Three Kingdoms*), and the epitaph on the monument of Priest Sedang. With these records as reference materials, I will delineate his life which was not bound to confrontation between trueness and secularity.

Wonhyo's secular family name was Sol, his given name being Sedang. Later he named himself Wonhyo, because his contemporaries called him "Saebyok," which has the same meaning as Wonhyo, "dawn." He was born under a sal tree in Chestnut Valley north of Pulchi Village, Apnyang County, Sangju (presently Chain-myon, Kyongsan County, North Kyongsang Province) in 617 (39th year of king Chinp'yong's reign). The record that Wonhyo was born not at home but in a wood, and not under a chestnut tree but under a sal tree, shows an adaptation in the legendary method of description aimed at glorifying him as the greatest Buddha born in Silla. Sakyamuni, it is said, died under a pair of sal trees in a northern Indian province.

Reaching the age of 20, Wonhyo willingly entered priesthood, remodeling his home as a temple which he named Ch'ogae-sa. At that time, Silla was engaged in war with two other kingdoms on the Korean peninsula and subject to incessant invasion from Paekche. In 642 (11th year of Queen Sondok's reign) Silla lost more than 40 castles to Paekche, even Taeya Castle near the capital. The critical situation compelled Silla to seek amity with T'ang China. The year 645 saw Silla's High Priest Chajang return from studies in T'ang and erect a nine-story pagoda in Hwangnyong-sa Temple for dedication to national defense. How did the critical situation facing Silla influence Wonhyo's studies of Buddhism?

Wonhyo did not learn Buddhism under the tutorship of any particular teacher. Some say that he learned it from Nangji on Yong-ch'wi Mountain, while others hold that he was a disciple of Priest Popchang in Hungnyun-sa Temple. Still another belief is that he learned the *Nirvana-sutra* from Podok, a Koguryo priest in exile in Silla. But a reliable literature recording Wonhyo's activities says that "Won-hyo was wise by birth and so he did not need a teacher." In short, he was free from any restraint and searched for truth in a free atmosphere.

In the fourth year of Queen Chindok's reign (650), Wonhyo set out on a journey to T'ang with his friend Uisang. He was 34 years of age. Five years before, Hsuanchuang returned to China from his 17-year studies of Buddhism in India, providing a turning point in translation of Buddhist scripture and Buddhist learning. Such Silla priests as Wonch'uk and Shinbang were active under him. The journey of

Wonhyo and Uisang however was not smooth. Their overland route took them to Liaotung, where they were mistaken for spies by Koguryo sentries and where they barely escaped captivity.

Four years later in Silla, King Muyol ascended to the throne, and in the seventh year of his reign(660) Silla destroyed Paekche in alliance with T'ang. During the reign of King Muyol a marvelous event befell on Wonhyo. He was married to Princess Kwa in Yosok Palace and begot a son. The Details are as follows:

One day Wonhyo wandered the streets chanting a mysterious song, "Who dares lend me an axe without a handle? I'll hew down the pillars supporting the heaven." No one on the streets knew what he meant in the song, but King Muyol interpreted it to mean that he was anxious for a noble woman and a bright son. The monarch let the monk stay at Yosok Palace, and the princess became pregnant.

It is true that the child between Wonhyo and Princess Yosok was Sol Ch'ong. It is also undeniable that Sol Ch'ong rated as one of the 10 wisest men of Silla, as he annotated the Confucian scriptures in the Korean language. The work held readership as late the Koryo years. However, the process of Wonhyo's begetting Sol Ch'ong reflects rich elements of legendary fiction. Especially mysterious is the passage that Wonhyo had resolved to "hew down the pillars which support the heaven."

The sea route to China was opened for Silla with the fall of Paekche. Uisang, who had once attempted a study in China with Wonhyo, again started his jounrey to that country in the year King Mumnu was enthroned (661). According to the *Sung Biography of Eminent Priests,* Wonhyo initially decided to join Uisang.

They were waiting for ship at Tangju in Haemun. A raging storm assailed and they sought a haven in a wayside earth mound. On the following morning, however, they found that it was an old tomb and they were lying baside a skeleton. The stormy rain became ever heavier and they could not set a foot outside. Before the night grew late, all sorts of ghosts came out. Wonhyo sighed and said, 'When Mind is generated, various laws arise; when Mind dies away, the earth mound and the old tomb become the same.'

Through several records available, we know that Uisang was successful in learning Huayen Buddhism under Priest Chinyen of T'ang during his second sojourn. However, there is no record which says that

Wonhyo attempted a study in China twice. Neither does *The Biography of Eminent Priests* confirm that he was engaged in study twice. Wonhyo already had turned 45 years of age, and by that time he had abandoned priesthood to return to the secular world. Therefore, it would have been impossible for Wonhyo to seek a study in China again.

It is considered that Wonhyo could initiate himself into truth all alone and rather spread his Buddhism to China than learning it in that land. In short, he was so great a priest. Concerning Wonhyo's plan for study in China, it is recorded in *Chiwolnok* that Wonhyo felt thirsty at night and drank water in the old tomb. On the following morning he found that what he drank was water gathered in a skull. In a moment, the record goes on to say, he realized the truth: "When Mind is generated, various laws arise; when Mind dies away, the skull is nothing different." But this is a slightly different story from the above.

This tale, as we can notice, has many legendary elements. However, it is a helpful reference material with which we can understand through what process Wonhyo reached truth and how he was interpreted by posterity. The saying, "The whole world springs from Mind," can be found in many parts of the *Huayen-sutra*. And the saying, "When Mind is generated, various laws arise; when Mind dies away, the earth mound and the old tomb become not two different things," is too similar to the paragraph in *Kishinnon*, "When Mind is born, various laws come into being; when Mind dies, various laws pass away.' The clause, "The earth mound (secularity) and the tomb (trueness) are not two different things," but coincide to Wonhyo's thought on harmony between trueness and secularity without obstacles.

Wonhyo's departure from the priesthood should not be construed as simple re-entry into the secular world. Several of his brilliant religious activities took place after he left the priesthood. Clothed in a secular dress and renaming himself Sosung Kosa after the secular style, Wonhyo lived a life which was not bothered by restricting conformity, whether it was true or secular. He did not care about his language, and had no hesitation about visiting a drinking house or a brothel. He also stayed at private residences, it seems, and sat in religious meditation, while at the same time, throwing himself to the battlefield. It is recorded that he interpreted for General Kim Yu-shin a letter of military secret from T'ang General Soo Ting-fang.

Borrowing a phrase from the passage in the *Huayen-sutra*, "Those who have no obstacles can transcend life and death with the truth," he named his trousers "No Obstacle," and wearing them, he wandered around all villages and hamlets, signing and dancing. His missionary work inspired even ignorant people who came to chant prayers to Buddha. Residing in Punhwang-sa Temple, Wonhyo worked on appending notes to the *Huayen-sutra,* but stopped the work in the fourth chapter which deals with missionary work. He was truly the greatest leader in popularizing Buddhism among the masses in Silia.

Most noteworthy among his brilliant religious activities were a series of lectures on the *Kumgang-sammaegyong-sutra* he delivered at Hwangnyong-sa Temple. One day the king invited noted scholars, including Wonhyo, to a mass at the royal palace. But his contemporary priests who liked to stick to accepted forms, naturally disliked Wonhyo's carefree manner, and they asked the king not to invite him. Some time later the king fell ill, and his illness lingered. This gave Wonhyo an occasion to have access to the king. He was asked to give a lecture on the *Kumgang Sammaegyong* to the king. Only Taean, who also practiced the truth of "no obstacles," could compile the scattered sutra; and only Wonhyo could append notes to it.

When Wonhyo completed the five-volume annotation, the king asked him to lecture on it at Hwangnyong-sa Temple. But priests who harbored jealousy to Wonhyo stole the manuscript. In three days Wonhyo restored the first three volumes and made them public at Hwangnyong-sa. This is the the three-volume annotation we now have. After the lecture Wonhyo declared, "When they needed 100 rafters some time ago, they omitted me. This morning they needed one large beam, I was the only person possessing the function," All those who censured him could not raise their faces in shame. This is a vivid reminder of what a great influence his practice of "No Obstacle" had on the Buddhist world in his day, which was bound with formality, and how great his learning and virtues were.

After destroying Paekche in alliance with T'ang, Silla finally exterminated Koguryo in 668 (eighth year of King Munmu), realizing the unification of the Three Kingdoms, its long-cherished desire. However, the reality was somewhat more complicated. By utilizing Silla, T'ang destroyed both Paekche and Koguryo and gradually exposed an intention to subjugate Silla, too. Shifting its diplomatic policy from pro-T'ang to anti-T'ang, Silla entered into war with the Chinese. Silla's resistance finally was a success in 677 (17th year of King Munmu) when it drove the T'ang government-general established in P'yongyang to Manchuria. Now unification became true in fact. Wonhyo died in 686 at the age of 70 (sixth year of King Shinmun), nine years after the actual unification. His body was laid in state by his son, Sol Ch'ong, at Punhwang-sa Temple.

A great thinker knows what problems his society faces. He gropes for the best means of resolving them by utilizing writing and action to awaken his fellow countrymen. The life of Wonhyo was truly perfect in this respect. He saw unification by Silla in his life time and the emergence of a brilliant culture in Korea on the basis of Buddhist harmony. His wisdom shone like the "morning star" as he could foresee a bright future for Silla Buddhism.   (Translated by Paik Seung-gil)

HWANG SU-YONG was born in Kae-
sung city in 1918. He first majored in
Economics at Tokyo University, but
after the liberation of Korea from the
Japanese rule in 1945, his academic
interest was directed to the study of
Korean art. He says that his love for
Korean art had earlier been fermented
under the personal influence of the
late Koh Yu-Sop, a pioneering art
historian in Korea.

He worked for the Korean National
Museum from 1947 to 1950, and was
appointed to a member of the Cultural
Property Commission, which post he
has been holding till today. In 1956 he
begun to teach at Tongguk University
as a professor of Korean art history,
his present position. He also served as
the Curator of the Korean National
Museum for three years on leave of
the university.

His major publications include *Fifty-
Three Buddhas of Yujomsa Temple*
(1967). *Report on the Restoration Project of Sukkulam Stone Cave* (1969)
and *A Study of Buddhist Sculptures
in Korea* (1973).

BUDDHIST SCULPTURE IN THE
SILLA PERIOD

Hwang Soo-yong

1. Introduction

Kyŏngju, a place conserving historical and cultural vestiges of
Korea, was the capital of Silla Kingdom over one thousand years ago,
witnessing a racial migration, the formation of a tribal society, the
establishment of an ancient state, and finally the unification of the
whole peninsula with the opening of the bright Silla era in the middle
of the seventh century. It was in Kyŏngju that one of the most beautiful
flowering of a new civilization in ancient history started, with the subsequent enjoyment of peace and stability during the span of several
centuries. Also, it was the place in which a concentration of physical
and spiritual efforts toward founding a new cultural heritage was
earnestly pursued, together with a sincere exertion to safeguard the
nation, which had been severely damaged by the long struggle among
the Three Kingdoms.

Buddhism, which had been imported into this land via the northern
part of the country around the later part of the fourth century, diffused
rapidly across the nation by both the land and sea routes. It contri-
buted greatly to the nation by being the foundation of the political and
religious life in this land, with the strong support of the pious believers.
However, the official recognition of Buddhism in Silla was much delayed compared with that in the other two neighboring kingdoms. The
reason for this was partly due to the fact that Silla (namely Kyŏngju)
was located a ittle remotely in the south-eastern corner of the country,
and partly that Silla held fast to its own tradition in thought and art
for a long time. It deserves our attention that Silla left evidences of its
resistance against the introduction of Buddhism, although she hardly
could have succeeded in preventing the mighty stream of Buddhism
from flowing into the Korean peninsula. In that sense, the difficulty
with which Koguryŏ Buddhist priests propagated Buddhism, and the
martyrdom of Ich'adon, a Silla monk, should not be regarded as in-

significant. At any rate, it was inevitable for Silla to have recognized Buddhism officially in the beginning of the sixth century, and see the spread of that religion in Kyŏngju and vicinity. Finally, the establishment of Buddhism as the official cult of the state was attained with the conversion of the king himself, who subsequently tried to make himself a model in cultivating and reforming the life of the people in accordance with the Buddhist teachings.

It is assumed that the role of Buddhism in Silla was more important than that in the other two rivaling states. Buddhism is believed to have been one of the fundamental incentives to the unification of the Three Kingdoms. The unification of the Three Kingdoms may be considered as the result of the political and military supremacy of Silla over the other two kingdoms, but at the same time it should properly be claimed as a natural consequence of spiritual solidarity on the part of the people in Silla. It is obvious that for the promotion of such a spiritual solidarity, Buddhism exerted a vital influence through its fusion with the traditional Sillan spirit. It was the period in which the main current shifted from disunion to unification, from war to peace. By being keenly perceptive of the domestic as well as international development of the times, Silla succeeded in turning such a situation to its national interest. Since Buddhism itself was a spirit connotative of unity and peace, it is no wonder that the spread of Buddhism in the Three Kingdoms proved to be the first step toward the spiritual unification of the people there. Thus, Buddhism finally found an ideal foothold for its future full blossom in Silla, which had won the final victory by taking advantage of the international situation as well as winning the hearts of the entire nation.

Silla was originally a small group of six villages dotting in the wide area of Kyŏngju. Yet in the course of time it gradually grew stronger and accumulated more experience in its foreign policies. It must have been the result of a steady effort and firm goal over the long period of time that such a small state situated in a corner of the peninsula should have succeeded in accomplishing the great task of the unification of the whole peninsula. Yet the role played by Buddhism at the crucial moment of the unification was also great, for Buddhism gradually attracted the mood and soul of the Silla people, who had long clinged to their own traditional beliefs. It led them to a new direction in thought and art. The leadership for this new task naturally fell on the Buddhist priests.

Therefore, the Buddhist priest played a leading part in the conquest of the national crisis, while the leaders of the people who had been enlightened by these priests were willing to sacrifice themselves for the cause of the country. This was the backdrop against which the *Hwarang* system was born in Old Silla. *Hwarangs* were fully aware of the international situation of the time and prepared themselves for the creation of a new history. At the same time on account of the enlightenment of Buddhism, the ordinary citizens were also ready to devote themselves to the cause of the country. Consequently, Buddhism conferred a great influence equally upon the ruling and the ruled classes. Having solidified its political system and established the foundation of the spiritual life of the nation with the aid of Buddhism, Silla finally realized a new historical era.

With such a period for its background, Buddhism in Silla was able to attain its official recognition first from the upper class, and then through the gradual conversion of the common people. The official recognition of Buddhism as a state religion led to the establishment of such great Buddhist temples as Hŭngryun-sa, Hwangryong-sa, Chiwŏn-sa, Silje-sa, Yŏnghŭng-sa, Samryang-sa, Punhwang-sa, as recorded in *The Samguk-sagi (The Historical Record of the Three Kingdoms)*.

It should be noted that of these temples, the founding of Hwangryong-sa, which was initiated by King Chinhŭng (a restorer of the Sillan glory), was a result of the special demand of the time. Priest Chajang was born of a royal family in Silla. Prior to his return to Silla after his five-year study in China, he visited Wŏnhyang, a priest of the Zen-sect, at his cell at Mt. Chongnam. It was in the twelveth year of the reign of Queen Sŏndŭk (AD 643). The Chinese Zen-priest told Chajang that according to his inspiration Silla's neighboring states would come and surrender to Silla if Chajang built a nine-storied *stupa* at Hwangryong-sa upon his return to Silla. Soon thereafter, Chajang's proposal to follow the advice of the Chinese priest was adopted by the king. The result was the founding of the nine-storied wooden pagoda at Hwangryong-sa at 225 feet high, one of the highest of its kind in the Orient. The unification of the Three Kingdoms was the supreme task for the Silla priests at the time. Therefore, the founding of Buddhist temples could hardly depart from being their major tactic. Thus, having officially been recognized after severe ordeals, Buddhism in Silla displayed its rapid adaptability to the national demand.

The sculpture of Buddhist images in the early Silla Period can hardly be understood without the knowledge of such a historical and religious background. In regard to the sculptural style and technique of the earlier Buddhist images of Silla, the influence of those made in the Southern and Northern Dynasties of China, Koguryŏ, and Paekje, all of which had been earlier receivers of Buddhism, was clearly indicated. Especially the influence by the Paekje Buddhist sculpture upon Silla's should be emphasized.

Up to now, however, the discussion on the early Silla Buddhist image in general has been made from its external stylistic aspect, and most of the foreign scholars' discussion of the Silla sculpture has also treated merely the same characteristics. Yet, it goes without saying that our research in the Buddhist sculpture from now on should be aimed of a deeper level. That is, our effort to grasp the entire and real picture of the Silla sculpture should be made from both external and internal aspects. The following sections deal briefly with the stone Buddhist sculpture of Old and Unified Sillas from this standpoint, with the exclusion of the works made of gilt-bronze.

2. Stone Images of Buddha in Old Silla

As was the case in the two neighboring kingdoms, the early Buddhist images in Old Silla, especially those imported from China are thought to have been those of small sized gilt-bronze Buddhas. It is also inferred that such gilt-bronze images immediately became the model for the wooden and plaster statues that were enshrined on the alter of the main hall of the temple, along with the gilt-bronze images. The Buddhist images of the triad at Hwangryong-sa, together with the already-mentioned great pagoda in it, was one of the three national treasures of Silla. Both of them were noted objects of ardent worship by the people. This trinity of Buddhas at Hwangryong-sa was the largest of its kind that had ever been produced in Korea. According to the record of the *Samguk-sagi*, the total amount of bronze and gold to be used in the making of this statue was 35,007 *kun* and 10,198 *p'un* respectively. Today the huge stone pedestals at the site of the ruined Hwangryong-sa are the only monument of the past glory left for the wonder of visitors to Kyŏngju.

It is supposed that in the wake of, or at the same time with, such gold-bronze images, and wooden statues (a single example of whose remnants had never been found in this land) there appeared stone figures of Buddha. Those stone images were the product of the transitional period, in which the Buddhist image began to undergo indigenization into the peculiarly Sillan type both in material and stylistic aspect. Originally the Korean stone images of Buddha had come into being in each of the Three Kingdoms in the late sixth century, almost at the same time with the rise of the stone pagoda. Although there might have been a slight difference depending on the situation in each kingdom, by AD 600 the stone image is generally believed to have been constructed in all the Three Kingdoms. Such a conjecture about the date is based on the assumption that it might not have been possible before the turn of the 6th and 7th centuries and the introduction of Buddhism into Korea in the late fourth century that the tradition of the Korean Buddhist sculpture could be solidified. By the end of the 6th century, it was possible for the stone image of Buddha and the Buddhist pagoda to be produced in Korea.

This pair of brilliance in formative art and the two great objects of Buddhist worship could be sculptured by cutting and polishing the white hard granite, which is produced in abundance everywhere in Korea. The present writer believes that the characteristics of the Sillan sculpture lie in the fact that the people of Silla could construct beautiful objects of worship for a foreign religion by utilizing their domestic material. Indeed the stylistic and technical peculiarities of the Silla stone sculpture were derived from this unique condition. This is why we should hold in esteem the motive and skill of the Sillan artisans who dicided to use granite as their main material. Korea is commonly known as "the country of stone pagodas," while Japan as that of wooden pagodas, and China of brick pagodas. This indicates not only the difference in the choice of the material of their Buddhist sculpture among these three countries, but also reflects the peculiar attitude of each nation to accept and adopt Buddhist formative art. This tradition was maintained unbroken afterward.

With the official recognition of Buddhism in Old Silla in the sixth century, the construction of Buddhist temples is believed to have started both on level land and in the mountain area almost concurrently. Needless to say, the conditions for building temples varies with the lay of the land. Therefore, it can be inferred that building of temples on level land in the capital and its vicinity followed the contemporary fashion, which included halls and pagodas in the precincts. As seen in the site of Hwangryong-sa, the temple had a pagoda facing southward, the main hall, the lecture hall, the corridor, and the middle gate to be used for usual occasions. Compared with this, the early temples erected in the mountains were naturally of small scale. Many of them followed the form of the stone cave shrine, which was quite different in shape from the temple on the level ground. It is the opinion of the present writer that at the beginning stage of the propagation of Buddhism, such a stone cave shrine in the mountain area might have been a common practice prior to, or coincident with, the establishment of regular temples on level land. The situation had been similar in India, China, or Paekje. Only in Korea was a slightly different type from those in these other countries seen. The granite in Korea, unlike the equivalent material in China or India, is so hard to fashion that the Sillan artisans found it difficult to cut a great cavity in huge natural rock in which to enshrine the separately sculptured Buddhist statues or pagodas. Accordingly, it is assumed that from the outset Buddhist images were curved on huge living rock in the mountains to which wooden and tiled roofs were added as cover. The present writer believes that the stone cave shrine at Shinsŏn-sa in Mt. Dansŏk, on which he has been focussing his investigation with great interest these several years, is a typical example of the early form of the stone cave shrine.

This Shinsŏn-sa is very important. This temple, which is located below the summit of Mt. Dansŏk some 16 kilometers south of Kyŏngju, presents a very significant similarity, in its location and distance from the capital of Silla, to Sŏkkuram stone cave shrine, which is situated near the crest of Mt. T'oham at an almost equal distance east of Kyŏngju. It is strongly desired that much more attention should be given to this stone cave shrine at Mt. Dansŏk by the students majoring in this field, as well as by the general public.

The Dansŏk stone cave shrine is a natural rock chapel composed of several huge pieces of living rock towering high in the shape of a U with its one side opening westward. Recent investigations confirmed that its roof had been of wood and tiles stretched between huge walls of rock. It is believed that the characteristics of the early stone cave shrine in Silla might be brought to light by the examination of the remains at this temple. Fortunately on the inner wall of this artificial grotto an inscription has been found. An effort by the present writer to decipher the inscription in 1968 and 1969 revealed that the name of the temple was Shinsŏn-sa and that the type of Buddha enshrined there was similar to the Maitreyas of the triad. The rock chapel is divided into the internal and external parts. On the northern wall of the internal room a standing Buddha (see *plate 1*), 23 feet high, is carved, while on the eastern and southern walls of the same room a standing Bodhisattva is carved respectively. Despite of weathering, the contour of those carved images is discernible. On the other hand, on the northern wall of the external room four figures of standing Bodhisattva are carved, and below them two more standing figures are depicted. Furthermore, on the same wall an image of half-cross-legged Bodhisattva in thinking posture, sole existing Sillan relic of its kind—is also seen. The image is facing southward with an unsophisticated, archaic smile (see *plate 2*). This stone cave shrine is the Maitreya cave shrine which was built in the Old Silla period (6th-7th centuries). The name of the temple, Shinsŏn, indicates *hwarang*. Since a *hwarang* was believed to be an incarnation of Maitreya, Shinsŏn-sa could mean a temple of Maitreyas, a temple of *hwarangs*. And this stone cave shrine may have been the very place which is referred to in *The Samguk-sagi* as "the stone cave in the central mountain where General Kim Yu-shin disciplined himself." This is a conjecture induced from the structure and internal evidences of the shrine.

Conversely, according to a recent research, Sŏkkuram stone cave shrine is inferred to have had a certain relation with the underwater tomb of King Munmu, a great hero who had accomplished the unification of Silla. Sŏkkuram is supposed to have been built after the completion of the said underwater tomb. A common belief among the Silla people was that King Munmu and General Kim Yushin not merely put their cooperative energy into the attainment of the unification of Silla, but also they were firmly determined to defend the nation against the invasion from the eastern sea even after their deaths. The union of the three elements—faith, history, and persons—was the real motivation of the production of the Silla masterpieces in sculpture. The worship of the Buddhist images is believed to have greatly encouraged the people to devote themselves to the protection of the country.

However, this is not a whole story about the stone images in the Old Silla period. There was another location in which a concentrated effort to construct the stone image was made. That was the whole area around the northern crest of Mt. Namsan in Kyŏngju. Belonging to this group are the extant stone Buddhist images scattered in both the east and west villages, and also at the northern foot of the mountain. Some of them have been removed to museums, but others are still left at the sites of the extinct temples. Among them the most noteworthy were the Samhwaryŏng Maitreyas of the triad, which were located on the northern crest (Changch'anggok) of Mt. Namsan. The name, original location, and construction method of these images of the triad, which are now collected at Kyŏngju National Museum, were brought to light by the investigation of the present writer. In addition to this, another group of the Maitreyas of the triad is located at Paeri in Mt. Namsan (see *plates* 3 and 4). This trinity of Maitreyas had originally been discovered at the site of Sŏnbang-sa, but later it was removed to the present location at Paeri. This was a product of the much later period than its counterpart at Samhwaryŏng, though its size is much bigger and its figures are all in standing position. In addition, another seated single stone Buddha (see *plate* 5) was discovered at Pulgok in the same mountain. This image, which seems to be much older than the above mentioned statues, is enshrined in a small stone niche, and shows the classical posture with the robe hanging down to the pedestal. Furthermore, another piece of seated stone Buddha (now in Kyŏngju National Museum) discovered at Inwangri, Kyŏngju, and a standing stone Buddha (now in the same museum) whose original location is unknown, are also thought to have been the works of the early Silla period. Though of small size, their style is quite old.

Besides these triad-style or single-style images, the half-cross-legged, thinking-posed Maitreya or Bodhisattva stone image is another rarity in the style among the Old Silla Buddhist statues. Especially the headless stone statue discovered in 1909 at Kŭmsanje near the east hillside of Mt. Songhwa, is a typical example belonging to this group. This noteworthy relic is inferred to have originally been at Samhwabang, the site of an ancient temple. This image seems to have been a later product than the already mentioned Shinsŏn-sa stone image. And the great stone image at the site of Pugjiri-sa in Ponghwa County, which has become an object of reexamination of late, is inferred to have been made in the middle of the seventh century, a much later work than the Songhwabang image. These stone images should receive as much attention as the relics of gilt-bronze statues. Especially desirable is research into the background from which the vogue of the half-cross-legged, thinking-posed images came into being in Old Silla.

Investigations conducted after the liberation of the nation in 1945 disclosed that a gilt-bronze Koguryŏ Buddhist image was unearthed in Pyongyang (see *plate 6*), and that a Paekje statuette made of agal-matolite was discovered at Puyŏ. Along with these two extant Buddhist images, a half-cross-legged, thinking-posed figure, which is carved as an attendant to the Buddhas of the triad on rock at Kayahyŏp in Sŏsan (see *plate 7*), suggests the probability that there had existed such a stylistic similarity as that of a half-cross-legged, thinking posture among the Buddhist statues in the Three Kingdoms.

However, the vogue of this half-cross-legged, thinking-posed style seems to have been more conspicuous in Old Silla. Even if the similar trend to worship the Maitreya image had prevailed throughout the Three Kingdoms and China, there must have inevitably arisen a modal difference in the construction of the Buddhist images in each of these ancient kingdoms. Probably such a modal difference resulted from the dissimilarity of the inner interpretation of faith by the people of each country.

At present in Korea, we have two gilt-bronze, half-cross-legged images of Buddha (see *plates 8* and *9*), some three feet high respectively, and lately have discovered two figures of the same size and type of Buddha carved on living rock. Accordingly, it is easily understood that the Buddhist image of this type was more popular in Korea than in China and Japan in the sixth and seventh centuries. More masterpieces of this type were produced in Korean then. Moreover, the image of this half-cross-legged style was imported into Japan. Therefore, it is noteworthy that the stone image of Maitreya, which *the Chronicles of Japan* described in its article of the thirteenth reign of Emperor Min-tatsu (AD 584) as the one imported from Paekje by a man named Shika Hukatami, has been conjectured to have been indentical with a half-cross-legged stone Buddha.

Furthermore, it is certainly an indication of the close cultural interchange between Silla and Japan that the two standing Bodhi-sattvas carved on living rock located at the already mentioned Sam-hwaryŏng bear a close resemblance to the sculptured works of the same type produced in the Hakho period in Japan. The traditional Japanese Buddhist image of the forty-eight bodies is very noted for its peculiar style. The fact that almost all of the extant images of this type, with the exception of very few pieces, were constructed in Japan indicates the rapid receptivity of the Japanese people.

The same fact can be pointed out for the stone sculpture in Old Silla. For reflecting undoubtedly the various stages of the Chinese influence, the Sillan stone image of Buddha, whether a work in round carving or a rock-cut statue, should be considered as the embodiment of the inner faith and the peculiar technical evolution of the Sillan artisans and people. This is the reason why in the investigation and appreciation of the ancient stone statues of Silla, not merely in its technical aspect, but also the insight into the faith or the spiritual aspect of the people, must fully be taken into account.

3. Sculpture in the Early Unified Silla Period

With the close of the long struggle to attain the unification of the Three Kingdoms and the start of the new order, the vigorous attempt to build Buddhist temples finally commenced. Even at the end of the Old Silla period, Kyŏngju was described as the capital in which "temples were spread like stars in the sky; pagodas were standing like flocks of wild geese."

Entering upon the new era of peace and stability, the magnificence of Kyŏngju accelerated day by day. The founding of Sach'ŏnwang-sa by King Munmu was an expression of his desire to protect the nation. Another temple, named Kamun-sa, which was also constructed by his initiative on the coast of the East Sea, was the embodiment of his wish to defend the nation against possible invasion even after his death. It is easily conjectured that a large number of new temples including Mang-dŏk-sa were founded soon after the unification, while the existing temples also greatly increased their prestige. Gradually the path was paved for the founding of a great Buddhist country.

In addition to these state-supported temples, numerous other temples which were started by individual princes or nobles began to appear in Kyŏngju. Of these temples the most important was Hwang-bok-sa, which was located on the northern hillside of Mt. Nang, one of the three famous mountains in Silla. The construction of those temples, which aimed to supplicate the prosperity of the nation, became a vogue gradually until the reign of King Kyŏngdŏk in the middle of the eighth century.

The golden age of the Sillan art really reached its climax under the reign of this art-loving king. The prosperity of Kyŏngju at the time seems to have been beyond our imagination. Ch'angan in China, Kyŏngju in Silla, and Nara in Japan were really among the worldwide great cities at the time. The cultural interchange among these three capitals and their contact with India and its neighboring countries were greatly instrumental in the expansion of Buddhism as a sole spiritual chain to unite the Oriental world. At the same time Buddhist sculputre, especially Buddhist images, which were most urgently needed as the object of worship, thrived remarkably, with the result that many masterpieces of stone sculpture were produced. Indeed, master works of Silla Buddhist stone images could never have appeared without such a background of national security and prosperity.

In the transitional period between the end of the Three Kingdom and the beginning of the Unified Silla there appeared excellent stone works of new type (see *plate 10*). These were the Buddhist images carved on the stone monuments located around Yŏngi, South Ch'ungch'ŏng Province. Of seven works which were examined for three years beginning in 1960, four pieces contain an intelligible inscription, which disclosed the names of the monuments. Also according to the inscription, it was brought to light that their founders had been subjects of the ruined Paekje Kingdom. All these works are of Amitabha worship, and the images are minutely carved on pencil stone. Especially noteworthy are the two images of a half-cross-legged, thinking-posed Buddha carved on the two stone monuments. This is evidence that the images of Amitabha and Maitreya were the main object of worship of those days. Such a parallel worship of the two different types of images still was practiced in the Unified Silla period.

For one thing, the two standing images of different type at Kamsan-sa are the product of the early eighth century. However, except for such Buddhist images carved on the stone monuments, which were mainly produced in the provinces, the Silla sculpture from the middle of the seventh century on, focused its effort on the establishment of temples in Kyongju and its vicinity. Though severely damaged, the huge rock-cut trinity of Buddhas installed on the crest of Mt. Sŏag in Kyŏngju is a great work. And the Kunwi Buddhas of the triad (see *plate 11*) discovered in the northern valley of Mt. P'algong in 1962 indicate that the Ambitabhas of the triad were in vogue in Silla of those days. The central figure of this triad seated on the square pedestal displays a hanging drapery of classical form. The two standing Bodhisattvas on either side bear a close affinity in style with the Paekje gilt-bronze images. When discovered, this Kunwi trinity of Buddhist images was widely reported and highly admired as 'a second Sŏkkuram' for its artistic beauty.

The fact that such a masterpiece has been buried and hidden unnoticed in the deep valley of the mountain is a good indication of the possibility that more of such works could be discovered in the future. Ponghwa and Yŏngju, two towns forming the northern bounderies of Old Silla, are noted for their preservation of good stone images. For example, the seated stone Buddha at Pukjiri, Ponhwa, could be regarded as one of the greatest works of its kind made in the later seventh century. Not very far from this statue is located the famous Pusok-sa temple, which was founded by Priest Ŭisang, a royal messenger of King Munmu.

Entering upon the eighth century, the reign of King Sŏngdŏk began. In the course of half a century after the unification, the Buddhist formative art, which had had its separate origin in each of the Three Kingdoms, now found a new integration on the new prosperous soil. Its development culminated in the establishment of Buddhist temples and pagodas.

In the Old Silla period, the northern crest of Mt. Namsan had been the center of the Buddhist temples in the Kyŏngju area. But now this temple area was expanded so far southward that the whole mountain was dotted with temples. No rock on which carving was possible could pass unnoticed. Regardless of its extent, almost every available space was used for the construction of temples. In the light of this, whether it was an image to be enshrined inside the hall or an image carved on natural rock outside, the stone image produced in Kyŏngju during the first half of the eighth century should rightly be regarded as the most wonderful piece that had ever been produced during Silla period.

Among the more typical works of that period are the standing statue of Amitabha (see *plate 12*) and the standing Maitreya Boddhisattva statue (see *plate 13*). These two statues were constructed by a Silla noble named Kim Ji-song for praying for the heavenly bliss of his departed parents. The inscription on their backs has disclosed that they were made in the eighteenth year of King Sŏngdŏk (AD 719). Through these two stone statues, each some two meters high, we can imagine what the representative Silla stone Buddhist images were like.

These two statues of Amitabha and Maitreya are also suggestive of the popular mode of worship of the day, as mentioned in the case of the images carved on the stone monuments at Piam-sa.

It is propitious now to mention the sculpture at Sŏkkuram stone cave shrine located on the hillside of Mt. T'oham (see *plate 14*). Sŏkkuram was begun in the middle of the eighth century. The shrine was a culmination of the continuous development of the Sillan stone cave shrine, whose origin can be dated back to the Three Kingdoms period. The long tradition of the Buddhist stone cave shrine, which had originated in India, finally gave birth to an excellent work on the hillside of a Silla mountain, a remote place in the southeastern corner of the Korean peninsula. Though of small size, this stone cave shrine consists of a main chamber and an anteroom which is used for worshipping and offering.

Kim Dae-sŏng, prime minister of Silla, in accordance with the wish of King Kyŏngdŏk, carried out the construction of Pulguk-sa on the western hillside of Mt. T'oham, and Sŏkkuram stone cave shrine on the eastern hillside of the same mountain. The former is said to have been set up to pray for the good health of Kim's living parents, while the latter for the repose of the souls of his dead parents. The construction of both temples are said to have started at the same time. What Kim Dae-sŏng meant by his dead parents seems to have been his royal ancestors, who had been buried in underwater tombs in the East Sea, including King Munmu, the hero who had accomplished the great task of unification. This is why the direction of the eyes of the great Sakuya Buddha seated at the center of the stone cave shrine actually corresponds to the location of Mnmu's underwater tomb near the coast of the East Sea.

This articifial cave grotto built of stone of various sizes is much different from those of the same kind in India and China in that the latter were made by carving a natural rock wall. On the contrary, though of small size, nobody will deny that our Sŏkkuram is one of the most beautiful specimens of its kind in the Orient. Especially the great seated Sakuya Buddha in cross-legged posture on the lotus pedestal at the center of the main chamber deserves admiration as the greatest and most beautiful stone image of Buddha that was produced in the Orient in the eighth century.

On the southern and northern walls of the anteroom, eight divine generals are carved, four on each wall. Yet their sculptural technique is somewhat clumsy, tough, and perfunctory. This seems to indicate that the carving of these divine generals was part of the last stage in the construction of this stone shrine, for the completion of which several decades had to be spent. On either side of the entrance into the main hall, an image of Deva King standing on the rock pedestal is carved in relief, with two heavenly guardians are standing on each side facing the opposite counterparts. The carving method of the suits of armor worn by these guards is interesting, but even more fascinating is the unusual treatment of the images of devils who are trampled under the feet of these guardians. The posture and facial expressions of these devils are very amusing.

The great Sakuya Buddha is enshrined a little backward from the center. On the surrounding walls to the left and right of the central image, the ten Bodhisattva disciples are standing; on the innermost wall the eleven-headed Avalokitesvara is carved. This standing image seems to be far superior to its counterparts made of wood or stone in China or Japan. Of the four Bodhisattvas, the one which is standing to the right of the entrance is especially beautiful because of its splendid feel of motion, elegant fall of the drapery, and graceful expression of various personal ornaments on her slender body. Big noses belonging to foreigners are humorously depicted along with the stern facial expression of the ten disciples. Furthermore, a variety of marked individuality in the posture of each person is realistically expressed.

When the Buddhist believer finsihed his worship of the main Buddha in the anteroom, perhaps he moved into the main chamber along the right side and offered his adoration to each stone image, as is the fashion inside the Indian pagoda. To meet this demand, the position, arrangement, and facial direction of each image must have been taken into account. On the upper walls above these images eight pieces of small seated Buddhas are enshrined in each separate niche. All of them are facing forward and are graceful, classical and solemn in their features and bearing. It is regretful, however, that two Buddhist statuettes enshrined in the niche and a stone pagoda installed in the main chamber were taken to Japan. It is sincerely hoped that these artifacts could be returned to their original place of installation as soon as possible.

The vaulted ceiling of the main chamber consists of 108 pieces of stone besides projecting imposts. These ceiling stones depend on a great lotus-shaped keystone at the center. According to *The Samguk-yusa* (*Remnants of the Three Kingdoms*), the installation of this lotus keystone, which is now cracked into three parts, was one of the hardest works in the construction of this shrine. In the latest repair work, a separate tiled roof was provided upon the anteroom. This was a return to the traditional method of the construction of the stone cave shrines since the Three Kingdoms period. With the reconstruction of this anteroom, the main chamber has come to preserve a more stable atmosphere and the danger of its being exposed to weathering has considerably lessened. However, more attention and study should be made for the preservation of cave's good condition. It should be remembered that the initial purpose of the founding of this stone shrine was to pray for the heavenly bliss of the departed King Munmu and his royal clan. This reminds us of the similar history of the establishment of Chinese temples initiated by the royal household in the T'ang period. Indeed, after long years of tradition and technical evolution, the Silla stone sculpture reached its culmination in the completion of this stone cave shrine. This shrine is really one of our most valuable treasures and rare example of the Oriental Buddhist sculpture. In addition to these pieces in Sŏkkuram, some other stone images of the eighth wonderful century, which were discovered in Mt. Namsan, are now collected at Kyŏngju National Museum.

With regard to the other stone statues of the eighth century except for those in Sŏkkuram and those collected at Kyŏngju National Museum, some are scattered at various sites of abandoned temples in and around Mt. Namsan. It has been known that some seventy temples of various sizes were erected on that mountain during the eighth and ninth centuries. At many of the temples, excellent stone pagodas and statues of the eighth century are extant today. Among them, especially notable are the huge seated rock-cut Sakuya Buddha at Sangsŏn-am, Samnŭngge, and the seated stone Buddha, which has recently been removed to Seoul National Museum from its original location at Sangnŭngge on Mt. Namsan. The latter is an excellent work with its well-preserved pedestal and halo.

Moreover, on the eastern and western hillsides of Mt. Namsan not a few relics remain. Especially handsome are the Buddhist images at T'apgok which are carved on the four sides of a huge rock. The standing Sakuya Buddha is a remarkable work modelled after the central

image in Sŏkkuram stone cave shrine. The rock-cut Buddhas of the
triad and the rock-cut Buddhas on the four walls at Ch'ilpul-am, and
the seated Avalokitesvara (see *plate 15*) installed at Shinsŏn-am (a little
upward thence) also follow this pattern. The seated rock-cut Buddha at
Yongjangge has been noted for its graceful lines and classical features.
In addition, the stone Buddha at Kolgul-am in Yangbukmyŏn, Wol-
sŏnggun, is assumed to have been a product not later than the early
eithth century, though it has undergone severe weathering. Among some
other superior works of the eighth century there is a seated stone Buddha on a huge pedestal in the shape of lantern, which is now situated
in Kyŏngju National Museum. Also excellent is the octagonal stone
pedestal at Changhangri in Yangbukmyŏn, Wŏlsŏnggun, around which
are carved Buddhist images with halos.

4. Sculpture at the Late Unified Silla Period

Sŏkkuram stone cave shrine, which was the essence of the eighth
century Sillan sculpture, is believed to have been completed during the
second half part of the eighth century. After the completion of both
Pulguk-sa and Sŏkkuram stone shrine, however, the royal power and
the national security of Silla gradually began to shake and be disturbed.
This resulted in the rise of the powerful local clans.

The decline of the Silla Buddhist art including sculpture, was an
extension of the general trend that could be seen all the other Oriental
countries. This declining trend of sculpture, by joining the force of
national instability, drove the Silla sculpture toward the wane. This was
caused by the extreme concentration of strength both of the government and the people on the founding of Buddhist temples. The policy
naturally brought the weakening of national power and the slackening
of the spirit of the nation. Despite such insecure circumstances, kings,
and the nobility still were engaged in erecting many temples on a small
scale at various places either in the capital or surrounding localities.
Most of them were not state-supported but instead were built for the
purpose of praying for the prosperity of individual royal or ruling class
families. In certain cases there was bitter rivalry between royal families
in erecting temples. This resulted in the diminution in the scale of temple construction, plus sacrifices in the stolidity of the sculptural technique.

Entering upon the ninth century, this phenomenon became more

remarkable, as the propagation of Buddhism extended far into localities. Among the notable local temples, which were erected in such
a climate after the ninth century, were Donghwa-sa, Pŏbkwang-sa,
and Haein-sa. Accordingly, the scale of the stone images or pagodas
constructed there had to be reflective of such a mood of the time.
However, it should be remembered that although the scale and vitality
in stone sculpture became diminished and weakened, the compensating
delicacy in the depiction of the detailed parts improved markedly.
Especially the showy decorative touches on the pedestals or halos
became outstanding features. For one thing, though on small scale, the
seated stone Virocana (see *plate 16*) at Piro-am in Donghwa-sa is very
impressive, in that the folds of the drapery are very closely expressed,
just as the delicate and detailed figures and patterns are minutely represented on the pedestal and the halo. The same thing can be mentioned about the relics at many temples of varied sizes located in such
mountains as Mt. T'aepaeg, Mt. Chiri, and Mt. P'algong.

At the same time, however, there appeared a change in the mode of
Buddhist images. In the seventh and eighth centuries the main image
enshrined at the main hall of the temple was that of Amitabha or
Maitreya, but from the ninth century on, it gradually shifted to the
Virocana image with the gesture known as the *jikwon mudra*. On the
other hand, such a Virocana image was also cast in a huge iron statue,
a Silla speciality in the ninth century.

Again, in the ninth century, many rock-cut images were also
produced. The characteristic type of this period are the Buddhas of the
triad or a single Buddha depicted on the spacious rock surface in bold
linear carving. Belonging to this type are the Buddhas of the triad and
the seated Sakuya Buddha at Samnŭngge in Mt. Namsan (see *plate 17*).
Besides those depicted in linear carving, the other examples of this
period are various sizes of stone Buddhist images carved on rock in Mt.
Namsan and the seated Buddha carved on living rock at the entrance
to Donghwa-sa. Also numerous examples of the same ninth century
products can be found in the vicinity of Kyŏngju other than on Mt.
Namsan. Belonging to them are the seated Buddha preserved at Kyŏng-
buk University in Taegu; the Buddhas of the triad at Dudaeri, Wŏlsŏnggun; the seated Buddha at Yŏngji, Wŏlsŏnggun; the images of
the ten disciples collected at Kyŏngju National Museum; the standing
Avalokitesvara at Kaesŏn-sa; and the images of eight divine gods or

guardians carved on the pagoda body or the sides of the pedestal, which can easily be found in and around Kyŏngju.

Finally, a brief mention should be made on the vogue in this period for erecting stone pagodas or lanterns around the tomb and carving the figures of twelve zodiacal gods in relief on the stone parapets of the tomb. The figures of twelve zodiacal gods had orginally been worshipped as the guardians of Avalokitesvara, but gradually in combination with the ancient idea that the twelve zodiacal gods were related to time and direction, they came to be expressed in the formative art in the Unified Silla period. In ancient tombs in China clay icons of the twelve zodiacal gods were buried with the dead body. However, the practice that stone images of such zodiacal gods should be installed around the royal tomb in accordance with the compass direction was an original idea of the Silla people. The earliest examples of the Silla stone zodiacal gods that had been made in the eighth century were discovered at the tomb of King Sŏngdŏk. They were standing statues in round carving and placed on the square pedestals to be installed separately at each compass direction. An example of this type (an image of monkey) is exhibited at Kyŏngju National Museum. Currently this type of independent image has been replaced by the images carved in relief on the stone parapets of the tomb. Among those existing stone figures of twelve zodiacal gods are those carved on the stone parapets of the tombs of Kings Kyŏngdŏk, Wŏnsŏng, Hŭngdŏk, and Hundok as well as that of General Kim Yu-shin.

Parenthetically, some examples of such stone parapets have been found installed around the square-shaped tomb, which is a departure from the usual type of the round-shaped tomb. Among the recent discoveries belonging to this group is the damaged Nŭngji pagoda at Mt. Nang, which is to be restored to the original state in the near future. Another example of such stone parapets installed around the square-shaped tomb is one at Kujŏngdong near Pulguk-sa. The mode of these stone images of twelve zodiacal gods is divided into two types: the image wearing military uniform and that in civilian attire. The former belongs to the majority. The sculpture of these zodiacal gods also followed the modal change which had been brought about in the Silla stone sculpture in general during the eighth and ninth centuries. Inevitably, products of this kind in the ninth century also turned out to be perfunctory in their style. In addition, there were images of twelve zodiacal gods carved on the stone pagoda. Representative examples of this type are found on the two three-storied stone pagodas at Wŏnwŏn-sa in Wŏlsŏnggun. The images of twelve zodiacal gods in civilian attire are carved in relief on the four flanks (three images for each) of the upper pedestal of the pagoda. The gowns are gracefully represented. Among the images of the same kind produced in the ninth century are those in smaller size, which have been removed to Kyŏngju National Museum from Oryuri in Wŏlsŏnggun, and those made of agalmatolite unearthed at the outer periphery of the tomb of General Kim Yu-shin.

5. Conclusion

Entering upon the second half of the ninth century, the sovereign power of Silla was weakened still more, and the rise of the dominant local clans brought about the emergence of the Later Three Kingdoms. The founding of Koryŏ was attained in the tenth century, while the kingdom of Later Paekje occupied the southwestern part of the Korean peninsula and declared its independence. The showdown between the two newly emerged countries was fought at Nyŏnsan with the victory of Wangkŏn, founder of Koryŏ, who in turn succeeded in making Silla surrender to him in peace. Thus, Silla was replaced by the Koryo Dynasty, and the reign of Wangkŏn began with the profession of his political ideal "to unite the Three Hans (three ancient regional divisions of Korea) under one roof." Concurrently, the capital of Silla was officially designated as Kyŏngju. It remained a historical place of the ruined dynasty. With the pledge of loyalty of the Sillan nobility to the new dynasty, the political and cultural theatre of the nation for the first time in the long history of Korea now moved to the central area. From here a new tradition of the Koryŏ sculpture was to start.

From this brief survey we have seen that although located in the southeastern corner of the peninsula, Silla maintained its history of one thousand years and developed a remarkable art and culture of its own through a harmonious integration of its peculiar traits and imported foreign elements. Although delayed in receiving Buddhism, Silla made the most rapid and fruitful advancement in absorbing and digesting Buddhist culture among the Three Kingdoms. The attainment of the unification of the Three Kingdoms by Silla should not be measured only by the political or military aspect. Instead, the contribution of Buddhism by way of its cultural enlightenment of the public should rightly be recognized. The two stylistic specialities, the half-cross-legged, thinking-posed images of Buddha and Boddhisattva were marked features in the history of the early Silla period. These two types were an embodiment of the Maitreya adoration, which had been in vogue in the Three Kingdoms period. The extant masterpieces of this group, which we can see today, are the result of this tradition. Then, entering upon the Unified Silla period, the images of Maitreya came to be parallel in fashion with the Amitabha image. Then the Amitabha image came to occupy the position of the central figure of the temples which were erected by the special patronage of the royal and nobility clans. Pulguk-sa temple and Sŏkkuram stone cave shrine were the full maturity of this tradition.

On the other hand, there was also a fashion of constructing the Avalokitesvara image. In this connection, it should properly be pointed out that all these seated images of Buddha make the gesture known as the *bhumisparsa mudra*. The fact that the seated stone Buddhas of Silla show this *mudra* does not indicate that all of them should be regarded as the images of Sakuya Buddha. In other words, the *bhumisparsa mudra* was a common gesture of the Buddhist images in the Unified Silla period.

Again, entering upon the ninth century, the transition in the mode of worship came to reflect the disturbed state of the society. This was seen in the vogue of the Virocana image. Subsequently, in proportion to the decline of natural power, the scale and technique of sculpture underwent a marked change. Even the facial expression of Buddha changed. The symbolic expression in the Three Kingdoms period and the realistic depiction in the eighth century were finally replaced by the gradually weakened, feeble and delicate delineation. This was an unavoidable sequel to the general trend of decadence in sculpture in India and China. However, the Silla stone images, whether of the round carving or of the rock-cut, are peculiar in that they were entirely domestic products made of domestic material. No wonder the Silla stone images of Buddha merit their value and admiration for their beauty and tradition.   (Translated by Choi Jong-soo)

An Explanatory Note on the Plates

Plate 1: The stone Buddha in the Dansŏksan stone cave shrine.

Plate 2: The seated stone Bodhisattvas in the half-cross-legged, thinking posture in the Dansoksan stone cave shrine.

Plate 3: The stone Maitreyas of the triad discovered at Samhwaryŏng, now collected at Kyŏngju National Museum.

Plate 4: The stone Buddhas of the triad at Pae-ri, Kyŏngju.

Plate 5: The seated stone Buddha at Pulgog, Kyŏngju (to be enshrined in the niche).

Plate 6: The Koguryŏ gilt-bronze Buddha in the half-cross-legged, thinking posture.

Plate 7: The stone Buddhas of the triad at Kaya Pass in Sosan.

Plate 8: The gilt-bronze Buddha in the half-cross-legged posture at Seoul National Museum.

Plate 9: The gilt-bronze Buddha in the half-cross-legged posture at Seoul National Mueseum.

Plate 10: The stone Buddhas with Keyu inscription at Piam-sa.

Plate 11: The stone Buddhas of the triad in the stone cave shrine in Kunwi.

Plate 12: The Kamsan-sa Temple standing stone Amitabha.

Plate 13: The Kamsan-sa Temple standing stone Maitreya.

Plate 14: The stone Buddha and Bodhisattvas, in the Sŏkkuram stone cave shrine.

Plate 15: The seated stone Avalokitesvara at Shinsŏn-am, Mt. Namsan, Kyongju.

Plate 16: The seated stone Sakya Buddha at Piro-am in Donghwa-sa Temple.

Plate 17: The seated Buddhas carved on the living rock wall at Samnŭnggye, South Kyŏngsang Province.

TAMURA ENCHO was born in 1917 in Nara Prefecture, Japan. He was graduated from Japanese History Department of Kyushu University in 1941. A Doctor of Literature which was conferred by the University for his study on the history of Buddhism in Japan, Professor Tamura at present teaches at Liberal Arts College of the University.

He authors *A Study on the Biography of Honen Jonin*, *A Study of the History of Buddhist Thought in Japan*, and *A Study of the History of Asuka Buddhism*.

The Influence of Silla Buddhism on Japan During the Asuka-Hakuho Period

Encho Tamura

1. The Three Stages of the Asuka and Hakuho Buddhism

Three distinctive stages can be recognized in the history of the Japanese Buddhism during the Asuka-Hakuho period (from the year of the introduction of Buddhism to Japan to the year of the transfer of the capital to Heijo). The first stage lasted eighty-five years from A.D. 538, in which Buddhism was introduced into Japan from Paekche, to A.D. 622, the year of the death of Shotoku Taishi. During the first half of this period, antagonism between powerful clans took place in regard to the acceptance of Buddhism. It was after A.D. 587 (Yomei 2, Jin-pyong-wang 9), in which the strong elements of anti-Buddhism were swept away, that the golden age of Buddhism came. Japan's first full-scale Buddhist temple, the Hokoji (called Asuka-dera), appeared at the site of Asuka, and was followed by the constructions of Buddhist temples by powerful families mainly in the areas of Yamato, Kawachi, and Yamashiro. All of the Buddhist leaders in this period were the priests from Paekche and Koguryo. Among them were Heja (Koguryo) and Hechong (Paekche) who were invited to the Hokoji, Kwanruk (Paekche), and Hekwan (Koguryo).

The second stage was from A.D. 622 (the year of Shotoku Taishi's death) to A.D. 670 (Tenchi 9, Munmu-wang 10). During this period, most of the Japanese priests who had been sent to China under the Sui Dynasty in the era of Shotoku Taishi returned to Japan although a sizable number continued to go to China under the T'ang Dynasty. In other words, in addition to the contact with Paekche and Koguryo, Japan started to have the direct contact with China under the T'ang Dynasty. So-Min, who stayed for twenty-four years in T'ang, Eon, who remained for thirty-one years, and Dosho, who introduced a Buddhist sect Shoron-shu, were priests of this period.

55

The third stage lasted forty years from A.D. 670 (the year Horyuji was destroyed by fire) to A.D. 710 (the transfer of the capital to Heijo). It was in this period that the whole empire of Korea was united under the Silla Dynasty and relations between Korea and Japan became very close. The messengers from both governments were sent to each other, and the learned priests or monks of Silla crossed the sea to Japan. Myongchong, Kwanji, Byontong, and Shinge, were among those learned priests.

At first the priests from Paekche and Koguryo played a dominant part for Buddhism in Japan. The second stage was the continuation of the first. But the Japanese learned priests also returned from their studies in China under the T'ang Dynasty, and the Japanese priests continued to go there during the period of this second stage. Here, it should be noted that there was no priest from Silla as well as no priest of Japan to Silla at the first and second stages. At the third stage, the T'ang Dynasty and Japan became estranged, and Buddhism in Japan received the firect influences from Korea under the Silla Dynasty which had united the whole peninsula of Korea by that time. In reference to the Japanese history of art, the period of the first and second stage corresponds to the Asuka period, and the period of the third stage to the Hakuho period.

Let us now proceed with a general survey of the Korean Buddhism during the period which corresponds to the Asuka-Hakuho in Japan. First of all, we come across a number of names of learned priests or highly respected priests of Silla, while there is little data which clarifies the deeds of priests of Paekche and Koguryo. It is certain, however, that there were many priests in both of the latter. The lack of real evidence is perhaps due to the fact that the Silla Dynasty united the whole of Korea, thereby dominating the other Kingdom's influence. The well-known priests of Silla (under the old Silla Dynasty and the new Silla Dynasty) were as follows: Wonkwang (532–630), Chachang (608–677), Wonhyo (617–686), Uisang (620–702), Tojing (640–710), and Kyunghung (contemporary with Tojing). Wonkwang and Chachang were active in the period coincident with the Asuka in Japan. The other four priests were contemporaries of the Hakuho period. Most of the priests studied Buddhism in China under the T'ang Dynasty (or the Sui Dynasty), and accordingly Buddhism of Silla during the 7th and 8th centuries was influenced by Buddhism of T'ang (or Sui). The continuous appearances of learned priests in Silla seem to prove that there was a well established ground for Buddhist studies as well as a great number of priests who were diligent in their studies.

It can no longer be thought that Silla Buddhism at the traditionally high level had no influence upon Japanese Buddhism of the Asuka period. Although there is no historical evidence that indicates that priests went to Japan from Silla, there is information indicating that the images of Buddha were sent to Japan from Silla during this period.

According to *Nihonshoki*, the images of Buddha were sent to Japan twice from Paekche and three times from Silla during the Asuka period. There is no record of Buddha image from Koguryo (refer to the Table 1). Some of them might be questionable because of the unreliability of historical data. But it is also unreasonable to assume that only five images of Buddha were brought to Japan from Korea in more than one century. It is quite possible that there were a number of cases some of priests from Korea brought some images of Buddha with them.

Now, as you may notice in Table 1, the images of Buddha from Paekche are clearly indicated as of Sakyamuni and of Maitreya, but the images from Silla have no description as to their kinds. However, it should be noted that the images of Buddha were sent to Japan from Silla, in spite of no priest having gone to Japan, and that the images from Silla exceed those from Paekche in number. On this matter it might be speculated that there were instances in which Buddha images from Paekche and Koguryo were not particularily recorded (in *Nihonshoki*), as they were being brought over by priests from both countries, while the Buddha images from Silla were recorded since only Buddha images were sent to Japan. Also it might be considered that because the images of Buddha of Silla were quite different from those of Paekche and Koguryo, Japan asked Silla officially to send some Buddha images to Japan.

As mentioned already, the first stage Buddhism of Japan was guided and influenced by Buddhism of Paekche as well as of Koguryo. At the second stage, it was also influenced by Buddhism of the Sui and T'ang periods of China. However, this does not mean that Buddhism of Silla had nothing to do with Buddhism of the Asuka period. It did give some influence through the images of Buddha upon Buddhism of the Asuka period. When it came to the third stage, i.e., the Hakuho period, Buddhism of Silla started to have an even greater influence upon Buddhism in Japan.

2. The Image of Siddhartha and the Seated Image in Meditative Pose

There is the well-known article on the introduction of Buddhism into Japan dated the tenth month of the 13th year of the Kinmei period in *Nihonshoki*. This article contains the message from the King of Paekche to the Emperor of Japan, in which we find the words quotated from *Suvarnaprabhasottamaraja-sutra* which was translated into Chinese by Uijung in the third year of Changan era (A.D. 703). Accordingly it is obvious that this article was written after A.D. 703. The editor of *Nihonshoki* decided the thirteenth year of the Kinmei period (A.D. 552) as the year of the introduction of Buddhism, discarding the theory held by the priests of Nara that the year prior to Emperor Kinmei coming to the throne (A.D. 538) was the year of the introduction of Buddhism.

This seems to have some relation with the T'ang Buddhist theory which claimed A.D. 552 as the year representing the beginning of the latter day of Law.

The article on the introduction of Buddhism into Japan in *Nih n-shoki* was taken from the book called *Origin of the Gengoji Temple and List of Assets*. According to the article, what Sungmyong-wang of Paekche sent to Japan was not a gilt bronze statue of Sakyamuni Buddha, but (1) an image of Prince Siddhartha, (2) a Buddha image at birth and a set of the attached articles, (3) a pack of sacred texts which were inferred to be *Jatakas*, i.e., the stories of Sakyamuni's former life as well as of Prince Siddhartha.

The image of Prince Siddhartha was the seated image in meditative pose. According to the article dated the 13th year of the Bitatsu period (A.D. 584) in *Nihonshoki*, Kafuka, who returned from Paekche, brought a stone image of Maitreya to Japan which was also supposed to have been a seated image in a meditative pose. It might be concluded, from this information that Sakyamuni before his attainment of enlightenment, was the center of attention very early in Japanese Buddhism. It seemed that images of Prince Siddhartha, being different from the other Buddha images, were more agreeable to the Japanese temperament. Since Buddhism, founded in India and imported through China and Korea, was foreign to the Japanese, so were the expressions and forms of garments of Buddha images. It is also suggested that *Jatakas*, the stories of Prince Siddhartha, was a special interest to the Japanese.

The fact that the location of the pagoda is the axis in arrangement of buildings of Buddhist monastry seems also to suggest that the early Japanese Buddhism was Sakyamuni centered. Right behind a center-gate stood a pagoda where the Buddha's ash was enshrined. We find this pattern of arrangement in the Hokoji temple in Asuka, the first Buddhist temple built in Japan, as well as in the Shitennoji temple in Osaka.

An admiration for Sakyamuni and an interest in his life-story were held by the Japanese through the Asuka period. The biographic story of Sakyamuni became known to the Japanese through *Jatakas*, such as *Busshogyosan* and *Taishi-Zuio-Honki-kyo*, and thus the seated images in meditative pose seemed to become especially agreeable to them.

Images of Prince Siddhartha were made in the form of seated images in meditative pose in the ancient China. Mr. Seiichi Mizuno made a study in this matter. He states as follows: The pattern of the seated images in meditative pose, holding up the one hand on the cheek and laying the one leg on the other knee, of the Chuguji temple and the Koryuji-temple which are very familiar to us, appeared first in the caves of Yun-Kang in Shansi, China. In the 6th cave, the scene of Prince Siddhartha parting from horse, Kanthaka, is carved, representing a passage of life-story of Sakyamuni. On the stone-monument by Kwank Wongkyong of Unmil Prefecture the Prince's groom, Chandaka, as well as his horse are carved, and its inscription reads "Taehwa 16th year (A.D. 492)" and "an image of the Prince in meditative pose." Seated images in meditative pose and its background scene during the Northern Dynasty may be considered to be based on the stories in *Bussho-kyosan*. On the one hand *Kako-Genzai-Ingakyo* which remains in Japan describes Prince Siddhartha's deeds as follows: the Prince meditates when he sees a diseased, when he sees a dead, when he sees a monk, and when he is to transform himself into a monk and so on. And corresponding to this story, a picture of the Prince sitting in meditative pose is drawn on a page of this Buddhist scripture. Since suffering and thinking were thought to be a characteristic of Prince Siddhartha, seated images as well as pictures of the Prince in meditative pose seemed to be regarded adequate to describe the Prince.

All of seated images in meditative pose were regarded to be the images of the Prince in meditation, from the Northern Wei Dynasty, during which this pattern of image first appeared, until the Sui Dynasty during which its popularity declined. On the other hand, images of Maitreya were designed in the form of sitting with crossed legs during the northern Wei Dynasty, and in the form of sitting on a stool (seat) after the last decade of the Northern Chi Dynasty. Seated images in meditative pose became regarded as those of Maitreya only after the Northern Chi Dynasty (A.D. 559–575), or at least, sometime after the Eastern Wei Dynasty and the last decade of the Northern Wei Dynasty. Thus seated images in meditative pose, such as Maitreya, were introduced first into Koguryo from North China, and from there spread to Paekche and Silla. These are the main points of Mr. Seiichi Mizuno's study.

Now, Buddhism was introduced first into Koguryo in the 2nd year of the Sosurim-wang period (A.D. 372), and then into Paekche from the Eastern Chin Dynasty in the 1st year of the Chimryu-wang period (A.D. 384), and finally into Silla from Koguryo in the 14th year of Pubhung-wang period (A.D. 527). Hence, it can be inferred that images sitting in meditation were brought to Korea out of esteem for Maitreya, after Buddhism had taken hold in the Three Kingdoms of Korea.

The Bodhisattva relief seated image with the one leg on the other knee at Shinsunam, Kyongju, Korea is carved on the surface of a huge rock cliff more than one hundred feet high. The height of the image is about 1.4 meters. The thumb, middle finger and the third finger of the left hand are bent while holding a plant in right hand. The left leg is on the right knee, and the right leg is stretched down to a small lotusbase. This image is thought to have been made about in the middle of the 8th century, i.e., the middle of Silla Dynasty. This is a very rare seated image among the Buddha images at Mount Namsan, Kyongju.

The three-Buddha-images in relief on rock cliff, at Yonghyon-ri Sosan-kun, Chung-chong-namdo are 2.5 meters high with a standing image of a Tathagata in the center and an image of Bodhisattva on either side. The image at the left side is a seated image with the one leg on the other knee in meditative pose. Its height is 1.09 meters. The upper half of the body is unclothed, while the slim waist is covered with a skirt. The fingers of the right hand on the right knee touch the cheek lightly, and the fingers of the left hand are placed on the right knee. The right leg is on the left knee, while the left leg is stretched down. The skirt hangs down to the tips of the left toes. These three-Buddha-images are carved on the surface of a huge rock, and seem to have been produced in the last decade of the era of the Three Kingdoms, i.e., about A.D. 600. It is difficult to verify the names of the three Buddhas since there is no similar example of this three image pattern.

The seated image with the one leg on the other knee, (relief on rock cliff) at Sosan is a stone-image of Paekche which was made in the early 7th century. The image at Shinsunam is a stone-image of Silla which was made in the middle of the 8th century. Comparing these two images I should like to point out the significant differences. The seated image at Sosan with the right hand touching the cheek and right leg on the left knee, is a typical seated image with one leg on the other knee in mediative pose.

The seated image at Shinsunam, however, is not in the meditative pose. In other words, the former is undoubtedly an image of the Prince, but the latter may not be regarded as an image of the Prince, but of Bodhisattva. In regard to Bodhisattva painted on the 2nd wall and the 5th wall of the main building of Horyuji temple, they should be classified as the seated images with the one leg on the other knee, despite several other theories. The form of the Bodhisattva on either wall, holding up his right hand, bending the 1st, 3rd and 4th finger, and holding a lotus with his left hand stretched down, resembles the form of the seated Bodhisattva image with the one leg on the other knee at Shinsunam which does not take a meditative pose.

Table 2 owes a great deal to Mr. Ko Nakayoshi's study on the seated images with the one leg on the other knee which exist today in Korea.

From this table, the following knowledge may be derived. First, seated images with the one leg on the other knee were found in the Three Kingdoms, Koguryo, Paekche and Silla. This fact seems to prove that seated images with the one leg on the other knee, as well as Maitreya-worship, spread in the Three Kingdoms.

Second, the first 16th seated images of Bodhisattva with the one leg on the other knee listed in the table, bronze or gilt bronze, are rather small in size. Except the No. 3 image, 80.2 cm. high and the No. 4 image, 94 cm. high, all the other images are less than 30 cm. This seems to indicate that those small-scale images were produced as objects of worship for individuals. Also these are appropriate to be called the images of the Prince.

Third, it is indicated that the seated images with the one leg on the other knee were produced mainly during the last half of the 7th century, or in terms of the Japanese history, within a century from the era of the Emperor Kinmei to the era of the Emperor Kotoku. With the exception of the No. 21 image which was produced after Silla united Korea, those images were produced during the time when the peninsula of Korea was still divided. Hence, it can be inferred that the production of seated images with the one leg on the other knee rapidly decreased after the unification of the Three Kingdoms. This sudden decrease seems to indicate that change occurred in Maitreya-worship in that period.

3. Hwarang of Silla and Maitreya Worship

Maitreya worship in Koguryo and Paekche is hard to clarify because the available information is so limited. However, it is possible to discuss, to some extent, the Maitreya worship in Silla. Maitreya worship in Silla can not be disucssed without considering the *hwarang* system. First, I should like to relate the esesnce of the Hwarang system, owing to a study by a historian.

During the Silla Dynasty, there were social organizations of youth of aristocracy. Their heads were called *hwarang*. Such an organization was a social club, but its members were to be fighters in case of natinal emergency. Also, the club was the center of the members' education. A handsome young man was chosen as *hwarang*. Wonhwa, the predecessor of the *hwarang* system, was a female, but during the era of Chinhung-wang(A.D. 540 to A.D.575), Wonhwa was abolished and the *hwarang* system was establsished. A *hwarang* was beautifully dressed and was revered by the followers.

The era of Chinhung-wang came after the era of Pubhung-wang during which Buddhism was introduced into Silla. In Silla, Buddhism was first accepted by aristocracy, the same as in Japan. Pubhung-wang and Chinhung-wang took positive attitudes toward the acceptance of Buddhism. The national development of Silla Dynasty was remarkable in the era of Pubbung-wang as well as that of Chinhung-wang. Pubhungwang set up the codes of law and officially recognized Buddhism. He put Ponkaya under his control and advanced into the area of the River Naktong. Chinhung-wang extended his territory acquiring the area of the upper reaches of the River Han which was within the limits of the Koguryo Kingdom. The *hwarang* organizations seemed to play an important role in the national development of Silla.

The Maitreya-worship formed a bond between the members of the *hwarang* organizations. It was believed that a *hwarang* was the incarnation of Maitreya, and that the members would receive Maitreyas's divine protection.

A monk, Chinja, of Hungryunsa Temple was a devout worshipper of Maitreya, and he prayed for Maitreya to incarnate himself into a *hwarang*. He finally came across a handsome boy near the Yongmyosa Temple who, it is said, was respected and loved by the King later on.

The incarnation of Maitreya Bodhisattva, according to *Maitreya-Incarnation-sutra,* would appear in this land after fifty six thousand millions of years, and attain the enlightenment under the Yonghwa tree. Living beings would be saved thereby. The land where the incarnation of Maitreya would appear would be free of hostile rebels, war, famine and other hindrances. A *hwarang* was believed to be the incarnation of Maitreya whose goal was to realize such an ideal land.

We find recorded that Chukjirang was believed to be the incarnation of Maitreya. This indicates again that the belief based on *Maitreya-Incarnation-sutra* took hold in Silla, Kim Yushin, the hero of the great Silla, became a *hwarang* when he was 15 years old. Members of this organization thus called themselves the men of Yonghwa tree exclaiming that Maitreya worship formed a bond between them.

Each *hwarang* organization had its own songs and held social gatherings, such as singing and dancing parties. Most of the songs were written by monks, who likewise seemed to assume the leadership in the *hwarang* organization.

Let us now consider what type of image was regarded by the *hwarang* organizations to be appropriate for Maitreya Bodhisattva. Evidences indicate that it was the form of seated image with the one leg on the other knee in meditative pose.

The *hwarang* organizations and the seated image in meditative pose have some elements in common. A *hwarang* was a handsome young man and the members were youths, while a seated image in meditative pose expressed the young prince Siddhartha. Hence, it is quite reasonable to infer that the men of the *hwarang* organizations associated themselves with a seated image in meditative pose.

In addition, on the stone-wall of the Shinsunam cave of Tansuksan mountain, the place where Kim Yushin trained himself, we find the ten carved images, both small and large scale, of Buddha and Bodhisattva. Among them is a seated image in meditative pose. As mentioned before, Kim Yushin was revered as the incarnation of Maitreya, and the members believed in Maitreya's divine aid.

It can not be said that all of the seated images in meditative pose of Silla listed in Table 2 were associated with the Maitreya worship by the *hwarang* organizations. But most of the seated images in meditative pose were produced within a century, beginning with the era of Chin-hung-wang during which the *hwarang* system was established, to the time of Kim Yushin when Silla united the whole empire of Korea, and after which time the production of seated image in meditative pose decreased. All these seem to support the idea that the *hwarang* organizations and the seated image in meditative pose had an intimate relationship.

4. Koryuji and Shitennoji Temples

According to *Nihonshoki*, the Koryuji temple, which was also called Hachioka-dera, was founded in Uzumasa in the 11th year of Empress Suiko period (A.D. 603). The article dated the 11th year of the Suiko period in *Nihonshoki* states that the Prince (Shotoku Taishi) gave a Buddha image to Kawakatsu Hata, thereby founding the Koryu-ji in which this Buddha image was the principal one.

It is also recorded in *Nihonshoki* that Silla sent an image of Buddha in the 24th year of the Empress Suiko period (A.D. 616). However, what kind of Buddha image it was is not described.

On one hand, according to The *Koryuji-Engi* (*THE ORIGIN OF THE KORYUJI*) edited in A.D.836, the Koryuji was founded in memory of Shotoku Taishi by Kawakatsu Hata in the 30th year of the empress Suiko period (A.D. 622).

The date of Shotoku Taishi's death is the 29th year of the Suiko period according to *Nihonshoki*. But according to *Jogu Shotoku Hootei Setsu*, it is the 30th year of the Suiko period, a more likely case. Thus, it seems that Kawakatsu Hata started to build the Koryuji in the year of Shotoku Taishi's death, and that he placed the Buddha image, which Shotoku Taishi had given him, as the principal image at the Koryuji.

As for the Buddha image, we find the following record in The *Ko ryuji Shizai Kotai Jitsuroku-cho* edited in A.D. 890: "a Golden image of Maitreya Bodhisattva, 2 feet 8 inches (Japanese measurement) high, the form of expressing the Prince who holds the devine wish." The so-called Hokan (diadem) Miroku (Maitreya image) placed in the Koryuji is 2 feet 7.6 inches high. Consequently, this image can be regarded as the previously mentioned golden image. Hokan Miroku is a wooden image, but it is certain that the image was gilt wood, for such traces have been found. As a result, we may infer that the Buddha image which was said to be given to Kawakatsu Hata was this Hokan Miroku, and that this seated image in meditative pose has been the principlal image of the Koryuji Main Hall since its establishment.

In *Fuso Ryakki*, we find the following passage: "the Empress Suiko, the 24th year, the 7th month, the King of Silla sent a gilt image of the Buddha, 2 feet high, to the Empress and it was placed in the Hachioka-dera temple. This image glitters. Extraordinary things happen at times." The statement corresponds to the article dated the 24th year of Suiko period in *Nihonshoki*. In *Yamashiro-shu Kadono-gun Kaedeno-Ohi-go Koryuji Raiyuki,* edited A.D. 1499, it is recorded that the image of the Buddha and two attendants were placed at the Koryuji and that they were: (1) Miroku, gilt bronze, seated image, 2 feet 8 inches high; (2) Guze Kannon, gilt bronze, seated image, 2 feet 2 inches high; (3) Yakushi, wood, standing image, 3 feet high. The gilt bronze image of Miroku is thought to be the Hokan Miroku which exists today. The gilt wood seems to be misconceived as the gilt bronze at that time. And the gilt bronze image of Guze Kannon is thought to be the Naki (weeping) Miroku, 2 feet 2.1 inches high, which exists today, provided that the wood was misconceived as the gilt bronze. According to *Raiyuki* the image of Guze Kannon was sent to Japan from Silla, and it states that "this image glitters and extraordinary things happen at times". This assertion of *Raiyuki* corresponds to that of *Fuso Ryakki* mentioned before.

In *Shotoku Taishi Heishi-Den Zokan-mon*, edited in A.D. 1314 by Hoku of Tachibana-dera temple, we find the following article: "the King of Silla sent a gilt image to Japan and according to the *Koryuji-Ki* this image is a Miroku (Maitreya), that is, the principal image of the Main Hall, and (1) Miroku placed at the center as the principal image, gilt bronz, 2 feet high and (2) Nyoirin Kannon placed at the east, gilt bronze, 2 feet 8 inches high and (3) Yakushi placed at the west, 3 feet high and all are placed in the same small shrine". It should be noted that in this passage the gilt bronze image of Guze Kannon (Naki-Miroku) is the principal image of the Main Hall, while in the article of *Raiyuki*, it was one of the two attendants. It is quite evident that "Nyoirin Kannon placed at the east, 2 feet 8 inches" referred to Hokan Miroku.

Since the establsihment of the Koryuji, the principal image of the Main Hall has changed from Miroku to Yakushi to the Buddha and two attendants, but at any rate the principal image of the main Hall was the image of Miroku seated in meditative pose with the one leg on the other knee was given to Kawakatsu Hata by Shotoku Taishi at the time of the establsihment of the Koryuji, and the other seated images with the one leg on the other knee from Silla were also placed in the Hall.

The Hata-Clan was a group of the Korean descendants from Silla. The material of the image of Hokan Miroku is a red pine. This seems to provide a key to help support the theory that this wood image was sent to Japan from Korea. Red pine trees are usually found in Korea, although camphor and cypress trees are not.

All of this indicates that Silla, the seated images with the one leg on the other knee, and Shotoku Taishi·were mutually related in the establishment of the Koryuji.· The Shitennoji temple of Naniwa has the similar history.

According to the article dated the previous years of Sushun coming to the throne in *Nihonshoki*, Shotoku Taishi, responding to the appeal of Umako Soga, joined with the other princes and officials against Moriya Mononobe. After some bitter battles, Moriya's forces were defeated and Moriya killed. The supression of this civil war facilitated the building of the Shitennoji in Settsu with the properties of Moriya.

There is a theory derived from an article of *Goshuin-Engi* which indicates that the Shitennoji was built first in Tamatsukuri in A.D. 587, and then moved to the east of Arahaka. A.D. 587 was the year in which Moriya was killed. Moreover, according to *Nihonshoki*, the Shitennoji was built first in Arahaka of Naniwa in the 1st year of the Empress Suiko period (A.D. 593).

According to this information, the Shitennoji was built by Shotoku Taishi in A.D. 587. But the third piece suggests that it was built in A.D. 593, and that its founder is unknown. Concerning the problem of the Shitennoji's location, the second evidence indicating the change of its location to Arahaka, seems to solve the problem; that the location indicated in the first evidence differs from the one indicated in the third instance.

Still, there is another theory that claims A.D. 623 (the 31st year of the Suiko period) as the year of the first establishment of the Shitennoji. In this year, according to *Nihonshoki*, Silla sent a messenger to Japan with an image of the Buddha and other articles for a Buddhist alter. The image was enshrined in the Koryuji and the other articles, including the Buddha's ashes, the small golden pagoda and several other items, were placed in the Shitennoji. It is inferred from this information that the major purpose of the messenger from Silla was to deliver condolences for Shotoku Taishi's death to the bereaved. Likewise it is thought that the image was placed in the Koryuji along with other articles in the Shitennoji for the memory of the late Shotoku Taishi.

Considering the number of theories with regard to the year of establsihment of the Shitennoji, particularly, if the last theory is to be supported, it should be said that the Shitennoji was not built by Shotoku Taishi, but built in the memory of the late Shotoku Taishi, as in the case of establsihment of the Koryuji by the Hata Family.

Referring to the article dated the 2nd month, 4th year of Taika period in *Nihonshoki* which states that, "Abe no Ohomi asks four monks to the Shitennoji and enshrines four images of the Buddha in the pagoda," Mr. Toshio Fukuyama claims that there are no other documents which prove unquestionably the existence of the Shitennoji earlier than this period, and that the Shitennoji at the present place and in the present scale was built in the early Taika period. This article indicates the time of the completion of the pagoda as well as the time of the service held for the Buddha images.

Let us proceed to the question: what was the principal image of the Main Hall (Kondo) of the Shitennoji at the time of the establsihsment of Shitennoji? There is a quotation from *Daido-Engi* in *Taishi-Den Kokon Mokuroku-Sho*. According to this, the principal images of the Main Hall were Amida (Amitabha) and two attendants, and they were brought over by Eko, a monk from T'ang. This corresponds to the article dated the 31st year of the Suiko period in *Nihonshoki*.

The *Goshuin-Engi* tells us that the principal image of the Kondo was the gilt bronze image of Guze Kannon in the middle of the Heian period. It is not unreasonable to consider that by this image of Guze

Kannon was meant the image of Maitreya as recorded in the above mentioned quotation from *Daido-Engi*.

In *Taishi-Den Kokon Mokuroku-Sho* the following article follows the quotation: "according to *Hongan-Engi* (i.e., *Goshuin-Engi*) the image of Guze Kannon Bosatsu (Bodhisattva) was brought over from Paekche, but this image had to be of Maitreya, and so the record in *Hongan-Engi* was false." In other words, it claims that the image of Guze Kannon was actually that of Maitreya. The belief that Shotoku Taishi was the incarnation of Guze Kannon seems to induce people to regard the Maitreya image as the Bodhisattva image.

As we have seen before, according to *Daido-Engi*, Amida and two attendants were the principal image of the Main Hall. But our question is whether it had been so since the time of the establsihment of the Shitennoji. In addition to Amida and two attendants, it is recorded in *Daido-Engi* that there was "the image of Maitreya, seated on lotus." This image of Maitreya was to be the seated image with the one leg on the other knee. Although Buddha image are generally seated on lotus, it is especially noted that Maitreya "seated on lotus" in this case. This seems to indicate that the lotus pedestal was remarkably elegant. The image was thought to be the seated image in meditative pose, sitting on the high lotus with the one leg hanging down. It is recorded in *Daido-Engi* that this image of Maitreya was placed (in the Kondo of the Shitennoji) during "the Ohmi-Court-Gyou-Tenno period," that is, the Emperor Tenchi period. Mr. Toshio Fukuyama claims that this Maitreya-image was not the principal image at the time of the establishment of the Shitennoji. He contends that the period of the first construction of the Kondo of the Shitennoji was not later than the Kotoku period. However, it seems to me that he is preoccupied too much by the letters "the Ohmi-Court-Gyou-Tenno (the Emperor Tenchi) period." The Emperor Tenchi, who was called Naka-no-Ohe-no-Ohji before coming to the throne, became the crown prince of the Emperor Kotoku at the age of twenty in A.D. 645 (the first year of the Taika period), and he remained at the office of the administrator as the Empress Saimei's regent. He did not accede to the throne right after the Empress' death. He remained in the office as the crown prince for six years, then finally acceded to the throne at the Ohtsu palace in Ohmi in A.D.668. He was dead by A.D. 671. Hence it follows that the Ohmi-Court-Gyou-Tenno period lasted only four years, if it is to be understood literally.

Another question arises here: should it be interpreted that the placement of the image of Maitreya in Kondo of the Shitennoji, recorded in *Daido-Engi*, occurred within this short period? Norinaga Motoori pointed out that, "Tenchi Tenno was said to be the one, not Kotoku Tenno, who establsihed the Code of Laws at the time of the Reformation of the Taika, because this was achieved by the crown prince Naka-no-Ohe-no-Ohji's idea and will, although it occured during the Kotoku period." He seems to assume the key position in the administration of state affairs. This was the case during the next Saimei period. Accordingly, it seems quite justifiable to interpret that "the Ohmii-Court-Gyou-Tenno (Tenchi Tenno) period" means the period of twenty seven years from the year when he became the crown prince to the year of his death. Likewise, it can be thought that the image of Maitreya was placed in the Kondo sometime during this period (from the Kotoku period to the Tenchi period). From all mentioned above, it can be inferred that the principal image of the Kondo was the seated image of Maitreya in meditative pose, since the Kotoku period, which is thought to be the latest possible period of the completion of the Kondo of the Shitennoji.

In *Taishi-Den Kokon-Mokuroku-Sho* it is recorded that "the principal image in the Kondo of the Shitennoji was of Maitreya in accordance with the article in *Daido-Engi*. On the other hand, there was a tradition that this image of Maitreya and Shotoku Taishi resembled each other in shape. According to *Goshuin-Engi*, the gilt bronze image of Guzekannon placed in the Kondo was made in memory of the late Shotoku Taishi in the highest esteem and deep attachment to him by the King of Paekche. Although it is quite doubtful that the image was dedicated by the King of Paeckhe, this tradition about the resemblance between Shotoku Taisi and the seated image in meditative pose should be noted. It seems to suggest that people associated their impressions of the very image of Shotoku Taishi in his life time with the seated image in the Kondo, and expressed their deep attachment to and respect for him.

As for the question of where this seated image was made, or where this image came from, we have no means to answer at present. The image does not exist today. But, at any rate, it is quite important to note that Silla, the seated image in meditative pose, and Shotoku Taishi have a close relationship to each other concerning the establishment of the Shitennoji. The principal image in the Kondo of the Koryuji, which was established in the memory of the late Shotoku Taishi, and the principal image in the Kondo of the Shitennoji, which had the relation with Shotoku Taishi, were both seated images in meditative pose. People who had the deep attachment to Shotoku Taishi saw his very image in the seated image. This association between the seated image and the late Shotoku Taishi was seen first at the time of the establishment of the Koryuji. It should be especially noted that the image was of Silla.

5. Shotoku Taishi and the Silla Dynasty

The Yamato court maintained a pro-Paekche policy while adopting an anti-Silla policy on the whole. Under the such circumstances, Shotoku Taishi was a rare man who tried to promote the pro-Silla policy while keeping the friendly relations with Paekche and Koguryo.

He had two teachers. Heja was his teacher of Buddhism and Kakka was of Confucianism. Also, Hata Kawakatsu was one of his close associates. Heja was a Buddhist priest from Koguryu who stayed in Japan from A.D. 595 (Suiko 3, Yongyang-wang) to A.D. 615 (Suiko 23, Yongyang-wang 26). This means that he was in Japan while Shotoku Taishi was engaged quite actively in the internal administration as well as in the foreign policy.

The motherland of Kakka is not clear. He seemed to be from Paekche since he had the title of *Paksa*, 'a man of knowledge.' It can be thought that the system of granting the academic title, *Paksa*, was established in Paekche in the 6th century.

The Hata clan was of Sillan descendants. At the time when the messenger and his parties from the Silla Dynasty visited Japan, Kawakatsu Hata was appointed as the government official to receive them. In short, Shotoku Taishi had the three men closely affiliated with him: one from Koguryo, another from Paekche, and still another of Sillan descent. One might think that this happened by chance. However, to my mind this suggests Shotoku Taishi's unique philosophy, if we consider the fact that the three countries in Korea were struggling against each other at that time. Those three associates seem to be concerned with the policies made by Shotoku Taishi as well as the gathering of informations about the foreign countries. Shotoku Taishi opened diplomatic relations with the Sui Dynasty for the first time in the history, and also adopted the policy for developing friendly relations especially between Japan and Silla.

Silla overthrew Mimana in A.D. 571 (Kinmei 32, Chinhung-wang 32). After that, the relation between the government of the Yamato Court, whose intention it was to restore Mimana, and Silla became strained. In A.D. 591 (Sushun 4, Chinpyong-wang 13) an army 20,000 strong was rallied in Chikushi, Kyushu for the restroration of Mimana. With the pressure of military forces, the Yamato court opened negotiations with Silla. But then the Empress Suiko came to the throne following the murder of the reigning emperor Sushun, and in A.D. 595 the general withdrew from Chikushi. The Yamato Court appeared to give up the policy toward Silla in terms of military forces, but the policy was unchanged. The troops crossed the sea to attack Silla in A.D 600 for the cause of supporting Mimana against Silla. After Japanese army withdrew, Silla attacked Mimana again. In A.D. 602 the Yamato Court appointed Kume-no-Ohji who was Shotoku Taishi's brother by the different mother, as the supreme commander for an army of 25,000 strong that rallied for the subjugation of Silla. However he died in Chikushi, and the government appointed his brother, Tagima-no-Ohji as the supreme commander. Once again personal misfortune intervened when his wife died. Soon thereafter, the fighting was stopped. Thus in the earlier time of Shotoku Taishi's administration, Japan and Silla were opposed to each other, even with war breaking out between the two countries. However, Japan and Silla became friendly around A.D 605 when Shotoku Taishi moved to the Ikaruga Palace. In A.D. 608 (Suiko 16, Chinpyong-wang 30) a great number of people migrated from Silla into Japan, as Silla was invaded by Koguryo. In A.D. 610 Silla sent a messenger to Japan, and on this occasion, the government of the Yamato Court welcomed him by appointing an official for receiving him and another official for dining with him.

In A.D. 611 a messenger was dispatched to Japan from Silla. In A.D. 616 Silla sent an image of Buddha, and in A.D. 621 sent another courtier to Japan. Throughout this period, Japan did not take military action against Silla. In A.D. 622 (Suiko 30, Chinpyong-wang 44), Shotoku Taishi died, and in the following year, messengers from Silla were sent to Japan, carrying with them an image of Buddha and some other articles for Buddhist shrine. But within the same year the

Mimana problem came to the fore again, and Japanese forces, tens of thousands strong, crossed the sea and attacked Silla. At this time, there were two parties in opposition at the Yomato Court. One encouraged moves to be taken to solve the problem, insisting on negotiation with Silla; the other supported the military measures. The government sent messengers first to both Silla and Mimana to open the negotiations. But then the militarist party became influential and the government sent an army to Silla. Soga Umako seemed to fail in keeping the militarist party under his control. At any rate, the pro-Silla policy was changed to the policy of taking drastic measures against Silla after Shotoku Taishi's death,.

On the one hand, Japan and Paekche became estranged after A.D. 608 when Japan's pro-Silla policy became obvious. From that year to the year of Shotoku Taishi's death, A.D. 622, a messenger from Paekche was sent only once to Japan in A.D.615 (Suiko 23, Mu-wang 16). Even on this occasion he did not seem to come on a particular mission to Japan, but merely accompanied the returning Japanese messenger, Mitasuki, who had been sent to T'ang.

Silla was ruled by Chinpyong-wang during those days. Buddhism was flourishing at his court, as might be inferred from the fact that his father's name, i.e., Tongryun-wang, was derived from Buddhist sutra and his mother was called Maya. He reigned for 53 years, from A.D. 579 to A.D.631. He established close relations with Sui, as the learned priests such as Chinmyung, Wonkwang, Damyuk and others, went to Sui. The culture of Silla was enriched by the contact with other mainland cultures. It can be said that Shotoku Taishi recognized in the cultures of Silla a civilizing agent of prime importance to his country, and therefore tried to maintain the friendly relations with Silla, controlling the militarist party against Silla at the Yamato Court.

As mentioned before, no priest was sent to Japan from Silla, not only in the era of Shotoku Taishi but up to that time. We can not say that Buddhism of the Asuka period was influenced directly by the Buddhism of Silla which differed from Buddhism of Paekche. However, as we have seen, it can not be denied that Shotoku Taishi changed the diplomatic policy of the Yamato Court by promoting the pro-Silla policy, and that this led to the messenger from Silla delivering condolences to his death. The images of Bodhisattva and other Buddhist articles for shrines, which were brought over with them, were placed in the Koryuji and the Shitennoji. Those seated images of Bodhisattva in meditative pose became the objects of worship in the memory of the late Shotoku Taishi, and eventually became the center of the Taishi worship which spread widely.

6. The Hakuho Period and Silla

In A.D. 660 (Saimei 6, Muyol-wang 7) Emperor Kao Tsung of T'ang sent his army to attack Paekche, complying with the request of Silla. Kim Yushin of Silla and his army attached Paekche at the same time. Saja fell first and Uija-wang of Paekche surrendered to Silla in July, thus overthrowing the Paekche Dynasty.

At this time, the Yamato Court decided to support Paekche, complying with its pleas. Saimei Tenno and Crown Prince Naka-no-Ohe moved to Chikushi and took the command of the army. More than ten thousand men and a great amount of food and arms were sent to Paekche. When the movement for the restoration of Paekche became active, and Yopung, the prince of Paekche, residing in Japan, was called back to his country to accede to the throne. But in A.D. 663, Japanese navies were defeated at the battle of River Paekchon-kang and the armed forces of Paekche were destroyed. The war was over.

With the defeat at Paekchon-kang, Japan faced a crisis: the chance of armed aggression of the allied forces of T'ang and Silla. The government stationed the armies for coastal defense and arranged signal fires in Tsushima, Iki, and Chikushi. Three fortresses were established in Chikushi for the defense of Dazaifu, two fortresses (one in Nagato and another in Yashima) for the defense of the inland sea of Seto, and another fortress near Yamato for the defense of the region of Yamato. Just before and after the fall of the Paekche Dynasty many people of Paekeche took refuge in Japan. Some of them were appointed to the important posts in the government as experts in the fields of military strategy, medicine, Confucianism and law. There seemed to exist a deep gulf between the families of the Paekche-descendants who settled down in Japan and the people of Silla who united the whole empire of Korea. It is quite legitimate to say that this anti-Silla sentiment of the people from Paekche influenced the Yamato Court in framing Japan's policy towards Silla. After A.D. 667 (Tenchi 6, Munmu-wang 7) the messengers from Silla were sent to Japan almost every year, but the Yamato Court was so cautious that they were received and entertained in

Chikushi, where the local government of the Yamato Court was located. It was only after A.D. 690 (Jito 4, Shinmun-wang 10) that the messengers from Silla were received in Naniwa. This particular attitude toward receiving the messengers from Silla seemed mainly due to Japan's defense strategy, and partially due to the opinions of the refugees from Paekche.

Nevertheless, the friendly relations between Japan and Silla were about to be developed at the same time, for a new situation which forced Silla to adopt the pro-Japanese policy was developing in Korea. In A.D. 668 (Tenchi 7, Munmu-wang 8), the allied forces of T'ang and Silla overthrew the Koguryu Dynasty. Immediately after that, the struggle between T'ang and Silla began. Silla asked T'ang for the military aid to unite the whole empire of Korea under the Silla Dynasty, and T'ang sent the armed forces to Silla complying with the request. However, T'ang had an intention of establishing its domination over the whole Korea from the beginning. After Paekche and Koguryu were overthrown, the armed forces of T'ang did not withdraw from Korea, but went into battle with the army of Silla. In A.D. 676 (Tenmu 4, Munmu-wang 16), Silla succeeded in driving back the enemy from the area of the River Han, and established its domination over the whole empire of Korea.

The relationship between Japan and Silla once was so strained that they fought battles with each other, but the conflict between T'ang and Silla accelerated the growth of friendly relations between the two countries. The change took place in A.D. 668 (Tenchi 7). In the 9th month of that year Bojang-wang of Koguryo surrendered to the allied forces of T'ang and Silla, closing the history of the Koguryo Dynasty. In this same month Silla sent the messenger, Kim Tong-um, to Japan. The Minister Nakatomi-no-Kamatari presented a boot to Kim Yu-shin, the hero in the cause of uniting the whole empire of Korea. Tenchi Tenno presented Munmu-wang with a ship. The Yamato Court appointed two officials to accompany the messenger home to Silla in the 11th month of the same year.

Subsequently, messengers from Silla visited Japan almost every year, and Japan sent her messengers to Silla. In A.D. 676 (Tenmu 5, Munmu-wang 16), the first Japanese ambassador and his assistants to Silla were appointed. It was said that in A.D. 709 (Wado 2, Sungduk-wang 8), the Minister Fujiwara-no-Fubito met with Kim Shinbok, the messenger from Silla, in the government building in the capital, and he told the messenger that no messenger from Silla had ever talked with the Ministers of Japan before, and that the reason he was talking with him was to promote the friendly relations betweenthe two countries. All the contemporary evidence suggests that Japan maintained the friendly relationship with Silla under the guidance of Fujiwara-no-Kamatari and his son, Fubito, during the Hakuho period. Excepting this time, the friendly relations between the two countries seemed not to be maintained. Japanese Buddhists took very positive attitudes for learning Buddhism of Silla during this particular time of the Hakuho period. Within this time, A.D. 670 to A.D. 710, Japanese priests who went either to T'ang or Silla and returned to Japan either from T'ang or Silla were twenty-four in all. Among them, eight priests went to T'ang and fourteen to Silla. The two priests, Dokyu and Shogyo took unknown journeys. If we exclude Doji and Gyozen who returned home after the change of the capital to Heijo, and if we exclude Chiho, Chiran and Chiyu whose existences might be questioned, Chiso, Gitoku and Jogan who seemed to have contacts with Buddhism of Silla, and Bensho who died abroad, from the list of the priests who learned Buddhism in T'ang, then we must say that there were no priests who returned home from T'ang within this period. On the contrary, with the exception of Yamada-no-fuhito-mikata who returned to secular life, all of the others (13 of them) about whom we do have reliable date, introduced the culture as well as knowledge of Buddhism of Silla to Japan. One further example corroborates this point. In A.D. 689 (Jito 3, Shinmun-wang 9), the messengers from Silla came to Japan in order to express condolences on the Emperor Tenmu's death, and with them Meiso and Kanchi who had learned Buddhism in Silla, returned to Japan. The Yamato Court gave one hundered forty pounds (in Japanese measurement) of cotton each to Meiso and Kanchi to be sent to their teachers and friends of Silla who took care of them.

During this period, the prominent Buddhist priests such as Wonhyo, Uisang, Tojing, Sungjang, Dunryun, Hyeton, Myongrang, and Sungjon were active in Silla. It was the time Buddhism flourished in Silla. In Kyonju, the capital of Silla, many Buddhist temples were constructed. Among them, there are 31 temples whose name and vestiges can be identified, and 30 temples whose vestiges are fairly clear.

The two pagodas were built at both sides, left and right, of the Buddhist monastry. This arrangement was originated in Silla during this period. In A.D. 679 (Tenmu 8, Munmu-wang 19), the construction of the Sachunwangsa Temple, in the hope of driving back the T'ang invasion, was completed, and in A.D. 682 (Tenmu 11, Shinmun-wang 2), Kamunsa Temple which was to be the temple for the late Munmu-wang was constructed. The former had the two pagodas of wooden buildings and the latter had two pagodas of stone biuldings. Those pagodas were built one at the east side and another at the west side in the precincts of each temple. The Yakushiji of Asuka seems to be built following this plan of arrangement.

Japanese Buddhist reacted quickly to the movements of Buddhism of Silla. They followed the Buddhists of Silla to regard *Mahaprajnaparamita-sutra* and *Suranaprabhasottamaraja-sutra* as the important scriptures. Hosso-shu (a sect of Buddhism) was also introduced to Japan from Silla. It can be also inferred that the art of carving images was introduced to Japan from Silla.

It has been generally accepted that the Hakuho arts were traced back to the T'ang art in the early years of T'ang Dynasty, but we should attach importance to the Japan's relations with Silla. For example, during the Hakuho period, only once the messenger was sent to T'ang in A.D. 702, while the Yamato Court took the positive policies to improve the relations between Japan and Silla. In short, I should like to propose to re-examine the influences of the Silla Buddhism as well as of the T'ang Buddhism upon Buddhism of the Hakuho period.

(Translated by Hakunin Matsuo)

Table I **Buddha Images from Korea**

Dynasty	A.D.	Tenno Year	Emperor Year	Image
Paekche	A.D. 552	Kinmei 13	Sung-wang 30	Sakyamuni, Gilt bronze
	A.D. 584	Bitatsu 13	Uideuk-wang	Maitreya, Stone
Silla	A.D. 579	Bitatsu 8	Jinpyong-wang 1	Buddha image
	A.D. 616	Suiko 26	Jinpyong-wang 40	Buddha image
	A.D. 623	Suiko 31	Jinpyong-wang 45	Buddha image & its articles
Koguryo	—	—	—	None

Table II **Seated Image (with the one leg on the other)**

No.	Name of Image	Height	Year of production	Place of production
1	Seated Bodhisattva Gilt Bronze	17.5cm.	6th Century	Koguryo
2	Seated Bodhisattva Bronze	28.5cm.	Last half of 6th century	unknown
3	Seated Bodhisattva Bronze	80.2cm.	End of 6th century	Silla
4	Seated Bodhisattva Bronze	94.0cm.	Early 7th century	Paekche
5	Seated Bodhisattva Gilt Bronze	21.0cm.	Last half of 6th century	Silla
6	Seated Bodhisattva Gilt Bronze	14.2cm.	Early 7th century	Silla
7	Seated Bodhisattva Gilt Bronze	16.6cm.	Early 7th Century	unknown
8	Seated Bodhisattva Bronze	16.4cm.	First half of 7th century	Paekche
9	Seated Bodhisattva Bronze	9.4cm.	First half of 7th century	unknown
10	Seated Bodhisattva Bronze	10.0cm.	End of 6th century	unknown
11	Seated Bodhisattva Bronze	10.0cm.	Early 7th century	unknown
12	Seated Bodhisattva Gilt Bronze	15.1cm.	First half of 7th century	unknown
13	Seated Bodhisattva Bronze	14.2cm.	Second half of 6th century	unknown
14	Seated Bodhisattva Bronze	12.2cm.	Early 7th century	Silla

15	Seated Bodhisattva Bronze	12.4cm.	Early 7th century	unknown
16	Seated Bodhisattva Bronze	23.5cm.	End of 6th century	Paekche
17	Seated Bodhisattva Stone	126cm.	Middle of 7th century	Silla
18	Seated Bodhisattva Stone	41.0cm.	End of 7th century	Silla
19	Seated Bodhisattva Rock Cliff	110cm.	Early 7th century	Paekche
20	Seated Bodhisattva Rock Cliff	280cm.	Middle of 7th century	Paekche
21	Seated Bodhisattva Rock Cliff	140cm.	Middle of 8th century	Silla

Table III
Priests studied abroad, in T'ang or Silla, who returned home during the period from the Tenchi era to the Monmu era

No.	Name	Year of departure	Ship	Year of return	Ship	Country	Reference
1	Joe	A.D. 653	—	A.D.665 (Tenchi 4)	T'ang ship	T'ang	Joe-Den
2	Myoi	—		A.D. 668		T'ang	Nihonshoki
3	Hosho	—	—	A.D. 668 (Tenchi 7)	—	T'ang	Nihonshoki
4	Dokyu	—	—	A.D. 671	T'ang ship	—	Nihonshoki
5	Kanjo	—	—	A.D. 685	—	Silla	Nihonshoki
6	Unkan	—	—	A.D. 685 (Tenmu 14)	—	Silla	Nihonshoki
7	Chiryu	—	—	A.D. 687 (Jito 1)	—	Silla	Nihonshoki
8	Meiso	—	—	A.D. 689 (Jito 3)	—	Silla	Nihonshoki
9	Kanchi	—	—	A.D. 689 (Jito 3)	—	—	Nihonshoki
10	Chishu	A.D. 653	—	A.D. 690 (Jito 4)	Silla ship	T'ang	Nihonshoki
11	Gitoku	A.D. 653	—	A.D. 690 (Jito 4)	Silla ship	T'ang	Nihnoshoki
12	Jogan	—	—	A.D.690 (Jito 4)	Silla ship	T'ang	Nihonshoki
13	Yamada-Fubito-no Mikata	—	—	—	—	Silla	Nihonshoki

78

14	Bentsu	A.D. 693 (Jito 7)	—	A.D. 696 (Jito 10)	—	Silla	Nihonshoki
15	Jinei	A.D. 693 (Jito 7)	—	—	—	Silla	Nihonshoki
16	Doji	A.D. 701 (Taiho 1)	—	A.D. 718 (Yoro 2)	—	T'ang	Shoku-Nihongi
17	Gyozen	—	—	A.D. 718 (Yoro 2)	—	Silla	Nihon-Ryoiki
18	Chiho	A.D. 703 (Taiho 3)	—	—	—	Silla T'ang	Sangoku-Buppo-Denzu-Engi
19	Chiran	A.D. 703 (Taiho 3)	—	—	—	T'ang	Sangoku-Buppo-Denzu-Engi
20	Chiyu	A.D. 703	—	—	—	T'ang	Sangoku-Buppo-Denzu-Engi
21	Bensho	A.D. 701–703 (Taiho era)	—	deceased abroad	—	T'ang	Kaifuso
22	Giho	—	—	A.D. 707 (Keiun 4)	—	Silla	Shokunihonki
23	Giho	—	—	A.D. 707 (Keiun 4)	—	Silla	Shokunihonki
24	Soshu	—	—	A.D. 707 (Keiun 4)	—	Silla	Shokunihonki
25	Jijo	—	—	A.D. 707 (Keiun 4)	—	Silla	Shonkuihonki
26	Jotatsu	—	—	A.D. 707 (Keiun 4)	—	Silla	Shokunihonki
27	Shogyo	—	—	—	—		Shokunihonki

AHN KYE-HYON was born in Seoul in 1927. He was graduated from Department of History, Tongguk University and continued his study of the history of Buddhism in Korea at the graduate school. He started teaching at Tongguk as an assistant professor in 1959. At present he holds a professorship at the History Department of the university. During the while, he went to Harvard-Yenching Institute to study history of Buddhism for a year, and visited India to inspect Buddhist relics in 1972 under the sponsorship of the Indian Council for Cultural Relations and also participated in the International Sanskrit Conference in New Delhi. He is now the curator of University Museum at Tongguk.

He has published *History of Ancient Buddhism in Korea* (1970) and among his many articles are "The Buddhist Cultural Relations Between Koryo and Mongol" (1959), "Yi Saek's View on Buddhism" (1965), "The Bodhisattva Thought of the Silla People" (1970) and "Monk Army in the Early Yi Dynasty" (1972).

Publication of Buddhist Scriptures in the Koryo Period

Ahn Kai-hyon

The art of printing, together with the celadon ware epitomizes the culture of Koryo. Printing developed as a result of the need and desire to supply and preserve Confucian and Buddhist texts and other books, but it was also greatly stimulated and influenced by the appearance of printed matter imported from abroad.

The art of printing developed in Koryo represents an important landmark in the history of printing. During the early period of Koryo, wooden blocks were used exclusively. In later periods metal types were gradually introduced. Among the books printed in Koryo Buddhist literature occupies the most prominent place. This should come as no suprise, since Buddhism constituted the ideological basis of Koryo life and thought. As early as 946 (the first year of King Jungjong), the state set aside 50,000 sacks of rice in order to provide funds for the promotion and popularization of Buddhist literature throughout the country. It ordered every Buddhist temple to establish a special foundation called the 'Treasury for Buddhist Sutras' that printed and preserved Buddhist classics. As Buddhist temples grew both in their economic strength and political influence in the later period of the Koryo dynasty, the pace of printing Buddhist literature was even more accelerated. Sometimes, a huge amount of Buddhist books was published as a state undertaking, while individual Buddhist temples vied with one another in printing holy books.

1. The Koryo Tripitaka

Tripitaka refers to a collection of Buddhist writings edited in accordance with certain standards. The Sanskrit word, *tripitaka*, originally signified three baskets(*pitaka*). Thus, Tripitaka denotes three baskets into which the three catagories of Buddhist literature—the sutras, commandments, and theoretical treatises—have been divided. As Buddhism spread to China, an enormous amount of Buddhist literature was translated from Sanskrit into Chinese. A monk of Eastern China, Tao-nyan (314–385) compiled a catalog of Buddhist sutras published since the Han period. Subsequently, his work was continued by various other persons, resulting in many different catalogs. Of these the most systematic and complete is the one published in 730(the eighteenth year of Kaiyüan of the T'ang dynasty) by Chi-sheng. This catalog, known as the *Kaiyüan Annotated Catalog,* lists a total of 5,048 books, dividing them into 480 boxes labeled from No. 1(Tian) to No. 480 (Ying), following the order in which the Chinese characters appeared in the *Book of One Thousand Characters.* Thus the first 60 boxes, bearing labels from No. 1(Tian) to No. 60(Nai), contain 600 books of *Mahaprajnaparamita-sutra.* In 800(T'ang, Chengyüan 16th year), Yüan-chao published the *Chengyüan Catalog* which listed additional 259 books not appearing in the *Kaiyüan Catalog.*

In China the first printed edition of *Tripitaka* appeared during the Sung dynasty. Of the various editions, the *Kaipao Printed Tripitaka,* also known as the *Shu Printed Tripitaka* is most highly valued as the finest fruit of Sung Buddhist culture. It has also served as model for all subsequent Chinese translations of the *Tripitaka.* This one contains all of the 5,048 books and 480 boxes of Buddhist scriptures listed in the *Kaiyüan Catalog.* It took twelve years, from 971(the fourth year of Kaipao) to 983(the eighth year of Taiping Hsingkuo), for completion. Somewhat later in the reign of King Chent'zung (998–1003) of the Sung dynasty, sutras listed in the *Chengyüan Catalog* were printed together with those which had newly been translated under the Sung dynasty.

a. The Old Koryo *Tripitaka*

After the introduction of Buddhism into Korea, a large quantity of Buddhist sutras was brought into the country in various shipments. None, however, could impress the people of Koryo more favorably, whether in scope or organization, than the *Kaipao Printed Tripitaka,* which was brought home to Koryo by Han Un-kong in 991 (the tenth year of king Sungjong). In 1022 (the thirteenth year of King Hyunjong), Hanjo brought from Sung 538 additional Buddhist works, supplementing the content of the *Kaipao Printed Tripitaka.*

The thirteenth year of King Hyunjong was a time when Koryo was enjoying a brief respite from the Khitan invasions which had been plaguing the land incessantly since his accession to the throne. Yet there was no certainty of when another invasion might start. Four years earlier, Hyunjong had an enormous national shrine called Hyunwhasa built in order to commemorate his parents who had been put to premature death on charge of having given birth to an illegitimate offspring. It was just half a year after the completion of Hyunwhasa that the Koryo general Kang kam-chan was able to defeat Khitans. Consquently, peace treaty was signed between the two countries. To Hyunjong who had had to face the ordeal of the struggle for succession to the throne alone as a young orphan, and then to cope with the scourge of constant Khitan invasions after his accession, the erection of Hyunwhasa in memory of his parents, and the successful repulsion of the Khitans which followed, was no conincidence. Seeking the salvation of his parents' soul became an obssession with him.

Hyunjong decided to elevate the dignity of Hyunwhasa even further by compiling and publishing a *Tripitaka* of his own, using as its basis the *Kaipao Tripitaka*. For this purpose he established at Hyunwhasa a special treasury for the printing of *Mahaprajnaparamitrasutra* and printed one by one such sutras as *Avatamsaka, Suvarnaprabhasottamaraja* and *Saddharmapundarika*. In building the temple and printing Buddhist books, Hyunjong was not only motivated by a wish to safeguard his country against foreign enemies with the help of Buddha, but also by a desire to demonstrate to everyone the cultural achievement of Koryo as an independent nation. Still another purpose to be served, undoubtedly, was the consolidation of political power in his hands with the help of the Buddhists.

The project of printing a new *Tripitaka* was started in the tenth year of Hyunjong and was finally completed in 1087(the fourth year of Sunjong). The *Tripitaka* comprising a total of 6,000 books was named the *First Koryo Pitaka*. The blocks which had been used for its printing were later transferred to Buinsa temple where they perished in the fire caused by the Mongol invaders in 1232(the 19th year of Kojong), together with the printing blocks for the *Koryo Supplementary Pitaka*.

b. Koryo Supplementary Pitaka

The *Koryo Supplementary Pitaka* was the work of Daekakkuksa

Uichon (1055–1101). It is composed exclusively of treatises and commentaries which are written on books of all three catagories: the sutras, commandments, and treatises. This was the first time in the Buddhist world that an attempt was made to publish such a supplementary pitaka.

From 1073, when the printing of the *First Koryo Pitaka* was nearing completion, to 1090, Uichon devoted himself to the task of collecting Buddhist commentaries not only from all parts of Koryo but also from foreign countries such as Sung and Liao. The three major categories of books—the sutras, commandments, and treatises—had been collected and printed in many different editions. There was, however, no authoritative edition of the various commentaries written on them, and there was a danger of losing the scattered works for good unless special efforts were made to preserve them. It was Uichon's idea to collect these and publish them for the benefit of posterity. It was for this purpose among others that Uichon undertook a journey to Sung and studied Buddhism there. The *New Complete Catalog of Various Religious Scriptures*, also known as the *Uichon Catalog*, which was published by him in the seventh year of Sungjong, was a complete listing of all the commentaries he had collected.

The first book of the three-volume catalog lists 561 kinds and 2,586 books of commentaries written on sutras such as *Avatamsaka, Mahaparinirvana, Saddharmapundarika, Lankavatara, Vimalakirtinirdesa, Suvarnaprabhasottamaraja* and *Mahaprajna*. The second volume contains 142 kinds and 467 books of commentaries on books of commandments such as *Brahmajala-sutra, Yi Kiao King, Dhamagupta-vinaya* and *Sarvastivada-vinaya*. The final volume covers 307 kinds and 1,678 books of commentaries on theoretical tracts such as *Mahayana sraddhotpada-sastra, Che Moho Yen Louen, Vijnaptimatrasiddhi-sastra, Yogacaryabhumi-sastra* and *Nyayadvratarka-sastra*. Most of the 1,010 kinds and 4,740 books listed in this *New Complete Catalog* are works of Chinese scholars, especially of the Sung period. But it also contains 119 kinds and 355 books written by the Buddhist scholars of Silla such as Wonhyo, Uisang, Taihyun, Kyungheung, Uijuk, and Woncheuk. Moreover, there are 39 kinds and 190 books by twelve Khiten Buddhist monks such as Hsian-lien, Chue-yüen, Fei-chuo, Fa-wu, and Lao-yen.

The *Uichon Catalog* is greatly valued even today not only because of its comprehensive and impartial character, but also because of the special service it has rendered in preserving at least the titles of commentaries written by the Silla and Khitan monks which have all perished.

After the completion of his catalog, Uichon set up at Heungwangsa temple a bureau for publication of scriptures, and undertook the project of printing one by one the commentaries listed in his catalog. Once published, this *Supplementary Pitaka* was distributed to all parts of Koryo and even overseas to Sung, Liao, and Japan.

The *Supplementary Pitaka* was a fine embodiment of Oriental culture. Unfortunately, these books printed by Uichon have not been preserved. In 1232, about hundred and thirty years after the publication of the *Pitaka*, Heungwangsa temple was burned in the confusion caused by the Mongol invasion and the government's attempt to remove its seat to the Kangwha Island. Over four thousand wooden printing blocks were reduced to ashes. A small number of them survived until the reign of King Sejo of the Yi dynasty when an attempt was made to repair them. It is from these renovated pieces that we can get a picture of what they were like in their original form, *Mahaparinirvana-sutra,* authored by the T'ang monk Fa-pao, *Treatise on Saddharmapundarika-sutra* by another T'ang Buddhist Huei-ching and *Treatise on Avalokite-shvara* written by Khitan scholar Ssu-hsio (all of which are now being preserved at Songkwangsa temple) cite Heungwangsa as the place of publication, and bear such year names as Suchang and Daian, the Khitan way of designating the year. This was the same method used at the time of Uichon. Therefore, one gets the impression that these books might have constituted a part of the *Supplementary Tripitaka* published by Uichon. On closer examination, however, these all turn out to be later printings based on the original. Although we have no record of the original editions, the following publications issued by the Publications Bureau of King Sejo are all reprints which had used as model Uichon's own editions.

Treatise on Yogacaryabhumi-sastra, 35 Vols. (Compiled by the T'ang monk, Chi-chou)
Treatise on Avatamsaka, 10 Vols. (Compiled by Li T'ong Hiuan, T'ang era)
Treatise on Mahayanasraddhotpada-sastra, 3 Vols. (Compiled by the Sung monk, Tseu-siuan)

Collected Commentaries on Dhamagupta-vinaya, 6 Vols. (Compiled by the Khitan monk, Ch'eng-yen)

Commentaries on Mahavairocana-sutra, 7 Vols. (Compiled by the Khitan monk, Chüe-yüen)

Original copies of the *Supplement to Tripitaka* printed by Uichon are extremely difficult to come by. A rare find is the original 40-volume Uichon edition published by the T'ang Buddhist Ch'eng-huan in 1094, now being preserved at Todaiji temple in Japan. The four-volume *Commentary on Che Mo Ho Yen Louen* authored by the Khitan monk Chi-fu was also printed by Uichon, and then was brought to Japan in 1105, six years after its publication.

The influence of Khitan Buddhism on the publication of Uichon's *Supplement* was tremendous. Although trade between the two countries suffered from political restrictions, exchange of Buddhist culture proceeded without any hinderance and bore very important fruits. In Khitan also the publication of the *Kaipao Printed Tripitaka* in China gave rise to a desire to compile and publish a *Tripitaka* of its own. The *Khitan Tripitaka*, the work which was begun under King Hsingtsung, was completed and distributed in the next reign, that of King Taotsung. This *Tripitaka*, divided into 579 boxes in all in its organization did not follow the *Kaipao Tripitaka* which had relied upon the *Kaiyüan Catalog*. Instead, it was guided by *A New Edition Cotalog of Pitaka* and edited by Ke-hung.

The Buddhism cultivated by the Khitan scholar-monks was different from the Sung variety. Influenced more by the Northern Chinese Buddhist school, the Khitan Buddhists had established a tradition of much more solid and precise scholarship. The *Khitan Tripitaka* which was the fruit of long years of their concentrated efforts contains such books as *Cho Mo Ho Yen Louen* and *Yi Tsie King Yin Yi* which in China itself had long been suffering from neglect. The latter is a dictionary edited by the T'ang monk Huei-lin which covers all of the Buddhist literature listed in the *Kaiyüan Catalog*.

The *Khitan Tripitaka* was brought to Koryo in 1063, about ten years after its publication. Among other Buddhist works which were brought to Koryo from Khitan there were many works by monks. *Treatise on Surandama-sutra* by Fei-chuo, *Supplement to Yi Tsie King Yin Yi* by Hsi-lin, and *Long Kan Shou Jing* by Hsing-chün are only some of the more widely known examples. The last item mentioned, a dictionary, enjoyed such great popularity that it was reprinted even in the Yi dynasty. Out of the Khitan Buddhist books known in Koryo Uichon had selected overthirty-nine kinds and 190 books for inclusion in his *Supplement*. It was in Uichon's edition that *Commentary on Che Mo Ho Yen Louen* au thored by the Khitan monk Chi-fu was introduced to Japan from Korea, and six volumes of *Treatise on Avatamsaka-sutra* by another Khitan monk, Hsien-lien, were brought into Sung where importation of books directly from Liao was strictly forbidden. The vital role which Koryo played in the exchange of Buddhist culture, in particular books, is most clearly illustrated by the fact that *Che Mo Ho Yen Louen*, originally a Chinese work included in the *Khitan Tripitaka*, was reintroduced to China in Uichon's printing. The ten-volume *Supplement to Yi Ts'ie King Yin Yi*, which the Khitan monk Hsi-lin compiled in accordance with the *Chengyüan Catalog*, was included not only in Uichon's *Catalog*, but also in the *Restored Koryo Tripitaka*. It stands out as a shining monument to the Buddhist culture of Khitan.

c. The Restored Koryo Tripitaka

In 1236, four years after the burning of the printing blocks for the first *Koryo Tripitaka* and the *Supplementary Tripitaka*, the task of republishing the *Tripitaka* was begun at Kangwha and Jinju with the establishment of the *Tripitaka* Publications Bureau. As is indicated in a statement by Yi kyu-bo issued in the following year, the republication project was undertaken as a result of the national wish of the Koryo people to repel the foreign invaders with the aid of Buddha's power. The project was finished in 1251 after sixteen years of dedicated work. A special pavillion was built outside the West Gate of Kangwha City in order to house the printing blocks. The *Koryo Tripitaka*, now being preserved at Haeinsa temple, is this *Restored Koryo Tripitaka*. It is not clear when the printing blocks were moved from Kangwha to Haeinsa. We only know that they were moved from Kangwha to Seoul in 1398 (the seventh year of King Taejo of the Yi Dynasty), and that in 1399 there was a printing of the *Restored Koryo Tripitaka* at Haeinsa.

When the printing blocks used for the *Restored Koryo Tripitaka*, popularly referred to as the *Koryo Tripitaka*, were examined in 1915, it was discovered that only a few blocks were missing. A well-known contemporary calligrapher, Kim Don-hee, was hired to write out the missing parts, and new blocks were carved to complete the set. Except for this, the original 81,137 blocks have been preserved intact since the time of King Kojong of Koryo. The total number of books included in the *Restored Koryo Tripitaka* number 1,511 kinds and 6,805 volumes. Of the five editions of *Tripitaka* issued since the time of Sung, the 5,740 volume Ssu-chi Edition of *Tripitaka* and the 6,362 volume Chi-sha Edition of *Tripitaka* are the only ones still to be found in complete sets. This makes the *Restored Koryo Tripitaka* the most comprehensive collection of Buddhist books after the 7,182 volume Hung-fa edition of the *Yüan Printed Tripitaka*. The 6,805 volumes are divided into 639 boxes numbered from No. 1 (Tian) to No. 639 (Dong), following the order in which these characters appear in the *Book of One Thousand Characters*. The contents of each of the boxes in detail are:

a. Box No. 1–No. 480.... Books listed in the *Kaiyüan Catalog*
b. No. 481–No. 510...... Sutras newly translated into Chinese during the Sung dynasty
c. No. 511–No. 515...... the Khitan book, *A New Edition Catalog of Pitaka*
d. No. 516–No. 520...... Royal publications of the Sung dynasty such as the *Chanted Hymn on Saddharmapundarika* selected by King Taitsung of Sung.
e. No. 521–No. 560...... Books selected from the *Chengyüan Catalog*
f. No. 561–No. 563...... Corrections to the *Koryo Restored Tripitaka*.
g. No. 564–No. 567...... *Mahaparinirvana-sutra*
h. No. 568–No. 570...... *Fo Ming King*
i. No. 571.............. Index to the *Restored Koryo Tripitaka*.
j. No. 572–No. 585...... *Fa-yüan Chu-lin*
k. No. 586–No. 628...... Sutras newly translated into Chinese under Sung.
l. No. 629.............. *Supplement to Yi Ts'ie King Yin Yi*
m. No. 630–No. 639...... *Yi Ts'ie King Yin Yi*

Although the sutras listed in the Chengyüan Catalog were included in boxes from No. 521 to No. 560, *Fo Min King* is encased separately into boxes No. 568–570, while the Khitan publications, *Treatise on Paramarthu* and *Che Mo Ho Yen Louen* are in boxes No. 554 and No. 555 respectively. The editor of the *Restored Koryo Tripitaka* was Sukee. He collated the first *Koryo Tripitaka* with the Sung edition of the *Kaipao Printed Tripitaka* and the Khitan edition of the *Khitan Tripitaka*, and corrected errors. It is for this reason that the content of the boxes from No. 1 to No. 480 of the *Restored Koryo Tripitaka* is somewhat differently edited, although the material is organized in exactly the same fashion as in the first *Koryo Tripitaka* and *Kaipao Printed Tripitaka*. The four-volume work, *Collected Treatises of Fo-tao Lun-heng*, contained in Box No. 464, gives a fine illustration of the care with which Sukee edited the words. This book, edited originally by the T'ang monk Tao-hsien, is a collection of essays on state policies in regard to Buddhism and Taoism from the time of Emperor Mingtsung of the late Han period, to the time of King Kaotsung of T'ang. But the Koryo, Sung, and Khitan editions of the same work differed both in content and organization. While the Koryo and Sung editions included the seven items relating to the time of Kaotsung of T'ang in the third volume, and ten items relating to the time King Taitsung and the *Conversion of a Taoist into Buddhism*, written by Kuo Hsing-chen in eight chapters of the fourth volume, the Khitan version's third volume contained ten items relating to the time of King Taitsung of T'ang. In addition, both the seven items belonging to Kaotsung time and the *Conversion of a Taoist into Buddhism*, were placed in the fourth volume consisting of 34 chapters. Considering the fact that Kuo Hsing-chen published his *Conversion* in the time of Kaotsung and that the essays in the *Collected Essays on the Ways of Buddha* are arranged in the chronological order, it is clear that the Koryo and Sung editions had the arrangement confused. Sukee, therefore, corrected the second Koryo edition on the basis of the Khitan model and filled in missing parts as well. In the case of works such as *Samyuktagama* contained in Box No. 270, he discarded the Koryo and Sung versions altogether and followed the Khitan version.

Sukee chose to rely primarily on the Khitan edition because of its excellence. Therefore, the *Khitan Tripitaka* played a vital role in the publication of the *Restored Koryo Tripitaka*. The thirty-volume *Special Record of the Collation of the Restored Koryo Tripitaka*, which was published as a part of the *Tripitaka*, contains a detailed record of how the work of collation was done and sheds much light on the now lost *Khitan Tripitaka*.

The *Koryo Tripitaka*, now being preserved at Haeinsa temple, has been recognized from an academic point of view, as the greatest, of all extant *Tripitaka* in Chinese translation. Not only was the *Khitan Tripitaka* excellent in itself, but also serious efforts had resulted in minimization of errors in printing. One of the special services rendered by the printing of the *Restored Koryo Tripitaka* is the preservation of such books as *A New Edition Catalog of Pitaka*, *Treatise on Paramartha*, *Mo Ho Lo Yen Louen*, *Yi Ts'ie King Yin Yi* etc. These had been a part of the *Khitan Tripitaka*, but they would have been lost for good to the Buddhist world had they not been included in the *Koryo Tripitaka*. The *Khitan Tripitaka*, now lost, is receiving recognition among Buddhist scholars, thanks to the inclusion in the *Koryo Pitaka* of parts of its contents.

Haeinsa also houses fifteen kinds of supplementary printing blocks for books such as *Tsong King Lou*, *Tsu Tang Chi*, *Treatise on Vajrasamadhi-sutra*, *A Collection of Zen Koan*, which were made by the *Tripitaka* Bureau of Kojong of Koryo. Though not formally included in the *Koryo Tripitaka*, they are still extremely valuable. In particular, the twenty-volume *Tsu Tang Chi*, edited by the Venerable Cheng-hsiu of T'ang period, is the oldest historical source on the Succession of Buddhist school, now that a complete edition of *Pao Lin Chuan* is no longer available. *Tsu Tang Chi* became known to the world again only thanks to the supplementary printing blocks of Haeinsa. Religious contact between the two states had proceeded in spite of the clashes of political interests and produced important results.

Toward the end of Koryo and beginning of the Yi dynasty, Japan sent eighty requests for *Tripitaka* in exchange for a promise to put an end to the Japanese pirates raiding coasts and to help return Koreans taken captive by these pirates. In 1423, the fifth year of King Sejong, she even placed request for the printing blocks for the *Koryo Tripitaka* now found at Haeinsa. Sejong, not being aware of their value, considered complying with the Japanese request, but was stopped thanks to the objections raised by his ministers. The Japanese representative, frustrated in his attempt, went into a hunger strike.

The *Restored Koryo Tripitaka* is not only an important part of the cultural heritage of the Korean people, but also a significant landmark in the history of *Tripitaka* printing and development of Buddhist scholarship. It was not by coincidence that James Legge, in publishing an English translation of Fa Hien's work *Fo Kuo Chi*, under the title *A Record of Buddhistic Kingdoms*, in 1896, used the *Koryo Tripitaka* version as his original text.

2. Books Published by Individual Temples

Besides the *Tripitaka*, which was published as a state enterprise, many books were published by individual Buddhist temples with the money donated by the devoted. These books shed much light on the religious life of the common folk and the degree of understanding they possessed of various Buddhist dogmas. As they usually give clear indication of the date and place of printing, and the name of the publisher, these privately published books are especially helpful in bibliographical studies. The illustrations which most of these books contain at the beginning of each book also serve as an important material in the study of Buddhist thought, art, and graphics.

a. Books at Haeinsa Temple

Haeinsa now has altogether 11,139 printing blocks which are not related to the *Koryo Tripitaka*. Most of these were made during the Yi dynasty period, but there are a few dating from the Koryo period. Among these, the *Sipmunhwajnngron* edited by Wonhyo was published in 1098 (the third year of Sukjong) by the monk at Haeinsa, Sunghun. The *Baikhwa-dojang-palhyonmun* edited by Uisang was printed in 1328, also by another monk belonging to Haeinsa, Chewon. Chewon also edited the *Hwaumkyung-Kwanjajeamposal-sosulpubmunbyol-hengso-byungjif-yakhae* and had it printed in 1331.

In addition, Haeinsa also published the *Longevity Dharani-sutra* and *Inchonbogam* in 1278 and 1290 respectively. It is not clear exactly when the *Collected Works of Uichon* was printed, but it was sometimes after 1132. The *Commentary on Avatamsaka-sutra*, edited by Chenghuan, was reissued on the basis of the original included in the *Koryo Restored Tripitaka*.

The *Surandama-sutra in Small Letters* published at Haeinsa in 1295 draws our special attention because it mentions in its postscript the Sung monk Chie-huan, and his work, *Commentary on Surandama-sutra*. The fact that Chi-huan's work was singled out among all the commentaries written on that sutra clearly indicates that this was the most widely used of them all. It is noteworthy that another commentary written by the same man, *Interpretation of Saddharmapundarika-sutra* (the Lotus-sutra), also has enjoyed special popularity in Korea since the Koryo days.

b. Books published by Other Temples

The composition of *Interpretation* by Chi-huan took place between 1119 and 1126. The author who had written commentaries on many Buddhist sutras from a Zen and Avatamsaka point of view, also tried to interpret Avatamsaka and Tien-tai as a unified whole. His understanding of Buddhism as a connected body of teachings was congenial with the Korean mind, and his commentaries were all written in clear and concise manner. This explains the great popularity which his books such as the *Interpretation of Saddharmapundarika-sutra* and *Interpretation of Surandama-sutra* enjoyed in Koryo. The *Saddharmapundarika-sutra*, which was published in 1240 most likely at Sungbulsa temple in Hwanghae Province, is not different in content from the *Interpretation*.

The tenth year of King Kongmin (1361) saw the publication at Wonam-sa temple in Chonju of *The Three Sutras on Buddhist Masters* which is composed of the *Sutra in Forty-two Chapters, Yi Kiao King* and the teachings of the Venerable Wei-shan. The *Bhadrapala-sutra* was also published in his reign at Manilsa temple. A collection of Dharani entitled *Sanskrit Book of Dharani-sutra* was issued by Kaetaesa temple in 1218. An even earlier work on Dharani was the *Ratnakaranda-dharani-sutra* published at Chongjisa temple in 1007.

The custom of burying the *Dharani-sutra* in the pagoda together with a relic of Buddha dates from the Silla times. But the *Ratnakaranda-dharani-sutra* instead of the *Won Keon Tsing Koung Ta Jo Lo Ni King* was placed in the pagoda in Koryo thanks to the influence of Ch'ien Hung-ch'u (940–978), king of Wuyüeh, who, following the example set by King A'soka of India, had 84,000 small pagodas erected, and who placed in them the *Ratnakaranda-dharani-sutra*.

For the purpose of spreading Buddhist faith, Manuisa temple published, around the time of King Chungsuk (1314–1330), *Inspirational Experiences of Buddhists*. In 1379, *Argument in Defense of Buddhism* written by Chang Shang-ying of Sung in 1110 in order to refute Han Tuei-chi's attack on Buddhism, was published. Yi Saek wrote a postscript to this *Argument in Defense of Buddhism* in sharp contrast to another late-Koryo man, Chung Dojun, who was a vociferous anti-Buddhist.

Books belonging to the Zen school of Buddhism and sayings of the Zen Buddhists constitute the largest number among books published in Koryo times and survived. The sayings of Kyunghan (1299–1375) was published in 1378 at Chiamsa temple under the title *Baikunhwasang-orokjip* and the sayings of Haekeun(1320–1376), *Naonghwasangjip* was printed in 1379. The most representative of the Zen books publish-ed in Korea, *Sunmunyumsongjip*, and *Sunmunbojangrok* were printed in 1243 and 1293 respectively. The former was authored by Haedam, the second generation of Jokye order, and the latter the work of Chonjung, the fourth generation of Paekryun order. The teachings and corres-pondence of the Sung monk Tsungkua were published in 1378 and 1387 respectively, the former at Chongryongsa temple of Chungju. The *Tseu Men King Hiun*, edited by Chi-hsien, was first introduced to Korea in 1348 but was not published here until thirty years later, in 1378. When the *Liu-Tsu T'an Ching* was published in Koryo in 1207, Chinul wrote the postscript at the request of Tamyon. The same book was reissued under the kings Chungryul and Chungsuk, in 1300 and 1316. All these editions were based on originals imported from Yüan. A careful com-parison of the 1316 edition with a Yüan edition of 1290 shows many discrepancies both in content and organization. This was due to the fact that there were many different printings of the same book in China itself. The relationship which the Koryo version bears to the Yüan original indicates the manner in which the Zen school of Buddhism spread to Korea.

After the introduction of the *Treatise on Vajraprajna-sutra*, a work edited by Huei-ting toward the end of the dynasty, the *Vajraprajna-sutra* became a popular subject of study among Buddhist scholars. The above-said *Treatise* was printed also in Koryo in 1378, the fourth year of King U-wang. The date of publication is given as the eighth year of Hsienkwang. Hsienkwang was the designation for the year being used in Northern Yüan at the time. The fact that Koryo was still following the Northern Yüan's way of counting years could have been a reflection of the sympathy which the people of Koryo felt towards Yüan King Chaotsung, who had been chased out of his country by the recently risen might of Ming, and towards his mother who was a Koryo woman.

c. Stories of Inspirational Experiences

Among the Buddhist books published in Koryo, there were many collections of stories dealing with inspirational experiences. Although these do not contain profound philosophy and usually run counter to commonsense experience, they can not be lightly dismissed since they provide us with graphic examples of how Buddhist faith manifested itself in real life.

The *Inspirational Experiences of Buddhists* was published in the reign of King Choongsuk at Manduksa temple in order to spread the Lotus Faith. Lotus Faith meant cultivation of the teachings contained in the *Saddharmapundarika-sutra* (Lotus-sutra) and practising them in real life. The ninety or so stories in the *Inspirational Experiences* had all been selected from Chinese sources and therefore mainly reflect the life experiences taking place in the Chinese context. Yet the same book also contains some stories drawn from the spiritual experiences of Korean Buddhists from the Silla times on. It was so popular among Koreans that reprints were made in 1534 and 1544 at Munjusa temple of Kochang and Sukwangsa temple of Anbyun. The *Inspirational Experiences* enjoyed special popularity probably because it told many stories concerning the Bodhisattva. The charitable qualities of that Bodhisattva were extolled not only in the *Lotus-sutra*, but also in the *Avatamsaka-sutra*. It was for the purpose of spreading the faith in Bodhisattva that Chewon of Haeinsa temple in 1331 selected special portions from the *Commentary on Hengwon Chapter of Avatamsaka-sutra*, authored by Ch'eng-huan of T'ang and published the above-mentioned *Hwaumkyung*. Twenty inspirational stories, which Chewon included with his own notes, were new ones not duplicating any of the known stories concerning the Bodhisattva. The five inspirational stories contained in the *Treatise on Vajoraprajna-sutra*, published in 1378, were also instrumental in spreading the Diamond Faith which seeks the salvation of the deceased.

d. Books Printed With Metal Type

The invention of metal type towards the end of the Koryo dynasty brought about a revolution in the technique of printing from wooden blocks. The preface to a Buddhist song book called *Nammyongchon-songjingdoga*, published in 1239, clearly indicates that metal types had been in use before that date.

Among the books printed in Koryo with metal types are *Baikun-hwa-sangchorok-Buljojikjishimcheyojol* and *Chongyangsunjong-simyo-bupmun.* The former, which is also known by another title, *Jikjishim-kyung* was edited by Kyunghan and was printed in 1377. The latter was also printed around that time at the request of a high official of Yüan, Piepu-hua who wanted to distribute the book widely among his people with the aid of the advanced printing technique of Koryo. This fact throws much light on the nature of cultural exchange which went on between the two states. In 1305 Koryo had to send at the request of Yüan one hundred monk-copiers. Clearly, the development of copying and printing techniques in Koryo was a matter of enormous interest to Yüan.

The technique of printing with metal type, which was thus intro-duced to Yüan from Koryo, was then brought to Europe by way of the Arab world. It was only in 1453 that the more advanced movable type of Johann Gutenberg was introduced.　　(Translated by Lee In-ho).

YOM MU-WOONG was born in 1941 in Kongju, Chungchung-Namdo Province. He was graduated from German Department of Seoul National University and its Graduate School. As an active literary critic and an editor of the quarterly *Changjak gwa Bipyong* (Creative Work and Criticism), he has been widely known. In addition to his literary activities, he teaches at Duksung Women's College.

He has many literary articles to his credit, among which are "The Present Condition of Farmers and the Current Literature", "On the Literature in 1930's", "The Liquidation of the Colonial Literature", and "A Treatise on National Literature in Korea".

The Life and Thought of Han Yong-woon

Yom Mu-woong

Han Yong-woon, Manhae by Buddhist name, is already well-known as one of the 33 representatives of the nation at the time of March 1 Independence Movement of 1919, as the outstanding poet of *The Silence of My Beloved,* and as one of the great monks of the recent past. There has also been a great amount of interest on his life and achievements, and since the 1960s a considerable volume of research on him has been published largely as independent books and articles. Recently a collection of his works has been compiled and reissued. But considering the depth of his personality and thought, we can only say that research on Han Yong-woon has just begun, and the problem of how to follow him today has not been given the extensive study it deserves. This article aims at surveying the personal, philosophical and literary developments of Han Yong-woon, and at a true assessment of his importance as poet, thinker and patriot.

1

Han Yong-woon was born on the 29th of August, 1879 in Hongju County (the present Hongsung County) in Chungchong Namdo Province as the second son of Han Eung-jun. As is well known, it was a time when the bureaucratic and feudal Yi Dynasty had lost the Confucian ideal of its early days, and was in a phase of fatal decreptitude resulting from the corruption of bureaucratic aristocrats and the internal abuses of the system. The Yi Dynasty had failed to absorb the progressive reform-oriented ideas of the "School of Practical Learning" that emerged in the 18th century, and had been weakened by repeated commoners' rebellions initiated by the Revolt of Hong Kyong-rae. Even worse, the country had become the target of the invasion of powerful Western capitalism. The Treaty of Kangwha Island concluded three years before Manhae's birth was another event signifying the surrender of a backward feudal nation to the invasion of Western imperialism.

But the corrupt feudal rulers, instead of trying to confront the invading powers, tried to comport with the intentions of one of the foreign powers, thereby suppressing the people's uprisings and ensuring personal safety and power.

Born in such an era, Manhae began his education in the usual way, which was to learn Chinese letters in his village academy. Up to the age of eighteen Manhae had learned all the regular Confucian textbooks, including the *Four Books* and the *Three Classics*. He is also said to have perused, during this period, the Chinese romances and plays such as, *The Romance of the Three Countries*, and he reputedly showed a special capacity for appreciation of such popular literature.

In 1896, his eighteenth year, he left his home to enter the Oseam Monastery in Soraksan Mountain. There for five years, he read Buddhist canons intensively. Researchers have so far made the following observations on Han Yong-woon's family background and his reasons for entering the Buddhist temple: that his family had belonged to the scholar-literati class for generations, his father, grandfather and great grandfather all having held positions of civil service; that his father and his elder brother had joined the voluntary loyal uprising led by Min Jong shik and were sentenced to death after defeat; and that Manhae had joined and fought in the Tonghak Movement at eighteen and had to seek shelter in the Oseam Monastery at Soraksan Mountain after the movement failed.

But we cannot help having some doubts about these contentions, not simply from respect for historical accuracy, but for a more accurate understanding of the formation of Manhae's personality. First of all, the question must be raised about whether his family had really been of the scholar-literati class for generations. Upon this point Mr. Ahn Byung-jik has already established appropriate doubts and offered his views. (cf. Mr. Ahn's "Independence Thoughts of Han Yong-woon".) Considering all, Manhae's family seems to have belonged, not to the bureaucratic aristocrats or the literati class, but to the "middle men" class with some culture and economic capability. His father probably had been a petty official of a provincial town. Later on in life Manahe had said, "When in my home-town I had heard a lot of wise words from my father. Looking up from his books, father used to call me up to him and taught me the words and deeds of the heroes and saints in history, and also told me about the circumstances of the world and the organization of states and societies." (Cf. his essay "From Siberia to Seoul".) Considering also his own activities of later life, we might surmise that Manhae's father had been a somewhat unusual member of the country intelligentia of the "middle men" class who did not have to keep himself bound by the traditional feudal, Confucian world philosophy. Not infrequently after the 18th century, some of the unsuccessful Yangbans were degraded into the farmer class, and some farmers advanced to the ruling class. Thus, the boundary between Yangban and the farmer class was partly eroded. We can easily imagine that Manhae's father might have stood somewhat on the boundary. Manhae's later activities are certainly not unrelated to such a family background.

We should turn now to the theory that his father and elder brother had died after taking part in the voluntary loyal uprising led by Min Jong-shik. In general, the voluntary loyal uprisings toward the close of the Yi Dynasty had had three great surges: the murder of Queen Min and the Topknot Act of 1895, the Protective Treaty of 1905, and Emperor Kojong's demise of throne and the disbandment of army in 1907. The uprising of Min Jong-shik took place from early March to late May 1906. Then, if Manhae's father and brother had died around 1896, as is popularly supposed, they could not have participated in the uprising of Min Jong-shik. It was such men as Kim Bok-han, Ahn Byung-chan, and Yi Se-yong who led a revolt in Hongju in early 1896. These men and their followers did not receive very heavy punishments after their arrests. The fact of their having led the revolt in protest against the murder of the queen has served as extenuating circumstances. Therefore, it is possible that Manhae's father and brother had received death punishments in consequence of the second uprising of the Tonghak Army in 1894, or of the uprising of Min Jong-shik's loyal revolt in 1906.

In regard to Manahe's joining the monastery, the prevalent theory is that he had joined the Tonghak Rebellion at age eighteen (1896), had accomplished brilliant military feats (including the theft of military funds to the amount of a thousand pieces of gold from the treasury of Hongju County), and after its failure had to hide himself in the Oseam Monastery as the temple cook. This contention is indeed very doubtful. It is a historical fact that beginning the winter of 1895 loyal uprisings took place in all parts of the country, and that the struggle was especially fierce in Hongju around February of 1896. The uprising that occurred in many parts of the country at that time was complicated in character, so that the government itself admitted it could not discern whether they were Tonghak revolts or indignant loyal uprisings. (cf. p. 152, Volume IV of *The History of the Era of King Kojong* by the National History Compilation Committee.) Anyway, it is evident that the armed uprising of the period was not a mere revolt of farmers such as the Tonghak uprising originally had been. Moreover, the military activities of Kim Han-bok and others of 1896 was not a revolt against the feudal oppression carried out for the purpose of abolition of the feudal system, but a struggle for maintenance of the feudal and Confucian ideals. Therefore, it is naturally doubtful that Manhae had joined the Tonghak revolt in the same year and assumed a leading role.

On the other hand, it seems plausible that he might have joined the indignant uprising of Kim Bok-han. If so, as it was in the early part of April that the indignant army leaders such as Kim Bok-han, Ahn Byung-chan and others were arrested by Magistrate Yi Sung-woo of Hongju County, it is possible that Manhae fled to Soraksan Mountain around this time.

During his five to six years in the Oseam Monastery, he studied the Buddhist scriptures, and also seems to have absorbed some modern culture. He read history and geography, and especially through the early modernized Chinese philosophers he became acquainted with the views of Bacon, Kant and other Western thinkers. Around this time he came down from the monastery with the hope of making a world tour, and went to Vladivostok. But because of persecution he had to return to Korea, after which he toured many places before venturing back to his hometown in early 1904.

But in the summer of 1904 he left his hometown again. His wife, whom he had married at fourteen by his parents' orders, gave birth to a son a few months after he left, toward the end of 1904. He never visited his hometown again, and when afterwards his son sought him out, Manhae is said to have been extremely cold to him. We can never know why he, who insisted on the monk's right to marriage, and who himself remarried in later years, had been so cold to his first wife and son until the end. Anyway, he became a monk on January 26 of the next year in the Baekdamsa Temple in Inje County, Kangwondo Province, when he was given the Buddhist name of Bongwan by priest Kim Yon-gok. Afterwards, he succeeded Manwha Sonsa of the Konbongsa Temple, and received the investiture name of Yong-woon and the Buddhist name of Manhae.

2

Manhae, born as the son of a country intelligentia with a strong sense of justice in a period of decay of the Yi Dynasty, thus settled down as Buddhist monk after more than ten years of schooling in Chinese letters and a brief period of active participation in affairs of the times. All the developments of his thoughts and deeds after 1905 were circumscribed by Buddhist monkhood. Therefore, if we are to come to an adequate understanding of Manhae, we ought to know Buddhism and especially the course of Korean Buddhism during his period.

After he became a monk, he studied the Buddhist scriptures intensively, and also immersed himself in meditation. For about six months, from May of 1908, he went to Japan, and there surveyed many temples in Tokyo and Kyoto. He observed the new developments in Japan, and also audited Buddhism and Western philosophy lectures for three months at the Gomazawa College in Tokyo. It was during this period that he met and became friends with Choi Lin, then a student in Japan. In the autumn of 1911 he went to Manchuria, but having incurred the suspicions of some Korean young men, was shot. He escaped near death and returned to Korea.

Anyway, Manhae learned about the rapidly changing world through his travels, absorbed modern knowledge, and concluded that mankind is something that marches forward toward civilization. With such realization at the basis of his life, he wrote the great dissertation keenly analyzing and condemning the backwardness, stagnation and hermitism of Korean Buddhism of the times, "For the Revitalization of Korean Buddhism".

The book, published in 1913, is not a theological exposition of the Buddhist truths from a scholarly viewpoint, but a proposition of practical methods for improvement of the state of Buddhism in Korea. Nevertheless, because of that very practical intent, this dissertation not only grasped the conditions of Korean Buddhism of the day accurately, but also accurately comprehended the truths of Buddhism itself. In it, all Manhae's education, thoughts and observations are made manifest in the form of criticism on the state of Korean Buddhism. Also clearly outlined in it are all his later developments as thinker, activist and man of letters.

In this dissertation consisting of seventeen chapters are set forth his concrete opinions on the problems Korean Buddhism of the day had to face and solve. The first to the fourth chapter deals with Manhae's concept of Buddhist truths which ought to be the basis for solutions of the temporal problems Buddhism faced at the time. It is this first part that is of most interest to us. This writer, being completely ignorant of Buddhism, cannot judge how accurately Manhae understood the Buddhist truths, and perceived the realities of Korean Buddhism. But there is no doubt that his world philosophy as set down in the form of Buddhism is truly outstanding. His philosophy as expressed in this dissertation can be summed up roughly in three ideas.

First, Manhae maintains: "Hereafter the world will not cease to progress, until it attains the true ideal of civilization." And he raises the question of whether Buddhism will be appropriate to the future civilization of mankind. If Buddhism is not appropriate to future civilization, he suggests Buddhism will not be able to survive even if there comes a religious reformer like Martin Luther. In this regard, Manhae contends, Buddhism is the very religion that is most suited to the ideal of civilization, and it is a religion of awakening and widsom. He raises the question. 'Why do we believe in a religion?' That is for no other reason than that religion gives men hope for the future. If not for such a hope everyone will be content to live in comfort day after day and would not bother about conscience and idealism and consequently the world will become a hell full of barbarians. It is with this in mind that Christianity invented the idea of Heaven, and Judaism and Mohammedanism that of God and eternal life. But these are from first to last a deception and a superstition. How can anyone lead people to awakening through deception?

Buddhism, on the other hand, is a religion that leads men to awakening away from the myths and superstitions that impose unjust limitations on the wisdom of men. Then, the question becomes, what is the way to teach the mass wisdom and give them hope without resorting to such unnatural concepts as heaven and eternal life? Buddhism teaches that there is in everybody's mind the ultimate potential (the Buddhist nature or the true self) for attaining the ultimate truth. "The mass have in each of them this invaluable treasure and yet are ignorant of this fact, so that our merciful Buddha preached to them for their awakening," Manhae said. Therefore, he further asserts, Buddhism teaches men to attain immortality in the true and eternal self, and illustrates the way to hope and attainment of truth not through superstition but through abnegation of that useless state.

Second, Manhae stressed that the Buddhist teaching is based on egalitarianism. Equality is the opposite of inequality. If we look at the world of visible phenomena, there is nothing in the world that is not unequal. Among the sages some have died young, some have been put to death, and some among the heroes have died in exile. Others have ended up as kings and presidents. Some in the world are strong, some are weak; some are virtuous, and some are vicious. To look at the world from the viewpoint of equality means to escape the bondage of the inequality of phenomena, and to look with the eye of truth. Manhae detected in modern liberalism and cosmopolitanism the historical realization of Buddhist inequality. He was convinced that the world will continue to progress until it reaches the complete realization of equality. Manhae maintains that the egalitarian ideal of Buddha extends not only to individuals and countries, but also to all things and events.

Third, Manhae explains that one other outstanding characteristic of Buddhism lies in salvationism. Well, what is salvationism? It is an idea opposed to selfish individualism whose chief goal is self-interest and individual happiness. There is a popular misunderstanding that Buddhism is a religion whose end resides in the awakening of the individual through meditation and asceticism. But Buddhism is a religion that stands in direct opposition to this kind of self-centeredness. Manhae stresses that the preaching of Buddha was full of mercy for the unawakened mass. One might surmise that such understanding of Buddhism is based on the scriptures of the Greater Vehicle Buddhism such as, *Prajna-paramita-sutra*. Anyway, through his new interpretation of Buddhism, Manhae became an enlightenment-minded progressivist, and he had absorbed modern liberalism and rationalism into the Buddhist concept of equality, while at the same time rejecting individualism that can easily accompany liberalism.

What we must not overlook is that Manhae's desire to destroy the stagnation and backwardness of Korean Buddhism around the turn of the century had been the soil on which his concepts of Buddhism were formed. From the first, he was against blaming the stagnation of Korean Buddhism on things like fate and providence, and emphasized that we human beings are the ones who cause things to happen and who lead affairs to success. Therefore, he stressed that for the proper progress of Korean Buddhism, it is imperative that the outmoded and inappropriate conventions be boldly demolished. As a matter of practice, he urged the closing of prayer rooms in temples, moving temples from the isolation on hillsides to populous towns, and lifting of the demand for celibacy of monks—all truly revolutionary ideas at the time. The basis of such concrete revolutionary propositions lay in his concept of Buddhism which can be summed up as progressivism, egalitarianism, and salvationism. For example, here is his passage on the practice of meditation or Zen:

> I find the practitioners of Zen very strange indeed. The meditators in the past tried to keep their minds quiet, but the meditators of today keep their dwelling places quiet. The meditators of the past kept their minds static, but the meditators of today keep their bodies static. If one keeps one's dwelling place quiet, one cannot but become misanthropic, and if one keeps one's body static, one cannot but become self-righteous. Buddhism is a teaching of salvationism and the leadership of the masses. Then, how can it but be wrong for a follower of Buddha to pass into misanthropy and self-righteousness?

Manhae also insisted that monks cannot spend all their time meditating and reading scriptures sitting in a temple, but should produce their own food by their own labor. From his following passage we find that Manhae had considerable knowledge about the theory of the value of labor and the economic basis of social inequality.

> Since several centuries monks have been greatly repressed and have not been given due regards as human beings. It is undeniable that one of the prime causes for it is that they were clothed and fed without earning them. This corresponds to the idea of profit sharing discussed by economists of today. It is needless to say that such profit sharers are harmful to fellow human beings and to their countries. It is the labor of weaving that gives people the right to wear clothes, and it is the labor of tilling that gives people the right to eat. Therefore, if one wears clothes without weaving, then he cannot but be wearing what other people have woven. If one eats without tilling, then he cannot but be eating something other

people have grown. In case one gets clothed and fed without weaving and tilling, then he must repay with a production of his own equal in value to what he wears and eats. It is only then that there will be no resentment between him and other people and that there will be no defect in the overall economy. If there is one who eats and wears garments without giving anything in payment, then he is simply consuming a portion of the efforts of those who till and weave, and from the viewpoint of the overall economy also there is a deficit of one man's labor. As the increase and decrease of the labor force of the mass and the development or retrogression of economy is in direct proportion to the number of profit sharers, profit sharers are the thieves of production. Therefore, it cannot but follow that they will be repressed by the producers and it is only logical that they will have no words of excuse for their plights. If one is supported by others without making a similar contribution of his own, then it means that one's rights of survival lies not with oneself but with others.

Here we find already clearly outlined in "For the Revitalization of Korean Buddhism" all of Manhae's philosophy. Therefore, the development from the Buddhist philosopher Manhae to the national independence fighter may be said to be a direct linear outgrowth. And his philosophy is not so much a result of quiet reading and meditation as of his fervent desire for breaking away from the hermitism and backwardness of Korean Buddhism of the times through his sturdy activism. We can read in Manhae's interpretation of Buddhism and his ideas for revolution of Korean Buddhism a succession to the thoughts of the School of Practical Learning and School of Modernization, and also influences of the modern Western thinkers. (In fact, in "For the Revitalization of Korean Buddhism" such thinkers as Plato, Descartes, Bacon, Kant, Rousseau and Hegel are either quoted or examined.) But above all, Manhae is a Buddhist, an inheritor of the tradition of monks Wonhyo and Jinul, a product of the turbulent Yi Dynasty in the process of dissolution caused by the feudal aristocrats' long exploitation of the masses, and of the legacy of invasion by the foreign imperialist powers.

3

It was also through active struggles, not through passive meditations, that Manhae discovered the historical realities of colonial Korea. That struggle took the form of a counter-movement against the intrigues of pro-Japanese monks led by Lee Whoe-kwang. Lee Whoe-kwang went to Japan in the August of 1910, around the time of the shameful annexation of Korea by Japan, as the highest priest of Korean Wonjong Buddhism. On the sixth of October of the same year an alliance was concluded with the Japanese Sodoshu Buddhism under the protext of propagation of faith. The contents of the agreement consisting of six articles in effect, subjugated Korean Buddhism under Japanese Buddhism, thus extending the Japanese domination of Korea to the area of religion. Manhae, infuriated by the intrigue of Lee Whoe-kwang and his followers, convened a monks' convention in the Songkwangsa Temple in Soonchon, Cholla Namdo on January 15 of the next year (1911). Together with Park Han-yong, Chin Jin-eung, Kim Jong-rae and Jang Kum-bong, he condemned Lee Whoe-kwang as a traitor to the sacred order. At this convention, elder Kim Kyung-woon of the Sonamsa Temple was elected the temporary supreme priest of the Injejong sect, and Manhae was selected to be his proxy. They held another monks' convention in Pomosa Temple in Dongrae, Kyongsang Namdo, and condemned the plot for subordinating Korean Buddhism under Japanese Buddhism, finally succeeding in crushing the intrigues of the Lee Whoe-kwang faction.

Shortly after that, Manhae published "For the Revitalization of Korean Buddhism" (1913) and "The Grand Code of Buddhism" (1914), and made a lecture tour of numerous temples in the Kyongsangdo and Chollado area where he delievered fervent speeches. He is said to have come to an awakening around 10 o'clock of the night of December 2 1917 while in quiet residence in Oseam, Kangwon-do at the sound of something toppling down by the wind and broken. This writer, being a complete stranger to Buddhist faith, cannot tell what he was awakened to at the time, or what awakening is, and whether it can come so suddenly as that. But it is very clear that Manhae came to divine the real substance of Japanese imperialism that bound Korean people in bondage through his struggle against the pro-Japanese intirgue of Lee Whoe-kwang's faction. That is to say, he discovered the reality of Korean Buddhism inevitably as a part of the reality of the nation, and that the inequality between imperialist Japan and colonial Korea was a fundamental detriment to realization of the Buddhistic equality. Anyway, after 1917, toward the age of forty, he had succeeded building himself into an active patriot, monk and a poet.

It is only too well known that Manhae took an active and leading part in the great national independence movement of 1919. With Choi Lin, he played a core role in the planning of the Declaration of Independence, and wrote the three pledges attached to the declaration composed posed by Choi Nam-son. On the day itself, he made a speech before the assembly of national leaders in which he said: "We who have come to make the declaration as representatives of the nation should realize how grave is our mission and must henceforth dedicate our united efforts for the achievement of complete independence." In addition, he withstood the court trials with unflinching firmness and served full three years' prison term on principles of, 1) not employing lawyers; 2) not taking private food; and 3) not requesting bail. His accurate logic and lofty intelligence is said to have brought a confession from the Japanese procurator in charge: "I admit the justice of your reasonings but I cannot alter the policy of our government." His philosophy for national independence is concisely expressed in his "Reasons for Independence of Korea" (or "Treatise on Korean Independence.") This was written on July 10, 1920 as an answer to the interrogation of the Japanese procurator. Manhae is said to have written the entire dissertation in small letters on tissue papers which he folded and twisted into paper ropes and sent out to the outside world inside his laundry.

This "Reasons for Independence of Korea" contains the same philosophy of Manhae expressed in "For the Revitalization of Korean Buddhism," enlarged and deepened through the acute perception of national realities. First of all, Manhae explains that the history of mankind is progressing toward civilization and peace, leaving behind ignorance and conflict. He analyzes the present stage in world history, in which imperialism and militarism flourishes, from the point of view of this progressivism. Then, he defines militarism as the most wicked black art that tramples upon mankind's happiness, and exposed the disguised peace propaganda of aggressors as follows:

> The so-called power nations, or in other words the aggressors, recklessly commit aggressions in flagrant violation of ethics and justice. Nevertheless, when they explain about their acts, they always paint themselves as angels of justice, claiming to conduct

the aggressions for the peace of the world or of a certain region and for the happiness of the victims of their aggressions. For example, Japan has annexed Korea by force and turned the twenty thousand Koreans into slaves, and yet claims to have made the annexation for the peace in the east and for the welfare and happiness of the Korean people.

Manhae, from his firm belief that civilization of mankind progresses and not regresses, says: "How can such militarism last forever? Facts, even more than theory, testify to its mortality." He cites as an evidence that imperialism and its tool, militarism, are becoming historical relics with the defeat of Germany in the First World War. From what cause did the German Kaiser, who had wielded such a vast military power, face total destruction all at once? Was it because of the superior military force of the allies? Although the allies claimed to fight against the militarism of Germany, they also employed such murderous weapons as warships and guns as their tools, thus making the allies half militarists in fact. Then why was the Kaiser defeated? It was because the German people, who realized keenly the wrongs of militarism and the bitterness of war, abandoned war of their own accord, broke the sword of militarism, and thereby brought about the suicide of German militarism, clearing the way toward peaceful new life in republicanism. Therefore, the outcome of the world war is not so much a defeat of Kaiser as a defeat of militarism; not so much the victory of the allies as the victory of the German people. Manhae analyzed the general situation of the world thus and said that "from now on the course of the future cannot but be defeat of militarism and success of national independence struggles and pacifism."

Consequently, in Manhae's judgment achievement of independence of Korea was inevitable, in view of the course of world history in which militant aggressionism was going the way of destruction. In addition, the spirit of independence and mental preparedness are sufficient conditions for independence of a nation even if the material civilization is not yet fully developed. Also, independence of a nation is not something that is given by someone else, but something accomplished if only the nation itself declares itself a people of an independent state. "The Japanese keep saying that material civilization is at an impoverished state in Korea, but unless they abolished their tyrannical rule and the discriminatory education they are enforcing for the purpose of degrading Korean people and keeping them ignorant, Korea will hardly be able to attain a high degree of civilization." Thus, Man--hae pinpointed the essence of the Japanese aggressionist policy which laughed at the Koreans for not having the capability and preparedness for independence, and on the other hand carried out all kinds of deprivation and suppression in order that Koreans might not be able to attain such a capability and preparedness. Manhae was one of the few people who had rightly divined the historical reality, that what had to be fought against in the first place was the Japanese colonialism itself rather than the cruel militaristic rule of the Japanese governor-general. It was because they did not rightly see this point that a considerable number of patriots tried to secure "independence of internal government" or "voting rights" or "self-government" by soliciting the grace of the Japanese imperialists. Some of the national leaders, who took part in the planning of the 1919 independence movement, even suggested naming the Declaration of Independence a Petition for Independence. Manhae opposed all such surrenders and insisted that total annihilation of colonial institutions was the sole solution:

> The Koreans, although they have been degraded to the status of slaves and animals under the inhuman rule, have accepted it for nearly ten years. This is partly because resistance was impossible because of the oppression, but more owes to the fact that they did not try to revolt against the rule of the Japanese governor-general. This is because more fundamental than the governor-general rule is the problem of annexation. In other words, the twenty million people of Korea were determined to achieve independence and self-existence by annulment of the annexation. Therefore, they did not think fit to retaliate, however, harsh the rule of the governor-general and to be grateful however mild it was. That is to say, they regarded the governor-general rule as a regional problem.

Manhae, based on this conception of the Japanese imperialism, expressed his firm optimistic view that "the movement for independence of Korea is like a round rock rolling from the top of a mountain; its momentum will not decrease until it reaches its destination." The ultimate basis for this optimism he found in the unlimited power of the people as evidenced in the March 1 Independence Movement of 1919.

4

After he came out of prison in March, 1922, Manhae impressed numerous Koreans with his fervent lectures. In May, 1922 he made a speech at the YMCA hall on the subject, "Philosophy of the Imprisoned." In October of the same year he lectured at the Chondogyo Temple under the title, "Six Paramita." In the April of the next year he lectured on "Self-help" in support of the foundation of a peoples' university. In 1924 he assumed the presidency of the Young Buddhists' Association, and also composed the novel *Death*. Then in 1926, he sent a shock wave through the literary world with the publication of his *The Silence of My Beloved*. He continued to write novels as *The Black Wind* (1935, serialized in the Chosun Ilbo), *Regret* (1936, serialized in the Chosun Choongang Ilbo), and *The Unblessed* (1938, in the Chosun Ilbo), and also composed poems in the Chinese tradition and short sijos. But *The Silence of My Beloved* alone is enough to secure his place in literary history.

Manhae's importance is as great in the history of Korean literature as it is in recent national history. Literary histories so far written have mostly neglected to give him due credit, or at most recognized his importance only as an exceptional figure in the literary world. This estimation of him exactly corresponds to his position in the literary world of his days. But it is needless to say, that he should not be deprived of his due share of estimation because he remained outside the literary circles in his lifetime; because he did not follow such imported literary trends as realism, romanticism and symbolism; and because he did not form literary leagues and publish coterie magazines. The fact that Manhae attained the depth and width in his literary works was perhaps made possible by his aloofness from the literary circles of the day, which were steeped in anti-social and anachronistic tendencies, an outcome of national subjugation.

That Manhae is the first modern poet of Korea and the greatest literary figure of the Independence Movement era has already been pointed out (cf. Paik Rak-chong, "Bourgeois Literature.") Literary historians have until now, agreed in regarding Yukdang Choi Namson's "From Sea to the Boy" as the first deliberate literary break from the song-like poems of the past, and accepted Kim Dong-in's expansive delusionistic contention that the readers met for the first time truly modern poetry in Chu Yo-han's "Fireworks" (1919). It seems to be a persisting literary custom in Korea to regard these two works as the epoch-making precursors in "new poetry" and "free poetry" respectively. But because Manhae did not belong to literary circles is no reason for underestimating him as a literary figure. In fact, Manhae is the first modern poet in Korea, because he was the first to realize thoroughly the realities of Korea which, from the state of an independent nation has been degraded to the state of a nation without sovereignty, and the first to embody his pains in the form of modern poetry.

The lessons we get from Manhae are many. Included among them should be the fact that he was a poet above and outside the literary circles. As is well known, modern literature in Korea, in its first phase, was led by Choi Nam-son and Yi Kwang-soo, which were followed by the coterie magazine period with the publications of "The Creation," "Ruins," "White Tide," and the importation of various Western literary trends, such as, symbolism, romanticism and naturalism. In the very early days, Korean literature was not without a fervor for national enlightenment but after the 1920s, with the so-called "cultural rule" of the Japanese, even that characteristic almost disappeared. The literary world became, for the most part, an assembly of petite bourgeois. Manhae's literature, born in such a period, is entirely free of the limitations of such a tendency in the literary circles.

The Silence of My Beloved, standing outside the literary trends of the days, sings of the Korean people's realities and dreams most poignantly. Every one of the 88 poems in the collection sweeps us into emotional purity. But perhaps we had better remember that for Manhae writing poetry was not his sole or chief occupation. To be sure, even from the purely literary point of view, the excellence of his works already have been amply illustrated by critics; but to know that he had combined thinking and activism being a monk and patriot, is important for an understanding of his poetry. If we studied and analyzed his poems only by the western methods of literary analysis, he may be no more than a poet of abundant metaphor, a religious and meditative or a deeply metaphysical poet. He was not, however, a poet of the period of specialization, but a poet raised in a period whose ideal was integration of politics, science, morals and literature. *The Silence of My Beloved* must be studied from the viewpoint of how it succeeds "For the Revitalization of Korean Buddhism" and "The Reasons for Independence of Korea."

All poetic works of Manhae revolves around one single focus. All thoughts, associations, metaphors and images start from that single focus and return to that focus. That is his "beloved." Many have already pointed out that one cannot pinpoint what exactly Manhae's "Beloved" indicates. What kind of a being is this "Beloved"? The poet discovers his beloved through parting with his beloved:

> Separation is the creation of beauty.
>
> There is no beauty like the beauty of separation, even in the ethereal gold of the morning, or the fiberless black silk of the night; not even in the deathless eternity of life, nor in the unwithering azure flower of the sky.
>
> Oh Beloved! If it were not for separation, I could not die in tears and then rise again in laughter.
>
> Ah, separation!
>
> Beauty is the creation of separation.
>
> ("From Separation Is Beauty Born")

Separation is the occasion that makes me realize the existence of the "beloved": I discover my beloved through separation. Thus, "beloved" has separation as the component part of his being, and therefore, the lover is not a lover without separation. (cf. "The First Lovers".) Of course this may be a paradox; but this paradox is the very basic structure that makes possible Manhae's literature and the source of his vitality. The Buddhist dialectics of reaching affirmation through negation, and preparing the way for a greater affirmation through negation of that affirmation, inspires infinite vitality to his poetry which revolves around one single theme.

> Is your voice silence?
>
> I can hear your strain very clearly when you do not sing.
>
> Your voice is silence.
>
> (first stanza of "Inverse Proportions")

Thus, Manhae recognized his era as the era of the beloved's absence, and his reality as a reality in which the beloved is silent. But to him, the silence of his beloved is itself the voice of the beloved, and the absence of beloved is the evidence of his existence. To those who recognize only the visible existences, and deem as history only the immediate observable phenomena, the silence of the beloved may mean his nonexistence; that the only way to live is to follow the ways of the world. But Manhae has accurately divined that to cling to the phenomena of the immediate reality is to live in bondage to falsehood and delusion.

> I know your silence well.
> I know that you are being silent, surrounded by the adoration of children not come to discretion, suppressing your sardonic smile.
>> (third stanza of "The Diamond Mountain")

> If love is free, then the choice of lover, too, must be free. But are not you always shackled by this pretty-named master, freedom? Have you, too, a lover? If so, I fear it is not a lover but your shadow.
>> (from the Foreword: "Unnecessary Words")

Here we can read Manhae's caustic attack on the litertaure and the literary circles of the day. No individual can be free when the nation is bound under the yoke of colonial rule. In an era when one's country is ruled by another country, everything in sight cannot but be an object of regret. Therefore, praise of nature, freedom of love, the supremacy of art are all meaningless acts of children not yet balanced by discretion. They are deluded by the pretty name of freedom and infatuated with their own shadows. Such is a way of following the ways of the world, and such acts help to perpetuate the existing conditions. True literature always tries to destory the faults of the present and to lead readers to the truths of the future. Manhae's poetry is great in that it not only heard the silence of the beloved, but that it showed us the wisdom and courage of waiting, in the firm belief that the beloved will return. In this regard the poetry of Manhae is the song of unending and brimming hope.

> But knowing full well that vain tears at parting would sap our love, I poured the strength of this inconsolable sorrow into the well of hope.
> As we dread farewells when meeting, so we believe in reunion from the moment of parting.
> Ah, my beloved has gone, but I have not let my beloved go.

The tune of love that cannot overcome the sorrow of its strain encircles the silence of my beloved.

> (last part of "The Sillence of My Beloved")

In another work, he wrote:

As those who never meet are not lovers, neither are those who never part lovers.

The lover gives me laughter at meeting; and at parting, tears.

Dearer are the tears of parting than the laughter of meeting, and dearer still than the tears of parting is the laughter of reunion.

Ah, beloved! How long will it be till our laughter of reunion?

> (last stanza of "The First Lovers")

Therefore, to Manhae separation is not the end of love but the beginning of a greater and stronger love. Love does not dimishish in proportion to the distance of the lover, but increases. (cf. "Measure of Love".) Although "I" am not worth a speck of dust compared to the beloved, the beloved is also a being that exists because "I" exist. The beloved is an absolute being, but exists through my existence all the same. "I" am included in the beloved, and the beloved exists through me. The beloved is the goal of absolute yearning that is not forgotten through my efforts to forget, but is the more vividly remembered for that. Also, it is not because "I" am determined to wait for the beloved that I wait for him, but because I desire nothing else. It is because the beloved is the sole meaning of my existence and the absolute foundation of the possibility of my existence, and in the highest stage is myself.

Others like to think of their beloved;
I want to forget mine.
But since memory intensifies with my efforts to forget,
I tried remembering, hoping to forget.

> (first stanza of "Hoping to Forget")

It is not because I will it so that I wait for you, but because I cannot do otherwise.

I wait for you not out of the bondage of virtue, but out of love.

> (first stanza of "Voluntary Chastity")

It is a nature common to mankind that one nation does not want interference of other nations. This is a nature unalterable, and a nation cannot curb its own desire for independence however hard it tried.

(from "The Reasons for Independence of Korea")

Therefore, the beloved is a being who has the thirsty longing for him as one of his attributes. Similarly, to long and wait for the beloved makes possible the continuation of my being. To forget the beloved is to forget myself, and to deny the beloved is to deny myself. It is the way to death. "I" am a shadow and part of the beloved, and the beloved is the source of my being; therefore, to be bound by the beloved is not a sacrifice to the "pretty name of freedom" but the recovery of the more fundamental self and the attainment of a truer freedom. Therefore, to Manhae separation is not an isolation from the beloved by force, but the beginning of the struggle for quest of the true lover. The process of longing and waiting for the beloved takes the form of incarnating and winning the beloved. In this process the great sorrow is transformed into a great joy, and the great despair is transformed into a great hope. The beloved makes me look for him through separation and proves his existence through his absence, speaks to me through silence, and makes me realize that falsity and illusion are the evidences of the existence of truth. Therefore, death is the sure final guarantee of the beloved's coming.

The objective of human life lies in true freedom. Therefore, how can there be diversions and pleasures in a life without freedom? So, nothing, not even life, is too precious to be consecrated for attainment of freedom.

(from "The Reasons for Independence of Korea")

Come into my death, beloved.
Death is ready for you always.
If anyone comes chasing after you you can just stand
behind my death.
Death is the union of nihil and omnipotence.
Death's love is both infinite and eternal.
Before death warships and guns are dust.
Before death the strong and the weak are friends.
Then those who chase after you cannot get you.
Come. It is time for your coming. Come quickly.

(last stanza of "Come")

Here we thrill to note that Manhae's waiting becomes an ardent appeal and a suffocating cry weighty as death. In this poem we experience a prophetic moment in which literature and religion become one; thoughts and actions, the Buddha and the unawakened, the strong and the weak. It is a situation in which warships and guns are like dust. Thereby, he became the first poet to transcend the limitations of his time. He broke out of the fetters of the realities of his time and sang of the true order of the times to come. He was the creator of the most beautiful and expressive poetry in the history of our literature.

5

After his fifties, Manhae participated in the establishment of Shinganhoe (in 1927) and served as the director of its Seoul branch and during the Kwangju Student Revolt of 1929 convened a mass convention. After he became the publisher and editor of the monthly, "Buddhism," in 1931, he energetically engaged in writing essays and dissertations on Buddhism. He also led the young men's Buddhist movement and the movement for popularization of Buddhism as the practical leader of the "Buddhist 卍 Party", a secret organization of young Buddhists. Many anecdotes come down to us which tell us of his uncompromising integrity and courage. But the makers of history were no longer the people of Manhae's generation, which was the generation of the 1919 Independence Movement. Therefore, we might say that *The Silence of My Beloved* is a product of its era, in that the concrete and active confrontation with the national circumstances as shown in "For the Revitalization of Korean Buddhism" and "The Reasons for Independence of Korea" could not but be expressed in the form of vision and prophecy. The social conditions and his physical age did not permit the vision and the prophecy to be translated into actual social action. Nevertheless, Manhae stood firm while the Japanese militarism engulfed Manchuria and infiltrated into China and raised the Pacific War, while his former fellow leaders of national independence movement, such as, Choi Lin, Choi Nam-son and Yi Kwang-soo forsook the nation and gave their co-operation to the Japanese. Manhae died of chronic palsy on June 19 of 1944, one year before the cruel darkness was to be lifted. In a later year, Chong In-bo commemorated the poet of *The Silence of My Beloved* with the following poem:

The pungent perfume of orchid is dull compared to yours.
The lustre of the brightest star is dimness beside your light.
Come back! spirit of my beloved, for this land is Buddha's realm again.

Who would dare say of his silence that it has lost fragrance and light today?   (Translated by Suh Ji-moon)

SUH KYUNG-SOO was born in 1925 and graduated from Liberal Arts College of Seoul National University in 1958. He has been teaching at Tongguk University since 1964 and at present is an associate professor of Buddhist Thought.

Professor Suh is the author of several books on Buddhism: *The Way of the Worldliness and the Way of Nirvana* (1967); *The Wisdom of Himalaya* (1968); *A Hundred Years of Korean Buddhism* and others.

KIM CHOL-CHOON was born in 1923 in Pyongwon, Northern Korea. He was graduated from History Department of Seoul National University. He is at present Professor of Ancient Korean History at the Seoul National. He has published many articles including "The Dual Organization of the Earlier Silla Society" (1952), "The Formation of Official Hierarchy in Koguryo and Silla"(1956), "Genealogy of the Earlier Silla and its Chronicle" (1962) and "Family Group in The Silla Period (1968)."

Korean Buddhism: a Historical Perspective

The Editor's Note: *In the following dialogue, Professor Kim Chol-jun of Seoul National University and Professor Suh Kyong-su of Tongguk University review the role of Buddhism in Korean history, analyzing some key personalities, ideologies and cultures which have affected life in Korea from Koguryo to the modern transformation period.*

SUH: Our purpose here is not to make a comprehensive survey of the relationship between Korean history and Buddhism, but to discuss some personalities, ideologies and cultures that have been characteristic of particular periods in our history. First of all, we will start off by examining how alien ideologies and cultures were introduced and accepted during the Three Kingdoms period, and then, specifically, how Buddhism, one of these alien ideologies, was introduced into the land and what kind of influence it had on our culture.

KIM: If we look at the King Kwanggaeto Monument of Koguryo, we find that it is a *menhir* (a standing stone) of the megalithic culture with its epitaph inscribed not in the Chinese but in the Korean style. This tells us that a feature of Chinese culture was accepted and adapted as the special property of Korean culture. Also, we find in the earthenware of Silla certain characteristics that are identical with those of the ironware of Koguryo. These facts tell us that the national character and the cultural soil of Korea were not inclined to absorb Chinese culture unconditionally, but that it was accepted and transformed into a new culture based on the inherent culture of Korea. In other words, an idiosyncratic culture was created when fusion occurred between our native and alien cultures.

A unique cultural soil, whether it is good or bad, is capable of creating a high standard of culture, if it lasts from generation to generation, preserving its tradition. In our case, attempts to manage and improve our society were made as early as the neolithic age; and here, again, we find a readiness to accommodate alien culture. An example of this is the Five Secular Admonitions developed by Priest Wongwang of Silla. There are some who find Confucian influence in the

119

Five Secular Admonitions, but the Admonitions are entirely different from the moral codes governing the Five Human Relations. For instance, the first of the Five Secular Admonitions calls for "loyalty to monarch" whereas that of the Five Human Relations refers to "affinity between father and son." Our "trust between friends" corresponds with "discrimination between husband and wife" of China. These are differences between Buddhism and Confucianism and between Korea and China. We can consider the Five Secular Admonitions as a unique feature of the Buddhism of Silla. The fact that the sequence and intent of the Five Secular Admonitions differ from those of the Five Huamn Relations means that there are corresponding differences in their content of social ideology.

SUH: As for the dating of the introduction of Buddhism into Korea, popular belief puts it in the second year of the reign of King Sosurim of Koguryo (A.D. 372). But this is only a date officially recognized by the government for administrative reasons, and we must realize that the actual spread of Buddhism among the people had occurred to a considerable extent before that time. It was in about the first century before Christ that Buddhism was introduced to China by way of Central Asia, and it is not hard to surmise that it could have reached Korea earlier than toward the end of the 4th century in view of the geographical proximity and the political and military situation then prevailing between Koguryo and China.

The fact that certain ascetics of Koguryo were corresponding with Tao Lin of China as early as eight years before the second year of the reign of King Sosurim, the officially recognized year of Buddhist introduction, is good evidence to substantiate this theory. The question of dating also arises in the case of Silla, where Buddhism is believed to have been prevalent among the people even before the arrival of A Tao, who is considered to be the first missionary to have reached the kingdom. In this connection, I think, that there is a need to re-examine the cultural foundation of our incipient ancient states, to which Buddhism was introduced.

When Buddhism was introduced into the Three Kingdoms, its doctrines, such as the Three Seals of Law, the Four Noble Truths, and the Chain of Causation and Deliverance, inspired the ancient societies with a good measure of belief in universal validity and egalitarianism. Especially, the doctrine upholding personal deliverance enhanced the awareness of personal identity and infused the people with the idea that everyone was equal before the law of Buddha. However, what is noteworthy is the fact that the Buddhism that was introduced into Korea was different from that of India, as it had already undergone considerable change before it went through the process of indigenization in Korea. A conspicuous feature of this process was that law of Buddha was the law of the state; that is, the non-secular law of Buddha was equated with the secular law of the royalty. Accordingly, I think that the Buddhism that was introduced during the formative period of the ancient unified kingdom came to exercise a dual function as it spread among the rulers and the ruled in different forms. That is, for the ruling class an image of Buddhism dedicated to national defense was created whereby the king was equated with Buddha, while for the common folk who had lost their myth a new myth was presented. At any rate, we might say that the idea of universality inherent in Buddhism emerged as a new and highly sophisticated ideology during the formative period of the unified state.

KIM: In the case of Silla, just as in the case of Koguryo and Paekche, solidarity between the ruling class and the people was well maintained with relatively few instances of discord until the kingdom was united. This means the continuation of a tradition of the age of tribal states which were less troubled with social inequities. In general, the gap between the classes becomes narrower when a high ethical standard prevails and the morals are rigidly adhered to. Therefore, the people believed in Buddhism together with the ruling class without experiencing guilt feelings or any sense of obligation, and, what is more, even slaves were allowed to participate in Buddhist rituals. I think this was due not so much to the social structure of the period as to the universal nature of Buddhism itself. As it was propagated throughout the local areas after being introduced into the Kingdom, Buddhims did not reject the traditional native deities of particular localities but duly recognized their status, absorbing them into the huge scale, as it were, of Buddhism. I think it was through a gradual process of concretization of these development that the uniquely Korean Buddhism came into being.

SUH: When Buddhism was introduced into Korea, it was not the case of directly transporting Indian Buddhism in its original form. By the time original Buddhism reached China, it had become a uniquely Central Asian Buddhism as it became fused with the native religion of the area during the three or four centuries of its existence in Central Asia. It eventually reached Korea after having been remolded in the Chinese style on its way through China. On the other hand, in view of the geographical distance involved at the time, would it not be possible that it came to Korea directly, without going through China? Take one of the seated Maitreya images of Koguryo or Paekche for instance. It has unique central Asian features which are never found in China or Korea. It is probable that the faith of Maitreya or Amita Buddha of Silla which had greatly appealed to the nobility as well as the common people was influenced by it. It was originally in India that scriptures related to the faith of Maitreya or Amita Buddha were published, but it was in Central Asia that the faith was solidified into the shape of a folk religion. I think it is possible that this religion found its way directly to Korea instead of going through China. Based on this observation, I think we must examine the inflow of not only Buddhism but also ancient cultures in a variety of dimensions.

KIM: In view of the international situation then prevailing, in which the northern nations centered around Koguryo and Puyo were set against the Hans of mainland China, it is possible that Chinese culture or Buddhism was not taken at its face value but was countered with resistance, so that it proceeded directly from Central Asia without going through China. Whether it came directly or indirectly, Buddhist culture spread through Koguryo and Paekche and was crystalized into its ultimate form in Silla. Korean Buddhism was formulated in this manner, and it was in many respects closely allied with the ruling class. But when the close ties were broken, there emerged a new force that took up a new common people's ideology. It was then that the faith of Maitreya or Amita Buddha could emerge, and the greater the social unrest grew, the stronger the faith of Maitreya or Amita Buddha became. Also, in this connection, when Silla was about to unify the Three Kingdoms, Koguryo and Paeckche were struggling with contradictory elements inherent in any ancient society. Therefore Silla, which had a elate start, took advantage of the situation and was able to make preparations for the unification venture. But then Silla itself had to go through similar travail toward the end of the dynasty and the beginning of the Koryo dynasty. The hierarchy of nobility in Silla ran into the resistance of the northern establishment toward the end of the period, so that its kinship communities either shrunk in influence or disintegrated. In this period of transition toward Koryo there occurred a considerable change in Buddhist philosophy, in the architectural style of temples and in the overall character and structure of culture.

SUH: Before we study Buddhist culture after the Unified Silla period, I think we would do well to examine what sort of influence Buddhism had on the transformation and development of the ancieht tribal state into a unified state, what kind of influence it had on the overall culture and what changes it brought about. Those who espoused the new Buddhist philosophy in those days were imbued with the elitism of a chosen people, and these elites belonged to a minority during the early period of transformation into the unified state. When they were closely allied with the ruling class, their elitism grew much stronger.

KIM: The views of the world prevailing in the tribal state were of two types. One was that the rulers entertained a strong elitism identifying themselves with the various tribal states centered around Koguryo and maintained their own social order, absorbing elements of alien cultures. We might say that this had something in common with the ideology of "benefiting mankind everywhere." The other was that the tribal heads created the myth of hero-worship as a means of demonstrating their own heroic greatness in order to aggrandize their ruling power. After Buddhism was brought in, such myths were replaced by Buddhist myths. That is, Buddhism let the ruling class keep its old myths almost intact as the tribal state was being transformed into an ancient state; on the other hand, though, to the common people who had lost their myth Buddhism provided a new culture and a new ideology, thereby playing the role of a prime moving force in leading the cultural sphere of that age. It was not just doctrines or consicousness that Buddhism brought with it but music, art and craft, and philosophy as well. It introduced the culture not only of China but also of India and Central Asia and even Europe, thereby contributing to the formation of a new social culture. Having thus brought diversity to the ancient culture of Korea, Buddhism reached a fairly well-organized stage in the field of art and craft and mural paintings in Koguryo, and then proceeding through Paekche it finally succeeded in creating symmetrical beauty in Silla. In other words, we might say that Buddhism not only brought in a religion and a philosophy but also played a vital role in formulating our ancient arts in the field of culture.

However, what is more important is the attitude of receiving foreign influence. For instance, the fact that King Chinpyong of Silla adopted the name of Chinjong for himself, after that of Shakyamuni's father, and the name of Maya for his wife, is a reminder that he tried to absorb the new culture while retaining the superior position and the traditional posture of his own kingdom in the building of a Busddhist kingdom. It was because Silla did not forsake its tradition from its age of the tribal state as it absorbed Buddhist culture that the symmetrical beauty of Silla's Buddhist art was achieved.

SUH: While the tribal state was being transformed into an ancient state, Buddhism provided a new ideology, influencing the royalty and the people at the same time. It brought in not only an ideology but also an artistic culture, providing a basis for new artistic creations. In absorbing Buddhist culture Koreans skilfully harmonized the foreign elements, rather than blindly imitating them, in creating the culture of Koguryo, and then proceeding through Paekche they completed the process in Silla.

Now, turning our attention to the final days of Silla, when a condition of anomie was created from social unrest of various kinds, did Buddhism play its role properly as a religion then? Among certain elements of the population at that time the faith of Maitreya or Amita Buddha was highly popular. Could Buddhism simply end up being no more than an involuntary faith like that of Maitreya or Amita Buddha? Furthermore, as the Koryo dynasty began, Buddhists took advantage of their status of nobility to amass considerable amounts of farm land under the control of temples, even to the extent of becoming corrupt. Even though they had opportunities to reflect upon themselves, they remained closely allied with the ruling class, being unable to exercise their proper religious functions and thereby inviting criticism from the outside. Just as the church in the Middle Ages in Europe was set against the state but nevertheless managed to preserve its integrity by constantly reflecting upon itself, the Korean Buddhists should have reflected upon their self-seeking corruptive practices, controlled and criticized them and should have stood on the side of the people, constantly pointing out the wrongs committed in the society. But it seems that Buddhism in the final days of Silla and the early days of Koryo lost a good deal of its inherent sense of religious mission amid the confusion of religion and politics.

KIM: I think this problem was not due to any defects in the doctrines inherent in Buddhism itself but to the complex social phenomena prevailing at the time, as well as to the fact that the Buddhists failed to fulfill their proper mission. Toward the latter part of Silla there emerged a powerful revolutionary force of the northern barbarians of Manchuria. At that time Buddhists were allied with the nobility in the capital and were preoccupied with the management of the temple economy, and so their strength was greatly reduced. This may be illustrated by the story of Choe Sung-no, a Buddhist-turned Confucian leader who was brought up in a Buddhist temple. When he assailed Buddhism, he did not criticize the doctrines or contents of Buddhism but sought to separate Buddhism from politics because the Buddhist religion had grown inordinately rich. Then there were defects in the social system, too. The rulers of Silla relied too much on the native establishment centered around Kyongju, the capital, insisting on having a form of government and culture based on its system of nobility and not paying any attention to developments outside of its boundary. So there occurred repercussions in various areas, starting a period of confusion in which attempts were made to form a new establishment away from Kyongju. Buddhism then was in no way capable of solving this problem.

SUH: Another aspect of the Buddhism of Silla that cannot be overlooked, together with artistic culture, is the thought of Won Hyo. But, first of all, we might examine Silla's artistic foundation or subject matter on which the production of great works were based as early as the 8th century. I think the doctrine of universality presented by Buddhism gave Silla a sufficient basis upon which to build an everlasting image in the skies of that kingdom. And I feel that the idea of stressing personal deliverance opened a way in which one could proejct himself in creative works.

KIM: One of the characteristics of our anicent culture was its scientific nature. A high level of scientific skill was required to maintain an ancient society. Skill played a vital role in controlling and understanding a number of tribes and their tribal hierarchies. The geographical data and the population figures were very accurate and detailed. These skills of the ancient society were directly applied to the construction and layout of temples and to artistic sculpture. Especially, in the field of fine arts in Silla, beauty was not something extemporaneous but something that was achieved by an elaborate and scientific process. The creative works of art such as the Main Buddha in the Sokkuram Grotto, and the Tabo (*Bahuratna*) and Shakyamuni pagodas in Kyongju are products of scientific accuracy. In other words, these crystallizations are a continuation of an aesthetic tradition dating from ancient times and based on science. On the other hand, the financial support extended to temples by the nobility and the age-old tradition of faith centered around rituals like pagoda circling were combined to create the new culture of Silla. The highly developed arts of Silla went through a formal change in the latter part of the dynasty, becoming unscientific and unprincipled, and in the Koryo period there occurred yet another formal change whereby art objects directly related to the life of the nobility were mass-produced.

Won Hyo was a great thinker in many respects. Only a man like Won Hyo could combine and digest the multifarious sects and schools to evolve a new system. That is, Won Hyo did not study Buddhism phenomenally but tried to understand it in its original historical process of development. This is why he was able to combine and make sense out of the Yuga and Chunggwan schools. In coping with the complex situation brought about by the introduction of Hinayana and Mahayana Buddhism into Silla. Won Hyo systematized a macroscopic method of studying Buddhism which held that no order would be established without systematizing the One Buddha Vehicle (*Ekabuddhayana*). Of course, even before Won Hyo, a man named Ko Duk, of Koguryo, set about the task of studying the toatlity of Buddhism, but it was later and only by Won Hyo that a philosophical approach was established and that the fundamental philosophical attitude of "thinking" was preserved intact even though the philosophy itself might change.

SUH: Won Hyo grasped the doctrine of universality of Buddhism in its macroscopic perspective. In other words, he took pains to make a comprehensive yet flexible summary of the teachings of Buddha and to present it to the general public. Therefore, Won Hyo played the role of an intermediary who tried to develop and pass on something new by bringing the different schools and sects together, and to do that he took up, first of all, the inevitable task of developing his own philosophy. Won Hyo made efforts to establish popular Buddhism by bringing Buddhism down to the level of the common people at a time when it was highly susceptible of becoming aristocratic. Would you say that he had certain special motives for it, or did his status have anything to do with it?

KIM: King Munmu, on his deathbed, instructed his son, King Sinmun, to present Kyong Il, a man from Ungju (Kongju) of the defunct Paekche dynasty, with the title of state priest. But King Sinmun changed the title and gave him the title of state elder instead. This is an example of unmitigated prejudice and provincialism against all outside the hierarchy of nobility centered around Kyongju. I think it was because Won Hyo was so keenly aware of such social maladies and defects that he was motivated to place himself on the side of the common people. His world view was not confined to a region called Silla, but consisted in exploring the universality and fundamental essence of Buddhism itself.

SUH: We might say that Won Hyo even transcended Buddhism and pursued truth as one dedicated to the quest of infinity at the very root of a religion.

KIM: The greatness of Won Hyo may be glimpsed from the *Primary* and *Secondary Commentary* (*Non* and *So*) in the Confucian anthology *Tongmunson*.

SUH: So much for the Buddhism of Silla. We may now proceed to the Koryo dynasty. As we briefly noted a while ago, a religion is bound to become corrupt if politics or economics intervene. So Choe Sung-no was only right, and his observation penetrating, when he called for the separation of Buddhism and politics. Wang Kŏn founded the

Koryo dynasty and formulated the *Ten Articles of Admonition*, giving Buddhism the status of a state religion. At the same time, the Buddhist church became corrupt, even to the extent of engaging in usury, as they had accumulated resources on a scale just as abundant as the nobility. As one who was aware of the economic malady caused by the rampant construction of temples in Silla, what sort of religious policy did Wang Kŏn have and what were his true intentions?

KIM: When Wang Kŏn founded Koryo, the immediate task he was confronted with was not the renovation of Buddhism as the first order of business. Rather, he abolished the system of nobility of the ancient society and implemented a welfare policy, decreeing that the people be taxed reasonably. Wang Kŏn allied himself with the wealthy class in the provincial areas when he set about enstructuring the political and social systems of Koryo. The wealthy class kept a close relationship with the Buddhist church. Therefore, he abstained from radical policy-making even though he knew about the excesses of the Buddhist temple. In the *Biographical Series* of the *History of Koryo*, Choe Ung is said to have remonstrated with the king on the excesses of the Buddhist church. But this occurred when the Buddhist faith was flourishing among the people and Wang Kŏn could not regulate them for political reasons, even though he knew about these excesses. This problem had to wait until the reign of King Kwangjong, when he came up with an alternative. That is, Kwangjong adopted a civil service examination system to replace the system of nobility, promoted study of the national classics, and suppressed the wealthy class that was detrimental to establishing his royal authority. In seeking ideological unity he encouraged Confucian scholars while promoting Buddhist philosophy, and thereby defined the spiritual foundation of the ancient period. Kwangjong took pains to innovate various social systems even though he was hampered by tradition. He sought to find a prime moving force in the sense of identity in the spiritual world.

In the meantime, temples and pagodas were built at such a rate that the expenses incurred in one year were about equal to those of the entire reign of Wang Kŏn, and this was criticized by certain elements. But he resolved the confrontation between the Northern and the Southern School, became the first monarch of the dynasty to read *Emperor T'ai's Manual of Government*, became a student of the Pop-an

(Fa-yen) sect, reading classics like *Manson Tonggwijip* and *Chong-gyongnok,* and sought to systematize the ideological foundation of the Chon-tae (T'ien-t'ai) sect and the Pop-an sect. All of this indicates that he was inclined to strengthen his royal authority. And then in order to link the doctrine of "Three Truths in One" of the Chon-tae school with his own view of unified ideology, Kwangjong dispatched Che Kwan and Ui Tong to China to obtain a letter from Chon-tae Tok-so (T'ien-t'ai Teh-sao) together with scriptures of the Chon-tae school. Then he tried to resolve the feud between the Doctrine sect and the Dhyana sect. This means that Kwangjong attempted to involve Buddhism in the task of realizing the unity of the establishment just as Yang Ti of Sui built the Peiching temple to uphold the doctrine of "Three Truths in One", and just as King Taejo of Koryo drew upon that doctrine at the time of the unification of the Later Three Kingdoms. However, when Kwangjong died without fulfilling these objectives, his son, Kyongjong, failed to carry out the policy of his father and Che Kwan and Ui Tong did not return from China, so that the Chon-tae sect had to be re-established by State Priest Tae Kak.

SUH: In the *History of Koryo* it is generally pointed out that the Revolt of Myochong gave rise to toadyism or *sadae* ideology, and the *Samguk Yusa* by Il Yon was supposedly written with the intent of refuting the *Samguk Sagi* authored by Kim Pu-sik. There is a view that these had something to do with the internal division prevailing in Koryo at the time. In this connection, I wonder if you could comment on the social conditions and the status of Buddhism in the middle of the Koryo period.

KIM: The Confucians were constantly opposed to the accumulation of as much wealth by the Buddhist Church as by the nobility, but then Kim Pu-sik, who could indeed be considered as representative of the Confucian circle, and most other Confucian scholars, had meditation halls like *naewon* built next to their homes. Because of such a discrepancy between their political and private life, they were not able to launch an all-out attack against Buddhism. The accumulation of wealth by the temple was stopped by the Warriors' Revolt (Musin-nan) rather than by the Confucians' opposition. After seizing control of the government, the warriors reflected on the culture formulated by the literati and in order to rectify it they recruited scholars like Yi

Kyu-bo and Yi In-no to attempt a political and social innovation. But they ran into serious trouble because their raising of private armies damaged the economy, thus repeating the economic malpractices of the Buddhist temple. At this time the Mongols invaded the country and the attempt to innovate the social structure and cultural life ended in a failure. However, in spite of their failure, the warriors' endeavor to explore the spiritual culture in its flourishing period, which was accomplished through the fusion of Buddhism with the inherently native Korean tradition, is truly meritorious. Thus, even as Koryo approached its end struggling with the problem of restructuring her social structure in a variety of dimensions, the Buddhists were in no position to present a solution to the political chaos, and so that task fell on the Confucians. But even though the Buddhists failed to come up with any solution to the social unrest prevailing at the time, they left behind them monumental achievements such as the publication of the *Tripitaka Koreana.*

SUH: The publication of the *Tripitaka Koreana* was the greatest achievement of the Koryo dynasty, and it should be regarded as an epoch-making event in the history of printing also.

KIM: The publication of the *Tripitaka Koreana* can be compared to the compilation in those days of the *Encyclopedia* that contained data collected from all literatures. Granted it was a project of national magnitude, but the fact that such a massive and intricate publication could be completed in times of war and confusion nonetheless proves the superiority of the Korean nation.

SUH: Now, by way of reviewing the Buddhism of Koryo, we might pause for an examination of some of the most imporatnt problems before proceeding to the next topic.

First of all, To Son's theory of geomancy which had a unique influence on the ideology of Koryo is now being re-evaluated. Shouldn't his theory be re-evaluated from the standpoint of Buddhism also?

KIM: When we talk about To Son, I think we ought to relate him to the activities of the wealthy class of the Later Three Kingdoms. When the influential class in the capital of Silla became corrupt and the local wealthy class stood up against it, those of the latter class turn-

ed their estates into choice sports (for siting tombs and other purposes)
and tried to rationalize the division among them. As this grew worse,
the common people became disgusted with it and yearned for the
stability of united people. Such an aspiration of the people began to
show up in the form of geomancy toward the end of Silla. To Son
synthesized these theories of geomancy and restructured them sys-
tematically. He made the people turn their attention from the center of
Kyongju in the south to Songak in the central area, and in effect,
directed the popular sentiment in a way beneficial to Wang Kŏn in
his bid to unify the Later Three Kingdoms. This gave Koryo the underlying strength to achieve her national consensus after her founding.
This is why To Son is frequently mentioned in discussions concerning
the Koryo dynasty. To Son's theory of geomancy made great contributions to bringing about solidarity between the rulers and the people
and to maintaining the health of the society of Koryo.

SUH: We might say that To Son was something of a prophet who
had the most accurate knowledge of the political and social conditions
then prevailing and of the geomantic situations involved and made
concrete and sensible designs out of such knowledge. That is, he put
the entire territory of Korea in perspective, gave it bones in strategic
locations, and compared the veins of rocks and other terrain features to
the blood vessels in the human body. The theory formulated by To Son
from a comparative study of Esoteric Buddhism and the Chinese classic
Hwi So (*Huei Shu*) fertilized the soil in which Buddhism took root,
and the ruling class and the people were thus brought together. His
contributions in this respect were great, but on the other hand he committed the mistake of confusing Buddhism with the theory of geomancy
and of presenting a distorted picture of the essence of Buddhism.

Toward the middle of the Koryo period, Myo Chong staged a
movement to relocate the capital at Sogyong (Pyongyang). How different would you say the aim of Myo Chong was from that of To Son
in its character and content?

KIM: Underlying the society of Koryo was Buddhist philosophy,
and no philosophy that did not uphold Buddhism could ever exist. I
feel that it was for this reason that To Son and Myo Chong became
Buddhist monks. In comparing the two men, To Son's theory of geo-

mancy, a theory of unity centered around Kaegyong (Kaesong), was an ensemble of folk theories of geomancy that aspired to unity at that time, whereas Myo Chong's theory was aimed at national territorial unification centered around the new city of Sogyong, away from the corrupt society of the nobility in Kaegyong that had become an entrenched establishment. When Myo Chong started a rebellion, the Sogyong element had grown powerful enough to challenge the Kaegyong element, and Myo Chong took full advantage of this situation to arouse the public sentiment in favor of his cause.

SUH: We can cite Sin Ton as another unorthodox priest in the history of Koryo, a Buddhist figure who sought to innovate the political and social life of that period. Sin was a man who took part in innovative politics and created a considerable impact through his activities in a relatively short time, rather than influencing the world of ideology itself.

KIM: Sin Ton was an impartial and nonpartisan personality brought onto the stage by King Kongmin, who tried to renovate the confused society in the latter part of Koryo, and by the neo-officials (*sinjinsa*) who tried to put an end to the excesses of the entrenched old establishment. However, his contribution to the Buddhist cause was not great. He nevertheless deserves priase in that the confused society toward the end of Koryo was purified, though for a brief period, and the crumbling royalty was almost given an opportunity to recover its authority through his activities.

SUH: Turning now to the beginning of the Yi dynasty, we find the Confucians in complete control of the government and beginning to persecute Buddhism. The confrontation between Confucianism and Buddhism was due not so much to their doctrinal differences as to the damage caused to the entire society by the illicit acculumation of wealth by the Buddhist Church. This can be verified from Chong To-jon's *Criticism of Buddhism* in which he pointed out the adverse effects not of Buddhism itself but of what it did to the government and the economy. In other words, even though Confucianism played a leading role in formulating the ideology of leadership, it could never supplant the basic philosophy of Buddhism. Nor could Buddhism be eliminated or extinguished because it was deeply rooted in the religious minds of the people even if it were not to enjoy the status of a national ideology as it did in Silla or Koryo. The policy of persecuting Buddhism gained nothing progressive in the formulation of ideology and culture; on the contrary, it only resulted in bringing about a conservative trend, partisan factionalism, stagnation and internal division. But even as the Buddhists were being oppressed by the Confucians in the middle of the Yi dynasty, there emerged such great priests as So San and Sa Myong. These two illustrious priests figured more prominently as patriots committed to the cause of national defense than as religious martyrs.

KIM: For all the persecution of Buddhists by the Confucians from the latter half of Koryo down through the Yi dynasty period, Buddhism which was a state religion of Koryo, was never to be eliminated. This is because a religion has a way of perpetuating itself like subterranean water, fused with the inherent ideology of the common people or, rather, of the society of the masses. The Confucians could reject Buddhism externally, but they could not encroach upon its interior. The question now seems to be: to what extent has Buddhism been able to increase this strength which has been preserved so tenaciously by the society of the masses?

SUH: Now, it seems that we have come to the stage where we need to more or less conclude this discussion. When the modern transformation period began, this country was exposed to a variety of developments characteristic of a turbulent period. And the international situation around her involving Japan, Russia and China fanned powerful winds of change to bring about social innovations.

After the regency of Taewon-gun, when there occurred a series of rebellions including the Imo Military Revolt, the Kapsin Reform and the Tonghak Rebellion, there also occurred a modern transformation movement in Buddhism which produced methodistic priests like Yi Tong-in, and the ideology of such illustrious priests as Kyong Ho and Man Hae (Han Yong-woon) exerted a profound influence inside as well as outside the Buddhist order and on the nation's struggle for independence. I wonder if you could comment on the general situation during this period and on some of the noteworthy nationalistic ideologists.

KIM: It was toward the end of the 18th century when the Yi dynasty ran into a blind alley. This was when the society of the masses became extremely feeble. Finally, the nation's sovereignity was taken away by Japan, and after the loss of the country there arose a patriotic movement to retrieve her independence. There were many patriots who fought to the very end for the cause of independence of their fatherland around the time of the Samil (March First) Independence Movement, but men like Sin Chae-ho, the historian, Pak Un-sik of the Confucian circle and Han Yong-woon of the Buddhist circle were the most representative figures. Han Yong-woon's *Justification for Korea's Independence* has become an invaluable document, and Sin Chae-ho and Pak Un-sik were in possession of an important philosophy which must be re-evaluated today. In a word, these three men demonstrated an unflinching spirit during the period of national tribulations.

SUH: In the case of Han Yong-woon in the Buddhist world, his *Theory of Restoration* did not consist in the mere removal of the old in Buddhism, but also in teaching it a new future-oriented posture. Such a reformist ideology was in part inspired by the modern transformation ideology coming from abroad, but some of his views were developed from a sensitive assessment of the changing times based on his Buddhistic self-awakening.   (Translated by Song Yo-in)

1. 如來立像(部分)　慶北 月城

2. 神仙寺磨崖佛像群　慶北 月城

3. 三花嶺石造彌勒世尊　國立慶州博物館

4. 慶州拜里石佛立像　慶北 月城

5. 慶州南山佛谷石佛坐像　慶北 慶州

6. 金銅彌勒菩薩半跏像　서울　國立中央博物館

7. 瑞山磨崖三尊佛像(発見당시의 外景) 忠南 瑞山

8. 金銅彌勒菩薩半跏像　서울 國立中央博物館

9. 金銅彌勒菩薩半跏像　서울 國立中央博物館

10. 癸酉銘全氏阿彌陀佛三尊石像　서울 國立中央博物館

11. 軍威三尊石窟 三尊佛　慶北 軍威

12. 甘山寺石造阿彌陀佛立像　서울 國立中央博物館

13. 甘山寺石造彌勒菩薩立像　서울 國立中央博物館

14. a. 石窟庵 內部　慶北 月城

b. 石窟庵　金剛力士像　慶北　月城

c. 石窟庵　十一面觀音菩薩像
慶北　月城

15. 慶州南山神仙庵磨崖菩薩半跏像　慶北 慶州

16. 桐華寺毘盧庵石造毘盧舍那佛坐像　慶北 大邱

17. 慶州南山三陵溪磨崖坐像　慶北 月城

韓國文化 시리즈　第3輯

韓國의　佛教文化

國際文化財團

1974

韓國文化시리즈 發刊辭

韓國과 韓國文化에 대한 관심은 1960年代이래로 國內外를 막론하고 현저하게 高潮되었다. 한국인 자신은 과거 오랜 時日에 걸쳐 그들의 先祖가 쌓아 올린 傳統과 文化의 特性이 과연 무엇이며, 그들로 하여금 어제의 슬기, 오늘의 矜持, 내일의 榮光을 가능케 해 주는 文化의 바탕이 어떤 것인가에 대해 새로운 檢討의 기회가 있기를 원했다. 이와 때를 같이하여 한국의 벗으로서, 東洋의 眞珠와도 같은 이 由緒 깊은 半島의 역사와 현실에 대해, 그리고 未來의 貢獻에 대해 많은 관심을 보여준 友好的 外國人士 또한 한국의 文化에 대한 호기심을 增大시켜 왔다. 그들은 한국이 오랜 기간 동안에 축적한 그 文化的 遺産이 현실에 어떻게 反映되어 있으며, 未來를 위해 어떻게 활용될 것인가에 대해 특히 알고 싶어하고 있다.

國際文化財團은 이러한 要請과 必要에 응하며, 아울러 本財團이 적극적으로 意圖하는 바 한국문화의 海外紹介 및 國際間 交流의 목적을 위해 「韓國文化시리즈」를 발간하기에 이르렀다. 이미 1970년에 한국에서 열렸던 「펜」클럽 한국本部 주최의 世界作家大會에 즈음하여 「한국文學의 諸譜」이란 一卷을 본재단에서 出刊한 바 있거니와 앞으로 계속하여 一貫된 編輯方針아래 한국文化의 여러 側面을 順次的으로 소개코자한다. 그 방침이란 한 마디로 해서 특정한 主題아래 相互聯關性을 지닌 무게있는 論文을 모아 한권의 책을 엮는 것인 바, 主眼點을 韓國人의 文化樣態, 思考方式, 傳統과 現實의 調和, 自己發見에의 노력 등에 두어 궁극적으로 「韓國의 理解」라는 一點에 귀착하게끔 하는데 있다. 그리고 이 一聯의 主題는 각 분야를 可及的 망라하는데 重點을 둘 것이며 지나친 아카데미즘을 止揚하여 일반 敎養人의 이해에 資함과 동시에 특히 外國人士의 韓國理解를 念頭에 두고자한다.

本시리즈의 또 하나의 特色은 위와 같은 意圖를 최대한으로 반영시켜 國文 및 英文의 두개 텍스트를 동시에 收錄하는데 있다. 이러한 노력이 한국문화의 國內外에 걸친 理解와 紹介를 위한 보다 효과적인 방법임을 自負하며 내용의 선택에 있어서도 유능한 한국학자에 의한 글은 물론이요, 한국에 理解가 깊은 外國人學者에 의한 論文에도 항상 유의할 것이다. 그리고 이러한 方針을 살리기 위해 斯界의 專門人士들로서 編輯委員會를 구성하여 최선의 成果를 거두고자한다.

1970년대의 찬란한 새 나라 建設에 步調를 맞추어 本財團의 위와 같은 努力이 조금이라도 보람있기를 염원하면서 關心있는 人士들의 많은 聲援과 鞭撻을 바랄뿐이다.

1973년 1월

國際文化財團

理事長　全　信　鎔

目　　次

序 文

全 信 鎔

本 文化財團은 우리 傳統文化의 再評價와 그 繼承의 方法問題가 최근 활발히 논의되고 있음을 보고 「한국文化시리즈」를 刊行하고 있거니와 그 제 1권에서 「한국文學의 諸譜」, 제 2권에서 「한국의 선비文化」를 다루었고 여기 제 3권에서는 「한국의 佛教文化」를 다루게 되었다.

西紀 4세기末 처음으로 高句麗에 傳來한 佛教는 그후 百濟·新羅의 순서로 소위 古代三國에 전파되었다. 불교 傳來初期는 三國이 각각 中央集權體制를 강화하므로 部族이나 氏族國家들을 통합하기 위한 征服戰이 빈번하던 불안한 과도기였다. 이같은 시기에 王族이나 貴族춘신의 소수 엘리트들에게 있어서 심오한 思想體系를 지닌 佛教思想은 통일국가를 형성하는 데 요청되는 새로운 統合理念을 제시하여주는 外來宗教思想이었다. 불교는 퇴색한 部族神話나 原始信仰을 지양하는 새로운 고급 종교로서 나타난 것이다. 더구나 西域으로부터 中國本土에 傳來되어 중국적으로 변용되는 과정에서 다분히 護國的 경향으로 기울어진 불교는 三國에 傳來된 후 당대의 王族이나 貴族같은 지배층의 의향에 들어맞았다. 發祥地인 인도에서 직접 傳來되지 않고, 西域과 中國을 경유하여 傳來된 불교이기 때문에 어느 정도의 變容은 막을수 없었다. 한편 과도기의 불안한 상황에서 고통을 겪어야하는 庶民들에게 불교의 慈悲精神은 한가닥 위안을 주는 새로운 구제의 기쁜 소식이었다. 部族國家의 崩壞와 함께 소박한 部族神話와 신앙까지 잃은 서민들에게 구제의 길을 보여주는 불교는 새로운 신앙을 불러 일으켰다. 그리하여 彌陀信

仰, 彌勒信仰같은 祈福的 要素가 농후한 신앙이 유행하였다. 印度的 來
世觀보다는 西域, 中國的 풍토에서 변용된 現世利益的 祈福信仰이 삼국
시대 서민층에게는 쉽게 受容되었다.

이와같이 불교는 삼국에 傳來되어, 新羅에서만 固有信仰과의 마찰이
있어 異次頓의 殉教를 낳았을 뿐, 별로 저항도 받지 않고 수용되어 土着
하면서 새로운 문화를 이룩할 土壤을 조성하였다. 그후 1600여년의 오
랜 역사의 흐름과 더불어 불교는 多方面에서 다양한 형태로, 문화의 꽃
을 피웠다. 哲學, 文學分野를 비롯하여 造型美術分野에서 독특한 美를
창조하였다. 특히 조형미술의 탁월한 솜씨는 오늘에 이르러 허다한 國寶
級 文化財의 대부분을 차지하는 佛教文化財가 그 優雅와 精巧를 세계에
널리 자랑하고 있다. 이 책에서는 한때 전성을 이루었던 新羅의 造型佛
教文化의 대표작들을 視覺的效果를 고려하여 사진과 함께 수록하였다.
造型美術의 전통은 그 淵源을 삼국의 불교문화에서 찾을 수 있고 三國
중에서도 百濟나 高句麗보다는 文化財의 수량이나 조형미적 가치에서나
대표적 지위를 新羅佛教가 차지하고 있기 때문에 新羅의 조형문화만을
集約的으로 다룬것이다.

불교의 傳教는 인도에서 西域으로, 西域에서 中國으로, 中國에서 韓
半島 三國으로, 그리고, 三國에서 日本의 순서로 이루어졌다. 三國에
傳來된 불교는 곧 고구려나 백제, 신라에 의하여 일본에 소개되었다. 일
본에서 최초의 寺院建築과 壁畵는 삼국에서 건너간 歸化人들에 의하여
傳授되었고 형성되었다. 그러므로, 日本古代文化를 말하려면, 반드시
三國의 古代文化를 먼저 말하지 않을 수 없다. 그래서 이 책에도 고대의
韓日佛教文化의 交流關係를 다룬 논문 한 편을 실었다. 그러나, 우리 문
화를 객관적 안목에서 예리하게 관찰할 수 있는 外國人의 글 한편 썩을
싣도록 한다는 방침에 따라 韓日佛教文化의 交流에 관한 논문은 古代史
를 연구하는 日本人學者에게 집필을 의뢰하였다.

新羅佛教라하면 선뜻 머리를 스치는 인물이 있다. 그는 唐나라로 求
法의 길에 올랐다가 도중 骸骨바가지에 든 물을 모르고 마시는 순간

〈一切唯心造〉의 이치를 깨치고 신라로 도로 돌아왔다는 인물, 그후 王
相들의 會衆에서 佛法의 奧義를 거침없이 說法하는 道人인가 하면, 閭巷
에서 표주박 장단에 無碍歌를 부르는 狂人의 행색을 하던 奇人이 있다.
그는 다름아닌 신라불교의 대표적 존재로 손색이 없는 元曉였다. 그와
瑤石公主 사이에서 태어난 제2세가 신라에서 첫손 꼽히는 儒學者 薛聰
이었다는 사실도 그의 인물만큼 기이하다. 또 元曉만큼 막대한 양의
著述을 한 碩學도 드물다. 그는 佛法의 깊은 이치를 깨달았고 동시에
그 이치대로 無碍行을 실천한 宗敎人이었다. 그래서, 그의 저술 가운
데서 한 편을 번역하여 여기 싣도록 했다.

　佛敎는 高麗王朝에 이르러 國敎的 대우를 받았고 승려도 귀족에 가까
운 지위를 누렸다. 禪宗과 敎宗의 兩大派뿐 아니라 선종과 교종내에서
도 여러 종파가 있어 百家爭鳴하는 전성기를 이루었다. 王子의 신분에
서 出家한 大覺國師를 위시하여 많은 王師·國師들이 배출되었다. 또 해
마다 燃燈會 같은 불교행사가 국가적규모로 개최되므로 불교는 상류층만
아니라 서민층에까지 널리 유포되었다. 그러나, 高麗佛敎 하면 그 文化
財的 가치를 세계에 떨친「八萬大藏經版」간행을 빼놓을 수 없다. 北方
民族의 南侵때문에 종종 王朝存亡의 위기를 겪었던 고려조가 護國을
佛法의 加被力에 의존하려는 종교신앙적 기원에서 조성된 국가적 사업
이었다 하더라도 당시(13세기) 여러지방에 유통되었던 방대한 佛經들을
集大成하였다는 것은 18세기 西歐의 百科全書派의 업적에도 비유될 만하
다. 또 正確性과 精巧性을 다른 유사한 藏經 刊行에서 찾을 수 없다는
점은 우리 조상이 인쇄기술에서 보인 훌륭한 슬기를 말하여준다.

　朝鮮王朝 5백년은 불교의 受難期였다. 철학적 입장을 전혀 달리했던
儒林의 선비들은 불교의 信仰自由를 용허하지 않았다. 더구나 儒林이
政界를 주름잡던 지배층을 형성하고 있었기 때문에 불교에 대한 탄압은
거의 일방적으로 감행되었다. 같은 유교의 禮節을 숭상하고 같은 철학
적 입장을 固守하면서도 의견을 달리한다는 이유만으로 他派에 대하여
가차없는 肅正의 칼을 휘둘렀던 儒林들이었다. 따라서 그들의 눈에는

佛敎와 그 僧侶가 反禮節로 보이고 더구나 철학을 달리하는 邪敎로 비
첬기때문에, 儒敎勢力이 지배하는 사회에서 불교와 승려들은 철저하게
疎外된 음지에서 어두운 세월을 보내야 했다. 그러다가 조선왕조에
衰亡의 징조가 보이고, 開化의 바람이 한창 불어 닥치던 20세기초, 실
의와 허탈상태에 놓여진 佛敎界에 〈파괴는 건설의 어머니〉라는 과격한
구호를 외치며 「佛敎維新論」序文에서 불교의 소생을 시도하였던 인물이
나타났다. 그가 바로 萬海 韓龍雲이다. 日帝의 總督政治에 끝까지 저항
을 계속한 그는 區廳 戶籍에 자녀의 入籍까지 거부하였다. 그는 불교가
가르치는 각오에서 우러나오는 不退轉의 의지를 가지고 불의에 대하여
저항하였다. 불타는 애국열과 불교에 대한 신앙적 정열에다가 그는 또
文學에서도 남다른 천재적 소질을 보여 주었다. 「님의 沈默」으로 대표
되는 그의 詩는 당시의 문단에서 가장 선구적인 新詩였다. 여기에 그의
문학에 관한 논설 한 편을 실었다.

끝부분에 韓國佛敎文化史의 景觀을 國史學者와 佛敎學者의 對談形式
으로 엮어보았다. 한국의 불교문화에서 元曉, 韓龍雲같은 대표적 거물
들이 등장하는 무대에서 그 인물의 특성을 보다 두드러지게 부각시키기
위한 의도에서 地平線이 그려진 背景的 의미로 對談을 넣었다. 멀리 울
창한 숲이 있고 가까이에 흐르는 江이 있으며 그 사이에는 여러가지 나
무와 아름다운 꽃들이 피어있는 한국의 그림을 상상하자. 그 그림에 地
平線이 그려져 있지 않으면 遠近의 秩序가 무너지는 불안한 느낌을 안
겨다 줄런지 모른다. 이 책을 읽는 분들에게 정리된 佛敎文化의 景觀을
주므로 불교문화를 보다 깊이 이해하는 데 도움을 주고자 한다.

끝으로 이 한권의 책이 나오기까지 애써주신 여러분들에게 衷心으로
謝意를 표하며, 또 이 叢書의 장래 기획에 기대를 걸어주기를 독자 여러
분에게 바라면서 序文을 마치고자 한다.

元曉의 思想과 生涯

洪　庭　植

1. 新羅 初期佛敎의 性格

신라에 불교가 공인된 것은 제23대 法興王 14년(527)의 일로서, 高句麗(372년 공인)나 百濟(384년 공인)에 비해 거의 150여년이나 뒤떨어진 일이다.　신라의 불교 공인이 이렇게 늦어진 것은 신라에 불교가 늦게 전해진 때문이 아니다. 신라의 불교 전래에 대해서는 현재 4종의 異說이 있는데, 　그중에서 받아들일 만한 것이 제 19대 訥祇王 때(417—458) 沙門 墨胡子(阿道)가 一善郡 毛禮의 집을 중심으로 불교를 펴기 시작했다는 기록으로(註 1) 고구려나 백제에 불교가 전해진 때와 큰 차이가 없다.

신라에 불교가 이렇게 일찍부터 전해졌음에도 그것을 국가에서 정식으로 받아 들이려고 하지 않았음은 신라 사회가 보수적이고 폐쇄적이었음을 의미한다. 좀더 구체적으로 말하면, 위치로 보아 대륙문화의 영향에서 멀리 떨어져 아직도 氏族的 사회 기반에 머물러 있었기 때문이다.

이러한 신라 사회에서 완강한 衆臣의 반대를 무릅쓰고 불교를 공인한 法興王은 신라에 처음으로 律令을 반포하고(王 7년) 중앙집권적 왕권을 강화한 분이다. 그리고 그의 불교 공인을 위해 殉敎한 異次頓은 불교 승려가 아니라 바로 王의 從姪이었다. 이러한 사실들은 律令政治에 입각한 중앙집권적 왕권을 강화하고 文物을 이르키는 데에는 불교사상이 적당하다고 생각되었음을 示唆한다. 그리고 이에 반대한 衆臣은 왕권의 강화를 경계하는 씨족적 보수세력이라고 해석할 수 있을 것이다. 法興王

은 불교 弘布의 뜻을,「蒼生을 위해 修福 滅罪할 곳을 마련하기 위한 것」[註 2]이라고 표현하고 있다. 그의 뜻을 실현하기 위해 목숨을 바친 異次頓은,「이 법을 행하면 온 나라가 泰安하고 진실로 경제에 도움이 된다」[註 3]고 말했다. 신라의 불교 공인은 실로 국가의 발전을 목적으로 한 興國利民에 뜻이 있었으며, 이것은 그대로 신라 初傳期불교의 성격을 규정짓게 된다.

法興王의 뒤를 이어 불교를 크게 이르킨 이는 제24대 眞興王이다. 그는 法興王때 着工되었던 興輪寺를 완공하는 외에, 祇園寺・實際寺・皇龍寺와 같은 大伽藍을 창건하고, 국민의 出家를 허용하며 僧職制를 만들어 教團을 국가에서 통제하였다. 眞興王의 이러한 興佛策으로 불교는 보수적인 신라 사회에 물밀듯이 퍼져 나갔을 것으로 생각된다.

그러나 眞興王이 불교를 크게 일으킨 것도 어디까지나 국가의 발전과 번영을 위한 것이었음을 잊어서는 안된다. 그 두드러진 예를 우리는 그가 창설한 청소년 수련단체인 花郞徒에서 볼 수가 있다. 花郞徒는 國仙 (1인)・花郞(數名)・郞徒로 구성되어 있는데, 최상 중심을 이루고 있는 國仙은 신라에 태어난 彌勒으로 받들어지고 있었다.[註 4] 불교적 〈메시아〉라고 볼 수 있는 彌勒佛에 대한 신앙이 국가를 걸머질 人材를 培養할 청소년 수련단체에 응용되고 있었던 것이다.

불교에서 彌勒佛이 下生할 龍華世界는 轉輪聖王이 다스리는 이상적인 국토이다. 彌勒 신앙과 轉輪聖王 사상은 밀접하게 결부되어 있다는 말이다. 眞興王은 자기의 두 아들을 轉輪聖王의 일종인「銅輪」과「金輪」으로 각각 불렀다. 이것은 그의 불교 興隆이 어디까지나 신라의 국가적 이상을 불교사상을 통해 실현해 보려는 것에 있었음을 나타내고 있다. 뿐만 아니라, 그는 인도 아소카(Asoka)王의 불교적 善政을 본받아 아소카王이 행한 〈법의 巡行〉과 비슷한 국내 巡狩를 했었다.

眞興王・眞智(金輪)王을 이은 眞平王・善德女王・眞德女王들도 모두 불교 興隆에 힘썼고, 신라에 태어난 釋迦族, 또는 利帝利族임을 자처하고 있었다.[註 5] 신라 초기 불교가 이렇게 왕족을 중심으로 국가적인 성격을 짙게 나타내고 있는데, 그들 뿐만 아니라 당시의 高僧들도 그들의 불교 사상에서 국가라는 것을 매우 중요하게 意識하고 있다. 元曉이전의 신라 高僧으로 惠亮·圓光·慈藏을 들 수 있는데, 이제 그들에게서 그러한 면을 잠간 살펴 보자.

眞興王때 高僧 惠亮은 國統(最高僧職)의 자리에 오르면서 곧 護國的의식인 仁王百高座와 八關會를 열었고(551), 眞平王때 중국유학을 마치고 돌아온 圓光은 세속 생활을 위한 五戒를 세웠으며, 승려의 신분으로, 비록 왕명에 의한 것이긴 하지만, 고구려를 멸하기 위해 隋에 援兵을 청하는 乞師表를 지었다. 善德女王 5년에 唐에 들어갔다가 同王 12년에 歸國한 慈藏은 皇龍寺에 구층탑을 세웠는데(645), 이것도 국가의 안녕과 발전을 빌기 위한 것이었다. 그는 大國統의 자리에 올라 승려의 紀綱을 바로 잡는 한편, 衣冠文物을 唐에 따를 것을 국가에 건의했다. 이 밖에도 그는 文殊菩薩의 住處가 강원도 오대산이며 신라 땅이 불법에 가장 인연이 많은 국토라는 것을 주장했다. (註 6)

三國時代의 신라 불교가 이렇게 국가적인 성격을 띠고 있는 것은 三國이 서로 국가의 存亡을 판가름할 정도로 치열한 전쟁을 遂行하고 있던 당시의 상황으로 미루어 보아 이해가 갈만하다. 신라 뿐만 아니라, 고구려나 백제의 불교도 모두 그러한 성격을 띠고 있었으며, 삼국 불교의 이러한 성격은 삼국간의 대립과 전쟁이 치열해질 수록 더욱 심해져 갔을 것이다.

그러나, 불교의 순수한 종교적 목적에서 볼때 이러한 국가적 성격이 과연 정당성을 주장할 수 있을까? 大乘佛敎에 의하면, 우리의 세속적인 현실은 有無·一異·染淨 등을 분별하는 妄念에서 緣起한 것이다. 따라서 그러한 분별심을 멸하여 맑고 고요한 眞如(tathātā)의 세계로 돌아감을 종교적 목적으로 삼고 있다. 그리고 有無·一異·染淨 등을 分別하는 것을 俗諦(Samvrti-Satya)라 하고 그러한 분별을 여읜 것을 眞諦(Paramārtha-Satya)라고 하여, 俗諦보다는 眞諦에 종교적 가치를 인정하고 있음은 물론이다. 이러한 견지에서 볼 때, 他國을 멸하여 自國

을 존립시키려는 어떠한 의도도 불교적으로는 바람직한 일이라 할 수 없을 것이고 이러한 의식은 불교에 대한 이해가 깊어짐에 따라 더욱 뚜렷해져 갔으리라 생각된다.

따라서 국가의 세속적 목적과 불교의 가치관 사이에는 일종의 〈갭〉이 생기고 그러한 〈갭〉은 점점 크게 벌어지지 않을 수가 없었을 것이다. 신라의 三國統一에 文筆로서 武功에 못지 않는 功을 쌓은 强首가, 불교는 속세를 떠난 外教이니 자기는 儒學을 하겠다(註7)고 말한 것은 주목할 만한 일이다. 이러한 견해는 불교의 진정한 뜻이 무엇인가를 잘 모르고 있는 데서 오는 지도 모른다. 그러나 어떻든 그러한 문제가 일어났다면, 이에 대한 解明이나, 교리적인 설명이 提起되었어야 했을 것이다. 만일 그렇지 않았다면 국가의 세속적 목적과 불교의 出世間的 가치관은 서로 어긋나, 신라 불교의 국가적 성격은 파탄에 이르고 말았을 것이다.

이러한 때에 元曉(617—686)라는 위대한 불교사상가가 나타나, 起信論의 「一心二門」說에서 놀라운 이론을 전개하여 이 문제를 해결 한다.

2. 起信論海東疏 宗體文의 吟味

元曉는 起信論에 대해서 많은 저술을 하여, 현재 이름이 알려진 것만 해도, 大乘起信論疏 2권(現存)·大乘起信論 宗要 1권·大乘起信論疏科 文 1권. 大乘起信論科簡 1권·大乘起信論別記 1권(現存)·大乘起信論私 記 1권·大乘起信論大記 1권 등의 7책을 헤아릴 수가 있는데 이것으로 起信論에 대한 그의 연구가 어떠했던가를 알 수 있다.

이 중에서 현존하고 있는 것은 大乘起信論疏와 大乘起信論別記의 2책 뿐인데 전자가 起信論에 대한 주석이라면 후자는 이 주석에 다시 이론적인 설명을 따로 附記한 것이다. 따라서 이 두 책은 서로 떨어질 수 없는 관계에 있으므로 이 둘을 합본하여 起信論海東疏記會本이란 형태로 전해지고 있는 것도 있다.

元曉는 起信論을 주석함에 있어서 ① 宗體 ② 題名 ③ 消文의 순서로 하고 있는데, 그 宗體를 밝히는 첫머리에서 「大乘(Mahāyāna)」을 다음 과 같이 표현하고 있다.

然夫大乘之體也 蕭焉空寂 湛尔沖玄. 玄之又玄之 豈出萬像之表. 寂 之又寂之 猶在百家之談. 非像表也 五眼不能見其軀. 在言裏也 四辯 不能談其狀. 欲言大矣 入無內而莫遺. 欲言微矣 苞無外而有餘. 引之 於有 一如用之而空. 獲之於無 萬物乘之而生. 不知何以言之 强號之 謂大乘.

大乘의 法體는 쓸쓸한듯 고요하고 맑은듯 玄妙하다. 현묘하고 다 시 현묘하니 어찌 萬物의 겉에 나올 것이며, 고요하고 다시 고요 하니 오히려 사람들의 말속에 있다. 겉에 나타나지 않으므로 五 眼으로도 그 몸을 볼 수가 없고, 말속에 있으므로 四辯으로도 그 모양을 말할 수가 없다. 크다고 말할까 하니 속이 없을 만큼 작 은 것에 들어 가고도 남음이 없고, 작다고 말할까 하니 밖이 없을 만큼 큰 것을 감싸고도 남음이 있다. 있는 것으로 칠까 하니 하나 같은 것(一如)이 그것을 써서 비우고 없는 것으로 칠까 하니 萬物 이 그것을 타고 나온다. 이것을 도대체 무엇이라고 불러야 할까. 억지로 이름 붙여 본 것이 大乘인 것이다.

大乘佛敎가 어떤 것인가는 부처님의 五眼(肉·天·慧·法·佛)으로도 볼 수 없고 四無碍辯(法·義··辭·樂說)으로도 설할 수 없다는 것이 다. 부처님도 볼 수 없고 설할 수 없는 것을 어찌 중생들이 그에 대해 서 이러니 저러니 말할 수 있겠는가. 불교는 虛無寂滅의 道라거나 불교 와 국가는 서로 아무런 도움도 되지 않는다고 생각하기 쉬운데, 그러한 생각에 一針을 加하는 듯한 말이다.

大乘의 法體는 도대체 어떤 구조를 가지고 어떤 작용을 나타낼 수 있 는 것이기에, 그렇게 부처님의 눈으로도 볼 수 없고 부처님의 辯才로도

말할 수 없다는 것일까? 만일, 그럴만한 뚜렷한 이유도 없이 덮어 놓
고 大乘은 그렇게 불가사의한 것이라고 말한다면 그야말로 헛된 과장이
오 盲信의 강요에 불과할 것이다. 그러나 元曉는 大乘의 法體가 그렇게
불가사의한 이유 즉, 別記의 문장에 곧 이어 다음과 같이 제시하고
있다.

其體也 曠兮其若太虛而無私焉 蕩兮其若巨海而有至公焉. 有至公故
動靜隨成. 無其私故 染淨斯融. 染淨融故 眞俗平等. 動靜成故 昇降
參差. 昇降差故 感應路通. 眞俗等故 思議路絕. 思議絕故體之者乘影
響而無方. 感應通故 祈之者超名相而有歸. 所乘影響 非形非說. 旣超
名相 何超何歸. 是謂無理之至理 不然之大然也.

그 法體는 광활함이 虛空과 같아 私가 없고, 호탕함이 大海와 같
아 公에 지극하다. 公에 지극하므로 動靜이 따라 이루어지고, 私
가 없으므로 染·淨이 융통해진다. 染·淨이 융통해지니 眞·俗
이 평등하고, 動靜이 이루어지니 오르내림의 차이가 있다. 오르
내림의 차이가 있으므로 感應의 길이 트이고, 眞·俗이 평등하니
思議할 길이 끊긴다. 사의할 길이 끊김으로 그것을 체득한자는
그림자와 메아리를 타고 모남이 없고, 감응의 길이 트이므로 그
것에 기도하는 자는 名相을 넘어 돌아감이 있다. 타는 바 그림자
와 메아리는 形體도 아니고 言說도 아니며, 名相을 이미 넘었거
니 무엇을 넘고 어디로 돌아간다는 말인가, 이야말로 이치가 없
는 듯한 지극한 이치이며, 그러지 않을 것 같으면서 크게 그러한
것이로다.

이 別記의 문장에는 낯선 불교 술어들이 쏟아져 나오고 이론이 까다
롭게 진행되고 있어 무슨 뜻인지 도무지 이해가 되지 않는다고 말할런
지도 모른다. 당연한 말이다. 元曉의 起信論疏를 冠하고 있는 그 宗體
文과 이에 대한 別記는 漢字로 겨우 240字(宗體文 122字, 別記 128字)

밖에 안 되는 短文이다. 元曉는 이 짧은 글속에 그의 起信論 연구를 결론적으로 집약해 놓은 것이다. 따라서 元曉 思想의 핵심적인 것이 집약된 이 주옥같은 글을 이해하기 위해서는, 元曉의 起信論疏와 別記의 全文에 나아가 그것을 깊이 연구해 보지 않으면 안된다. 따라서 자세한 내용은 原文을 직접 읽어 줄 것에 기대하고, 다음에 간단히 그 요점만을 소개하고자 한다.

大乘佛敎에는 두가지 철학체계가 있다. 하나는 龍樹(Nāgārjuna 150—250)와 提婆(Āryadeba 170—270) 등에 의하여 전개된 中觀思想(Mādhamika)이고, 다른 하나는 彌勒(Maitreyanātha 270—350)·無者(Asaṅga 310—390)·世親(Vasubandhu 320—400)등에 의하여 전개된 唯識思想(Vijñaptimātratā)이다. 起信論은 이들을 각각 眞如門과 生滅門이라고 부르고 있다.

眞如門에 의하면, 一切는 生滅함이 없이 본래부터 고요하다. 오직 妄念에 의하여 有無·一異·染淨·動靜과 같은 차별이 있을 뿐이다. 따라서 중생은 본래 열반에 들어 있어, 번뇌를 여읜 뒤에 열반에 든다는 것은 잘못된 생각이라고 한다. 다시 말하면 생사와 열반은 둘이 아니라는 것이다. 이에 대해서 生滅門에서는 一切는 阿賴耶識(Ālayavijñāna)이라는 染心에 의하여 일어난 것이라고 한다. 따라서 열반은 阿賴耶識의 滅盡에 의하여 얻어지는 것이므로, 生死와 열반은 차이가 없을 수가 없다고 한다.

眞如門과 生滅門은 이렇게 서로 立脚地가 다르다. 元曉는 그들의 차이를 크게 네가지로 보고 있다. 첫째, 그들은 교리적 영역에 있어서 서로 정반대를 이루고 있으니, 진여문이 사물의 本體적인 면(理, 體), 즉 眞에 속해 있다면, 生滅門은 사물의 現象적인 면(事·相), 즉 俗에 속해있다고 말할 수가 있다. 둘째, 진여문은 生死(俗)와 열반(眞)을 평등한 것으로 보는 데 대해서(通相), 생멸문은 그들에 차이가 있다고(別相)보고 있다. 세째, 생멸문에는 法을 이르킬 생성능력이 있지만 진여문에는 그것이 없다. 네째, 진여문과 생멸문은 술어 사용의 면에 있어서도 서로 차이를 나타내고 있다는 것이다. 眞如門과 生滅門은 그들 사이에 이렇게 본질적인 敎理差를 갖고 있기 때문에 서로 대립하지 않을 수 없는 상태에 있다. 인도와 중국에서 中觀思想과 唯識思想이 대립하여 시끄럽게 諍論을 벌리고 있었음은 이 때문이다.

그러나 이들이 아무리 대립적인 교리차를 갖고 있다고 해도, 다같이 大乘佛敎인 이상 중생의 마음(心)을 法體로 삼아 그 최대의 治用을 목적으로 하고 있다는 점에 있어서는 다를 수가 없을 것이다. 起信論이 着眼한 점은 바로 이 點이다. 그리하여, 「一心에 의하여 眞如·生滅 二門이 있다」고 하여 그들 사이를 가로막고 있는 대립적인 요소를 완화하는 데에 최선을 다하고 있다.

기신론의 이러한 노력으로 진여문과 생멸문은 상당히 접근하여, 특히 생멸문이 阿賴耶識이라는 染心을 멸하여 一心의 本源에 돌아 갔을 때, 일체의 染相을 여읜 그 淸淨한 생멸문의 心體는 진여문의 眞如와 동일한 모습을 띠게 된다. 따라서 이때 진여문과 생멸문은 和合하여 불가사의한 大乘의 法體를 이루게 된다.

진여문과 생멸문이 이렇게 一心의 本源에서 화합하면, 그다음에는 어떠한 현상이 일어나게 될까. 染·淨을 동일할 것으로 보는 진여문의 기능은 생멸문에 작용하여 그에게 眞俗을 평등한 것으로 보게 해줄 것이다. 그러면, 생멸문이 갖고 있는 독특한 생성의 능력은 眞俗差別의 制約에서 자유로워져 자연히 불가사의한 業을 일으키게 될 것이다. 이와 함께 진여문도 眞에서 俗으로 나오게 된다.

진여문이 眞에서 俗으로 나오면, 이곳은 생멸문에 속한 영역이므로, 動靜을 다르다고 보는 생멸문의 기능이 强盛해져, 이것이 진여문에 작용하여 그에게 오르내림의 차이를 알게 해 준다. 그러면 言說分別을 부정하는 완고한 진여문에도 말이 통하게 되어 자기 본자리에 내려가게 될 것이다. 이와 함께 생멸문도 俗에서 眞으로 들어가게 된다.

眞에 들어가면, 다시 진여문의 기능이 强盛해져 俗으로 나오고, 俗에 나오면 다시 생멸문의 기능이 강성해져 眞으로 들어간다. 그리하여 진여·생멸 二門이 和合된 大乘의 法體는 眞에서 俗, 俗에서 眞으로 실로 圓融無碍하게 生動하게 되는 것이다. 이러한 大乘의 종교적 경지를 나는 眞俗圓融無碍라고 부르고 싶다.

眞俗圓融無碍에 이르는 이론적 과정이 起信論에는 뚜렷하지 않다. 그곳에는 다만 體·相·用의 三大가 大乘의 종교적 목적(義 ortha)으로 설해져 있을 뿐이다. 그러나 元曉의 起信論疏·別記, 특히 위에서 소개한 疏 宗體文에 대한 別記에는 그것이 집약적으로 아로새겨져 있다. 別記의 문장은 前文의 末句를 後文의 머리에 두는 承遞法을 써서 빙빙 도는 구조를 띠고 있어 얼른 내용을 파악하기가 어렵다. 따라서 먼저 그들을 계통을 찾아 갈라보면 다음과 같은 두 갈래가 된다.

大乘의
法體
{
(Ⅰ) ⓐ광활함이 허공과 같아 私가 없음→ⓑ染·淨이 융통해짐→ⓒ眞俗이 平等함→ⓓ思議할 길이 끊김→ⓔ이것을 체득한 자는 影響을 타고 모남이 없음.

(Ⅱ) ⓐ호탕함이 大海와 같아 公에 至極함→ⓑ動靜이 따라 생김→ⓒ오르내림의 차가 있음→ⓓ感應의 길이 열림→ⓔ이것에 祈禱하는 자는 名相을 넘어 돌아감이 있음.
}

大乘의 法體를 이루고 있는 이 두 갈래 부분에서, 「광활함이 虛空과 같아 私가 없다」는 귀절(Ⅰ—a)은 眞如門에 해당되고, 「浩蕩함이 大海와 같아 空에 至極하다」는 귀절(Ⅱ—a)은 생멸문에 해당된다는 것은 누구나 元曉의 起信論疏를 읽어본 사람이면 쉽게 느낄 수가 있을 것이다. 진여문은 주로 허공에 비유되고 생멸문은 주로 바다물에 비유되기 때문이다. 이 두 귀절이 「大乘의 法體」라는 主語에 대해 述部로 연결되어 있음은 진여·생멸 二門이 一心을 중심으로 和合해 있음을 나타내고 있다.

그 뒤를 잇는 (Ⅰ)의 문장(ⓑ에서 ⓔ까지)에는 진여문이 眞에서 俗으로 나오는 논리적 과정을 시사함이 있고, (Ⅱ)의 문장(ⓑ에서 ⓔ까지)에는 생멸문이 俗에서 眞으로 들어가는 이론적 과정을 示唆함이 있다는 것은 위에서 잠깐 소개한 바를 통해서 어느정도 짐작이 가리라고 믿는다. 別記의 문장이 承遞法을 쓰고, 각 문장은 그 자체안에서 다시 진여문에서 생멸문, 생멸 문에서 진여문의 순서로 語句가 배치되어 있는데, 이것은 문장구조상으로도 「圓融無碍」의 뜻을 표현하기 위한 것으로 볼 수 있을 것이다.

특히 別記의 ⓐ文에서 진여문을 「無私」로, 풀이하고 생멸문을 「至公」으로 풀이하고 있음은 주의할 필요가 있다. 그러므로 해서 진여·생멸 二門이 和合할 때 無私는 至公에 直結되어 「無私奉公」과 같은 강력한 현실참여의 뜻을 표현하기 때문이다. 그리고 생멸문에 속한 문장중에서 「感應의 길이 ˚열리며(d), 이것에 기도하는 자는 名相을 넘어 돌아감이 있다(e)」고 말하고 있는 것도 주의할 필요가 있다. 佛法에는 반드시 종교적 힘이 있으니, 이것은 爲政者는 名相을 떠난 순수한 마음으로 그것에 歸依할 것을 가리키는 말이 아닐까?

疏의 宗體文은 別記의 이러한 이론적 근거에 입각해서 大乘의 法體가 불가사의함을 설하고 있는 것이다. 「大乘의 法體는 쓸쓸한 듯 고요하고 (a) 맑은 듯 玄妙하다(b)」는 그 첫 문장에서 ⓐ文은 진여문을 가리키고 ⓑ文은 생멸문을 가리키고 있다. 진여문은 言說을 떠났으므로 고요하고, 생멸문의 覺心은 不生不滅인데도 生滅을 이르키므로 玄妙한 것이다.

「玄妙한 것이 다시 玄妙하니 어찌 萬物의 겉에 나올 것인가」라는 문장은 생멸문의 「맑은 듯 玄妙하다」는 말끝을 이어 그것이 至極하여 眞에 들어 간 것을 나타낸다. 그러므로 부처님의 五眼으로도 그몸을 볼 수가 없을 것은 물론이다. 「고요한 것이 다시 고요하니 오히려 사람들의 말 속에 있다」는 문장은 진여문의 「맑은 듯 아득하다」는 말끝을 이어, 그것이 지극하여 오히려 俗에 나옴을 나타낸다. 그러므로 부처님의 四辯으로도 그 모양을 말할 수가 없는 것이다.

따라서 그것을 「大乘」이라고 부르고 있지만, 사실은 그럴 수가 없는 것이다. 크다고 말할까 하니 속이 없을 만큼 작은 것에 들어가고도 남음이 없고, 작다고 말할까 하니 밖이 없을 만큼 큰것을 감싸고도 남음이 있기 때문이다. 또 그것을 有라고 볼까 하니 하나같은 것(一如)이 그것을 써서 비우고, 無라고 볼까 하니 萬物이 그것을 타고 나오는 것이다. 이것을 도대체 어떻게 불러야 할까? 억지로 이름 붙여 본 것이 大乘인 것이다.

元曉의 起信論疏를 冠하고 있는 宗體文과 別記는 이와 같이 眞俗圓融無碍한 大乘의 종교적 경지와 그에 이르는 이론적 과정이 주옥처럼 집약되어 있다. 中觀·唯識의 대립과 諍論은 여기에 이르러 비로소 하나로 和解하고, 佛敎의 眞俗價値觀에서 일어나는 모든 문제가 여기에 이르러 비로소 근본적으로 해결된다. 大乘의 이 〈다이너믹〉한 경지를 보고도 누가 다시 불교를 虛無寂滅의 道라고 말하겠는가?

3. 著述活動과 無碍의 實踐

元曉는 저술과 실천생활을 통해 그의 思想을 유감없이 발휘하고 있다. 그는 한국에서 뿐만 아니라 전 불교국을 통해서도 보기 드물 정도로 많은 저술을 하고 있어, 오늘날 史料에 남은 著述名만 해도 무려 100여부 240여권을 헤아리고 있다. 이중에서 현존하고 있는 것은 다음과 같다. (20부 25권 정도).

法華經宗要	1권,	大慧度經宗要	1권
涅槃經宗要	1권,	無量壽經宗要	1권
彌勒上生經宗要	1권,	阿彌陀經疏	1권
金剛三昧經論	3권,	瓔珞本業經疏	(권下)
菩薩戒本持犯要記	1권,	菩薩戒本私記	(권上)
起信論疏	2권,	起信論別記	1권
中邊分別論疏	(권2),	二障義	1권

遊心安樂道	1권,	大乘六情懺悔法	1권
發心文		華嚴經疏	(권5)
十門和諍論(斷片)		判比量論	(跋文)
解深密經疏序文(斷片)			

　이러한 저술들은 거의 모두가 한결같이 위에서 살펴 보았던 眞俗圓融無碍의 입장에서 저술되고 있어, 元曉는 그러한　思想을 확립한 다음에 그것을 弘傳할 목적으로 붓을 든 것이 아닐까 생각될 정도이다. 그가 즐겨 쓴 저술 형식은 經·論의 대의만을 摘記하는「宗要」라는 것인데, 이것은 그가 經·論의 逐字的 해석 보다는 그속에 깃든 생명에 찬 사상성에 보다 관심이 많았음을 의미한다.

　元曉의 현존 저술중에서 학자들의 관심을 많이 끈 것은 十門和諍論인데, 이것은 中觀·唯識의 대립에서 비롯된 여러가지　教學的인　諍論을 十門에 분류하여 和諍한 것으로 보인다. 따라서 이것은 그의　眞俗圓融無碍 사상에서 二門 대립을 극복한 和諍적인 면을 別述한 것으로 볼 수 있을 것이다. 오늘날 겨우 몇장만이 남아 그 전모를 볼 수 없음은 심히 애석한 일이다.

　元曉의 저술중에서 가장 큰 〈센세이션〉을 일으켰던 것은 金剛三昧經疏(3卷)라고할 것이다. 이것은 그가 국왕을 비롯하여 百官·僧侶·俗人이 법당을 메운 皇龍寺에서 자신의 佛教學을 과시했던 것이며, 이것이 중국에 전해져서는 그곳의 飜經 三藏들이「論」이라고 부를 정도로 존중받았던 것이다.(註 8)

　이것도 元曉의 眞俗圓融無碍 사상에 입각해서 저술되고 있음은 물론이지만, 元曉의 起信論疏와는 특히 밀접한 관련을 보여 주고 있다. 따라서 元曉의 起信論疏 및 別記가 大乘의 殊勝한 종교적 경지를 밝혀 주어 사람들로 하여금 안심하고 그것에 믿음을 일으키도록(起信)하는 데에 목적이 있다면, 金剛三昧經疏는 그러한 종교적 경지, 다시 말하면 金剛三昧에 이르는 실천원리 즉 一味觀行(角乘)을 설하는 것이라고 말할 수가 있다. 이런 견지에서 이 두 저술은 원효사상을 불교라는 종교로 定立시키는 두 근간적인 요소라고 할수 있을 것이다.

元曉의 彌陀淨土에 관한 저술로 현존하는 것으로는 無量壽經宗要(1권)·阿彌陀經疏(1권)·遊心安樂道(1권)가 있다. 이 세 책도 대의를 밝히는 첫 부분에 모두 元曉의 起信論疏·宗體文과 비슷한 구조를 가진 문장이 있다. 그리하여 그런 이론적 근거 위에서,「動·寂이 모두 한바탕 꿈이니, 깨달음으로 말할진댄 此岸·彼岸이 없으며, 穢土·淨土가 본래 一心이며, 생사·열반이 둘이 아니다.」라고 논단하고 있다. 따라서 元曉의 彌陀淨土 사상은 그의 眞俗圓融無碍 철학을 특히 일반인을 위해 신앙적 형태로 표현한 것이라고 볼 수 있을 것이다.

元曉의 저술에서 중요한 것을 몇개 예로 들어 보았지만, 그는 이렇게 저술을 통해 그의 사상을 체계화 하며 弘傳하고 있다. 그러나 단순히 저술활동에만 머물러 있었던 것은 아니다. 실제생활을 통해서도 또한 눈부시게 그것을 보여 주고 있다. 元曉의 行狀을 전해주는 중요한 자료로는 현재 宋高僧傳(元曉傳·義湘傳)·三國遺事·誓幢和尙碑 등이 있다. 이제 이러한 자료를 통해 眞俗에 걸리지 않는 그의 일생을 살펴볼까 한다.

元曉의 俗姓은 薛씨요, 어렸을 적 이름은 誓幢이라고 했다. 元曉라는 이름은 그의 自號인데, 당시 사람들은 그를 모두 國音으로 「새벽」이라고 불렀다 한다.(註 9) 그는 眞平王 39년(617) 湘州 押梁郡(지금의 慶尙北道 慶山郡 慈仁面)의 佛地村 북쪽에 있는 밤나무골(栗谷) 裟羅樹밑에서 태어났다.(註10) 그가 집을 떠나 숲에서 태어나고, 또 그가 난 밤나무를 裟羅樹라고 부르는 것은 그를 신라에 태어난 제일의 석가로 보려는 설화적인 뜻이 있는 것으로 생각된다. 석가여래가 열반에 드신 곳은 拘尸那揭羅의 두 裟羅樹(Sāla)가 나란히 서있는 곳이었는데, 元曉는 지금 그 裟羅樹밑에서 태어나고 있는 것이다.

元曉는 그뒤 관채(丱䯻)의 나이(20세 전후)에 기꺼이 出家하게 되는데,(註11) 出家하면서 자기 집을 절로 만들어 이름을 初開寺라 하였다 한다.(註12) 이 무렵 三國은 치열한 전쟁을 수행하고 있었으며, 신라는 끊임 없이 백제의 침공을 받는 약한 위치에 있었다. 善德女王 11년(642)에는 백제에게 獼猴城을 비롯한 40여 城과 大耶城까지 攻取당하고 있는 형편 이었다. 따라서 신라는 적극적인 親唐外交에 나아가고, 高僧 慈藏은 唐에서 돌아와 皇龍寺에 護國의 구층탑을 세우고 있었다(645). 이렇게 긴박한 국내 정세는 젊은 元曉의 佛敎學 연구에 어떠한 영향을 끼치고 있었을까?

元曉의 불교 공부는 어떤 스승에게 사사하여 그의 學統을 잇는 그러 한 것이 아니었다. 그의 불교학에 대해서, 靈鷲山의 朗智에게 배웠다고 도 하고, 興輪寺 法藏의 門人이라고도 하고, 고구려의 亡命僧 普德에게 涅槃經을 배웠다고도 하지만, 元曉의 行狀을 전하는 중요한 문헌(註13)에 는, 「태어나면서부터 영리하여 스승을 따라서 배운 것이 아니라」고 말 하고 있다. 그는 아무런 구속을 받지 않고 자유롭게 求道의 길을 행하 고 있었던 것이다.

眞德女王 4년(650, 唐 永徽 1년)에는 동료 義湘과 함께 入唐의 길에 오른다.(註14) 그의 나이 34세 때의 일이다. 당시 중국 불교계에는 玄奘이 17년간의 天竺求法을 마치고 돌아와(645), 譯經과 佛敎學(唯識)에 새로 운 전기를 마련하고 있었으며, 圓測 神昉과 같은 신라僧들이 그 밑에서 활약하고 있었다. 그러나, 元曉와 義湘의 求法의 길은 여의치 못하였다. 그들이 육로로 遼東에 이르렀을때 고구려 戌羅에게 諜者로 잡혀 겨우 빠져나오게 되는 것이다.(註15)

신라는 그로 부터 4년 뒤 太宗武烈王이 王位에 오르고, 同王 7년(660) 에는 唐과 힘을 합하여 백제를 멸하게 된다. 이 太宗武烈王 때에 元曉 에게는 놀라운 사건이 하나 있게 된다. 그것은 그가 瑤石宮의 寡公主와 결혼하여 아들을 낳게 되는 일인데, 그 내용은 대개 이러하다.

어느날 元曉는 터무니 없이, 「누가 나에게 자루없는 도끼를 빌려주지 않겠는가. 하늘을 받치고 있는 기둥을 잘라버리리라」는 이상한 노래를 부르면서 거리를 돌아다녔다 한다. 그러나, 아무도 이 노래 뜻을 알아

차리는 이가 없었는데, 太宗武烈王이 이 말을 듣고, 「귀한 부인을 만나 어진 아들을 얻고자 하는 것이라」고 하여 그를 瑤石宮에 묵게 하였던 바 과연 公主에게 懷姙이 있어 아들을 낳게 되었다는 것이다. (註16)

元曉와 요석공주와의 사이에 薛聰이라는 아들이 하나 있었다는 것은 사실이다. 그리고 그 薛聰이 신라 十賢의 한사람으로서, 그가 國音으로 訓鮮한 六經文學이 고려때까지도 傳授되고 있었던 것은 틀림없다. (註17) 그러나, 元曉가 薛聰을 낳게 되는 그 경로에 관한 위의 이야기에는 다분히 설화적인 요소가 포함되어 있는 것으로 생각된다. 특히 그가 말한 「하늘을 받치고 있는 기둥을 잘라버리리라(我斫支天柱)」는 귀절은 우리에게 무엇인가를 생각하게 하는 바가 있다.

백제가 망하여 唐에 이르는 海路가 열리자, 일찌기 元曉와 함께 중국 유학을 꾀했던 義湘은 文武王 1년(661, 唐 龍朔1년)에 다시 入唐의 길에 오른다. (註18) 宋高僧傳 義湘傳에는 이때 원효도 처음에는 그와 뜻을 같이 하고 있었던 것으로 되어 있다.

義湘과 元曉는 唐에 건너갈 목적으로 海門 唐州界에 이르러 배를 기다리고 있었다. 이때 모진 비바람을 만나 길가 土龕에 몸을 숨겼던 바, 아침에 일어나 보니 土龕이 아니라 古墳의 骸骨 옆이었다 한다. 그러나, 비는 더욱 심히 오고 땅은 질어 한 발자욱도 더 나아갈 수 없었으므로 埏甕에 몸을 붙이고 있었다. 그러자 밤이 깊기도 전에, 온갖 귀신들이 나타나는 것이 아닌가. 이때 元曉는 歎하기를, 「마음이 生하니 여러가지 法이 생하고, 마음이 滅하니 土龕과 古墳이 둘이 아니로다. (心生故種種 法生 心滅故龕墳不二)」라고 말하고 발걸음을 돌렸다 한다.

義湘이 唐의 智儼 門下에서 華嚴學을 배우게 된 것은 2회째의 入唐 企圖끝에 성공한 것이라는 것은 여러 문헌에 보인다. (註19) 그러나 元曉가 2회나 入唐을 꾀했다는 것은 現存文獻에서는 찾을 수가 없다. 위의 宋高 僧傳 義湘傳에서도 그것이 그들의 2회 째라고는 말하지 않고 있다. 또 원효의 나이 당시에 이미 45세에 해당되고, 시간적으로도 退俗한 뒤의 일이므로 그가 그때 入唐을 꾀했으리라고는 생각하기 어렵다.

따라서 이 이야기도 설화적인 것으로서, 원효의 불교는 중국에서 배운 것이 아니라 無師自悟하여 오히려 중국을 가르쳤다는 그 위대함을, 義湘의 入唐이 이루어진 2회째의 사건에 부쳐 표현한 것이 아닌가 생각된다. 더구나 이 이야기가 指月錄에는, 고분에서 밤중에 목이 말라 시원한 물을 마셨던바, 새벽에 깨어보니 해골 바가지에 고인 물이라 홀연히 깨닫기를,「마음이 생하니 여러가지 法이 생하고 마음이 멸하니 髑髏가 不二라」고 하여 이야기의 내용이 약간 다른 것이다.

이와 같이 이 이야기는 설화적인 성격을 다분히 띠고 있는데, 어떻든 이것은 元曉의 깨달음이 어떤 것이 었으며, 그것이 후세 사람들에게는 어떻게 이해되고 있었던가를 아는데에 좋은 자료라고 할 것이다.「三界는 오직 마음이라(三界唯心)」는 말은 華嚴經 등의 여러 經・論에 자주 나오는 말이다. 그러나, 그 설화속의「心生則種種法生이오 心滅則髑髏不二라」는 귀절은, 起信論의「生滅因緣」項에 나오는「心生則種種法生이오 心滅則種種法滅이라」는 귀절과 너무나도 비슷한 점이 있다. 그리고「心滅則髑髏不二」라는 귀절에서「翕(俗)과 墳(眞)이 둘이 아니라」는 대목은 원효의 眞俗內融無碍 사상에 상통하는 바가 있지 않은가.

元曉의 退俗을 단순한 退俗으로 보아서는 안 될 것 같다. 그의 눈부신 종교적 활동은 실로 이때 부터 전개되고 있기 때문이다. 破戒한 뒤 元曉는 俗服으로 갈아 입고 이름도 小姓居士라고 고친다음,[註20] 眞俗에 걸리지 않는 생활을 했다. 말을 함부로 하는가 하면, 술집이나 倡女의 집에도 거침없이 들어가고, 여염집에 묵는가 하면 山水에 坐禪한다.[註21] 戰陣속도 드나들었던 모양으로 文武王 2년 唐將 蘇定方이 金庾信에게 보낸 軍事機密文을 解讀해 주었다.[註22] 그는 또 華嚴經의「一切無碍人은 一道로 생사를 超出한다」는 귀절에서 이름을 따서 만든「無碍瓠」를 두드리면서 千村萬落을 돌아 다니며「노래와 춤으로써 포교하니, 몽매한 凡夫들도 모두 부처님의 이름을 알고「南無佛」을 염하게 되었다」한다.[註23] 일찌기 그는 芬皇寺에서 華嚴經에 疏를 짓다가 제4 十廻向品에서 붓을 꺾었다고 하는데[註24] 이것은 그가 이렇게 대중속으로 파고드는 것으로써

十廻向의 진정한 뜻을 삼으려고 한 것이 아니었을까? 그는 신라 대중
불교운동의 巨峰이라고 할 수 있을 것이다.

원효의 이러한 눈부신 종교적 활동중에서 특기할 만한 것은 그가
皇龍寺에서 행한 金剛三昧經의 講說이라고 할 것이다.(註25) 어느때 국왕
이 仁王百高座法會를 열어 국내의 碩德을 초청한 일이 있었다. 이때
元曉도 추천 되었지만, 형식에 사로잡힌 당시의 승려들에게 그의 종횡
무진한 행동이 달가울리가 없었다. 따라서 王에게 譖하여 그를 받아
들이지 않게 하였다. 그뒤 왕후의 병이 좀처럼 낫지 않는 것이 인연이
되어 金剛三昧經을 설하게 되었는데 이때 책장이 흐트러진 金剛三昧經
을 復原한 사람은 역시 無碍行을 하던 大安이었고, 그것에 疏를 지을
수 있었던 것은 오직 元曉뿐이었다.

원효가 疏 5卷(廣本)을 지음에 國王은 그것을 皇龍寺에서 講說하게
하였던 바, 시기하는 무리들이 그것을 훔쳐 감추어 버렸다. 元曉는 다시
3日만에 略疏 3권을 지어 이것을 皇龍寺에서 발표하니, 이것이 현존하
는 金剛三昧經論 3권이다. 元曉는 講說을 마치고, 「옛날 100개의 서까
래를 구할 적에는 내가 빠졌지만, 오늘 아침 하나의 대들보를 가로지르
는 곳에서는 오직 나만이 할 수 있다」고 외치니 元曉를 비방하던 무리
들이 얼굴을 들지 못하였다 한다.(註26) 元曉의 無碍行이 형식에 사로잡혔
던 당시의 敎界에 어떻게 생각되고 있었으며, 그럼에도 불구하고 그의
學德이 어떠했던가를 엿보게 하는 좋은 이야기라고 할 것이다.

唐과 연합하여 백제를 멸한 신라는 文武王 8년(668) 마침내 고구려까
지 멸하여 민족적 숙원이던 三國統一을 실현한다. 그러나 신라를 이용
하여 고구려와 백제를 멸한 唐이 이제는 신라까지 멸해 버리려는 본색
을 들어 냈기 때문에 이에 신라는 親唐에서 反唐으로 정책을 전환하여
唐과 다시 전쟁을 벌리게 된다. 신라의 필사적인 反唐戰은 마침내 성공
하여 文武王 17년(677) 唐이 그의 安東都護府를 평양에서 滿州 新城으
로 옮겨 감으로써 名實相符한 신라의 三國統一은 실현된다. 이 삼국통일
이 이루어진 때로부터 9년뒤인 神文王 6년(686)元曉는 70세를 一期로

穴寺에서 入寂하고[註27] 그의 遺骸는 아들 薛聰에 의하여 芬皇寺에 봉안된다.

위대한 사상가는 항상 자기가 처한 사회의 문제가 무엇인가를 잘 알아야 한다. 안 다음에는 그것을 해결할 최선의 길을 모색하여, 저술과 같은 효과적인 모든 방법을 통해서 사람들을 깨우치고 또 실천에 옮겨야 한다. 이 중에서 하나라도 빠지는 것이 있어서는 안될 것이다. 元曉의 일생은 실로 이 모든 점을 다 充足시키고 있다. 신라의 민족통일이 그의 일생중에 이루어지고, 그의 和靜思想을 바탕으로 찬란한 민족문화가 통일신라에 전개된다. 元曉의 叡智는 이렇게 밝은 앞날을 전망했던 신라불교의 「새벽빛」이 었다고 말할 수 있을 것이다.

註

1) 遺事 卷3 興法제3 阿道 基羅
2) 遺事 卷3 興法제3 原宗興法 厭髑滅身
3) 海東高僧傳 卷1 釋法空傳
4) 遺事 卷3 塔像제4 弥勒仙花 未尸郞 眞慈師
5) 眞平王의 諱는 白淨, 善德女王의 諱는 德量, 眞德女王의 諱는 勝曼임
6) 遺事 卷3 塔像제4 五臺山五萬眞身등
7) 三國史記 卷46 强首
8) 宋高僧傳 卷4 元曉傳
9) 三國遺事 卷4 元曉不羈
10) 同上
11) 宋高僧傳 卷4 元曉傳
12) 三國遺事 卷4 元曉不羈
13) 三國遺事 卷4 元曉不羈; 誓幢和尙碑
14) 三國遺事 卷3 前後所 舍利
15) 三國遺事 卷4 義湘佛教
16) 三國遺事 卷4 元曉不羈
17) 三國遺事 卷4 元曉不羈
18) 三國遺事 卷3 前後所 舍利
　※三國遺事 卷4 義湘佛教에는 永徽初; 宋高僧傳 卷4 義湘傳에는 總章 2년
19) 三國遺事 卷3 前後所 舍利; 三國遺事 4卷 義湘佛教
20) 三國遺事 卷4 元曉不羈
21) 宋高僧傳 卷4 元曉傳

22)　三國遺事　卷1　太宗春秋公
23)　三國遺事　卷4　元曉不羈
24)　同上
25)　宋高僧傳　卷4　元曉傳
26)　宋高僧傳　卷4　元曉傳
27)　誓幢和尙碑

新羅의 彫刻

—— 慶州의 石佛을 中心으로——

黃 壽 永

1. 序 論

  민족의 오랜 역사와 문화의 자취를 가직하고 있는 慶州는 민족의 이
동에서 部族의 형성과 고대국가의 건설에서 나아가 마침내 7세기 중엽
에 이르러 韓半島의 통일을 이루므로써 빛나는 新紀元을 이룩함에 성공
하였던 新羅 千年의 古都이다.
  우리 古代史에서 가장 빛나는 새로운 역사의 창조는 이곳에서 이루어
졌으며 그에 따르는 民族史의 光輝는 다시 數世紀에 걸친 평화와 안정
을 가져왔었다. 오랜 세월의 三國鼎立에서 입었던 민족의 傷痕을 다시
아물리고 국토의 수호와 민족문화의 새로운 건설을 위하여 物心의 힘을
한곳에 모았던 곳이기도 하다. 한편 4세기 후반부터 국토의 북으로부터
들어온 불교는 海陸을 통하여 生域에 보급됨에 두터운 믿음으로 받았으
며 國家政教의 바탕을 이룩함에 공헌하였다. 그러나, 新羅는 불교 공인
이 유달리 늦었다. 그 까닭은 신라가 韓半島 東南隅에 偏在하였던. 지
리적 여건도 있었을 것이나 한편 그만큼 신라가 오랫동안 고수하였던
그 자신의 전통과 사상과 예술이 있었기 때문일 것이다. 그러나, 세계종
교인 불교 東漸의 흐름을 막을 수는 없었다 하더라도 그 저항의 흔적만
은 주목되어야 할 것이다.

일찌기 불교를 전하려던 高句麗僧의 수난이나 신라 異次頓의 殉教史實을 소홀하게 넘겨서는 아니될 것이다. 그러나, 신라 또한 6세기에 들어서서는 불교를 공인하지 않을 수 없었으며 그 후 불교는 燎原의 불과 같이 신라의 서울인 오늘의 慶州를 중심으로 확대되었다. 그리하여 마침내 불교를 國教로 삼았고 國王은 친히 이에 歸依하므로서 세계 進運에 발맞추며 國內人心의 쇄신과 教化에 솔선하였던 것이다. 이같은 新羅에 있어서의 불교의 역할은 三國중 다른 두 나라에 비할 때 한층 중대함이 있었다고 보며 그것은 나아가 三國統一의 근본동력의 하나를 이루었다고 생각된다. 三國의 통일이란 군사적 정치적 힘에 의한 승리라 하겠으나 동시에 그것은 신라 국민의 정신적 內實의 귀결이기도 하였다. 그같은 정신적 내실을 형성함에 있어 불교는 신라가 오랫동안 간직되어 오던 고유한 정신내용과의 융합을 통하여 더욱 강력한 힘을 獲得하였던 것이다. 때는 분열에서 통일을, 전쟁에서 화평을 志向하던 時代였다. 이같은 國內外의 추세를 신라는 잘 통찰하고 나아가 그것을 국가이익에 一致시킴에 성공하였던 것이다. 무릇 韓半島에서 불교의 전달은 벌써 그 自體에 통일과 평화를 내포하고 있으므로 그 三國에의 보급은 앞으로의 정신적 통일을 향한 첫 단계이기도 하였다. 그리하여 불교는 마침내 국제정세를 잘 파악하고 國內人心의 歸一을 얻어 최후의 승리를 걷운 신라와 一體가 되었던 것이다. 일찌기 국가형성에 앞서서는 徐羅伐 넓은 땅에 六村을 이룩하여 그들의 단결로서 對外策을 마련하면서 차차 성장하여 왔던 오랜 年輪이 그들에게는 앞으로 大成에 이르는 길이기도 하였다. 그리하여 韓半島 一隅에서 축적되었던 物心의 큰힘은 마침내 點火되고 動力化하여 통일의 大業을 이룩함에 성공하였으니 그를 위하여서는 오랜 세월과 끊임없는 노력과 不動의 목표가 있었던 것이다. 그리하여 최후의 瞬間에 이르러 불교 그 自身이 이룩한 역할이 또한 중대하였으니 固有한 信仰을 오래 간직하여 오던 신라 民心의 動向은 불교에 의존하였으며 새로운 사상과 技藝가 또한 그에 따랐으니 그 담당자는 바로 僧侶였다. 그러므로 그들은 먼저 國難克服을 위한 핵심

에서 그들의 역할을 다하였으며 그들의 教化에 힘입은 지도자들은 나라
를 위하여 身命을 받침에 주저함이 없었다. 그것이 바로 古新羅에 있어
花郞制度 성립의 시대적 배경이니 그들로 하여금 世界情勢에 눈뜨게 하
고 나아가 새 역사 창조를 위한 自覺과 任務를 다하게 하였던 것이다.
동시에 일반 國民에 대한 教化 또한 이같은 國家 최대과업에 獻身함에
기여하였으니 불교는 얼마 안가서 支配階層에서 서민에 이르는 上下
에 均霑함에 이르렀던 것이다. 그리하여 마침내 鐵火와 같이 연마된 新
羅의 國家體制와 그 上下는 위에서 말한 민족사의 新紀元을 그들 손에
서 이룩하는 데 성공하였던 것이다.

　신라의 불교는 이같은 시대를 배경으로 삼아서 그 국토에 전달되어 먼저
支配階層에 의하여 공인되었으며 그 百姓에 의하여 歸依되었던 것이다.
그리하여 불교가 공인되면서 곧 시작된 것이 大刹의 건립이었으니 三國
史記에 보이고 있는 興輪寺 皇龍寺 祇園寺 實際寺 永興寺 三郞寺 芬皇
寺 등이 그들이다. 그중에서도 皇龍寺가 신라 中興祖인 眞興大王에 의
하여 이룩된 까닭은 그만한 시대적 요청에 副應되어서의 일임을 알아야
하겠다. 新羅의 「眞骨貴人」은 慈藏은 중국유학 5년만에 귀국에 앞서서
終南山 圓香禪師를 찾았다. 때는 신라 善德女王 12년(643)[註1]이었다. 禪
師는 그를 찾아온 慈藏에게 觀心으로서 公의 나라를 보니 (「以觀心觀公
之國」) 皇龍寺에 九層의 窣堵波(stupa)를 세우면 海東의 諸國이 모두
公의 나라에 항복하리라고 하였다. 그는 귀국하여 이것을 국왕에 건의
한 것이 곧 동양의 大塔인 高2백25척의 皇龍寺九層木塔이 건립되기에
이르는 直接 契機가 되었던 것이다. 불교 僧侶도 삼국의 통일이 그들
의 최대의 과제이었으며 國刹의 건립 또한 이같은 大前提에서 벗어날
수는 없었던 것이다. 이같이 신라의 불교는 오랜 수난을 겪어 공인되고
난 뒤에는 가장 빠른 受容相을 보였으며 또 그같은 국가적 요청을 따라
서 加速化되었던 것이다. 新羅初期의 佛像彫刻은 이같은 시대와 믿음을
떠나서는 理解할 수 없다고 생각한다. 비록 그 初期佛像의 樣式이나 技
法에서 중국 南北朝의 그것과 高句麗 百濟 등 불교수입의 선진국과의

交流相은 얼마든지 지적할 수 있으며 또 後者는 더욱 강조되어야 마땅
할 것이다. 그러나, 그길은 樣式的 논의는 어디까지나 物的이며 外形的
인 것임에는 아무도 異議가 없을 것이다. 지난날의 外人에 의한 古新羅
의 조각에 대한 논의는 이 범위를 크게 벗어나지 않았으며 또 벗어날
수도 없었다고 생각한다. 그러나, 우리는 전진하여야 하겠고 심화되어야
함은 비단 佛像研究에 있어서만이 아니다. 內外의 兩面에서의 고찰만이
그 眞相을 깊이 꼬집어낼 수 있으며 物心兩面에서의 통찰만이 그 자태
를 全容에서 파악함에 긴요할 것이기 때문이다. 이하 章을 바꾸어 古新
羅와 新羅統一期에서의 신라의 彫像 그것도 金銅像은 일단 제외하고 石
佛을 중심으로 삼아서 간략하게 논의하려는 까닭이다.

2. 古新羅의 石佛

三國이 모두 그러하였거니와 초기의 佛像 특히 중국에서 전달된 불상
은 모두 작은 金銅佛이었다고 생각된다. 그같은 金銅佛은 곧 木造 또는
塑造의 모범이 되었을 것이며 큰 法堂에의 奉安은 金銅佛뿐 아니라 이같
은 재료에 의한 造形이었다고 생각된다. 史上에 유명한 皇龍寺三尊佛은
그 앞에 세워진 上記한 大塔과 더부러 新羅三寶가 되어서 그 종말에 이
르기까지 나라의 두터운 보호와 국민의 깊은 믿음을 받아왔던 것이다.
이같은 皇龍寺의 丈六三尊像은 일찌기 한국에서 鑄成된 최대의 것이었
으니 그 所要金銅의 量은 三國史記 眞興王 35年 春 3 月에 기록이 되어
서 「鑄成皇龍寺丈六像. 銅重 3 萬 5 千 7 斤. 鍍金重 1 萬 1 百98分」이라 하
였다. 오늘 이 皇龍寺 廢址에 남은 이들 塔像址의 巨石의 臺座와 心礎
石의 크기는 無二의 막중한 기념물로서 古都를 찾는 사람들을 놀라게
한다.

이같은 金銅佛이나 오늘에 單 一軀도 아니 전하는 당대의 木像등에 이
어서 또는 그들과 나란히 石像이 발생되었다고 생각된다. 그것은 佛像
彫刻이 토착하는 과정이며 新羅彫刻으로서의 재료적 양식적 특색을 보

이는 첫길이기도 하였다. 한국의 石造佛像은 石塔과 거의 때를 같이 하여서 6세기 후반에 이르러 各國에서 발생한다. 혹은 나라에 따라 다소 時差가 있었다하더라도 600年頃에는 성립한다고 생각한다. 이같은 年代의 추정은 4세기 후반에 불교가 도입된 후 2세기의 時間이 경과하여서 비로소 한국조각이 그 自身의 傳統地盤을 構築할 수가 있었던 까닭이기도 하다. 2세기의 과정이 마침내 스스로의 손으로 그 국토 도처에서 풍부하게 생산되는 花崗岩을 주목하고 驅使하여 이 白堊의 견고한 자연소재를 깎고 다듬어 불교미술의 兩大 예배대상이며 따라서 造形의 雙璧인 塔像을 이룩함에 성공하였던 것이다. 필자는 이같은 自身의 소재를 발견하여 그것을 主材料로 삼아 그 당시의 새로운 外來宗敎인 불교의 예배대상을 고루 造形한 곳에 우리 고대민족미술의 소재적 특징이 주어졌으며 그 樣式과 技法의 差別相이 또한 비롯하였다고 생각한다. 그러므로 花崗岩을 이같이 主材料로서 채택한 工匠과 그 계기를 중시하려는 것이다. 한국을 「石塔의 나라」라고 할 수 있는 것은 일본의 木塔 中國의 塼塔에 대하여 재료적 차별 뿐 아니라 각국이 모두 佛敎造形을 受容하면서 얼마안가서 그 자신의 특색을 발휘하였으며 그 전통의 系脈을 이어나갔기 때문일 것이다.

6세기에 들어 古新羅에 불교가 公認됨을 따라서 伽藍은 平地와 山地두 곳에서 거의 때를 같이하여 건립되었다고 생각된다. 말할 것도 없이 평지와 산지에서는 지형에 의한 制約이 따르기 마련이다. 따라서 國都를 중심으로 삼은 평지에서의 伽藍 건립은 당시의 配案方案을 따라서 堂塔兼備의 건립이 있었을 것이다. 그리하여 皇龍寺址에서 보는바와 같은 南面한 一塔式 伽藍에 金堂은 말할 것도 없거니와 講堂과 다시 이들을 둘러서 廻廊이 있고 中門으로서 출입케 하였던 것이다. 이에 비하면 초기의 山地伽藍은 자연히 그 규모가 작기도 하였거니와 그 다수가 石窟寺院의 형식을 따라서 시대와 장소에 따르는 變相을 나타내기도 하였다. 이것이 필자의 견해인 바 그것은 비단 신라 뿐 아니라 불교전달의 당초에 있어서는 본격적인 寺刹이 경영되기에 앞서서 또는 그와 병행되어서 이같은 山地伽藍이 주로 石窟寺院의 형태를 취하였다고 생각한다.
그것은 인도나 중국이나 또는 백제에 있어서도 동일하였다. 다만 한국에
있어서는 石窟造成을 위하여 上記한 바 화강암이 인도나 중국의 造材와
는 달리 硬度가 높았기에 天然의 巨岩을 穿鑿하여서 塔像奉安을 위한
一大空間을 구성하지는 못하였고 따라서 磨崖佛像을 그 처음부터 造成
하면서 그들을 木造瓦葺의 架構로서 덮는 방식이 채택되었다고 생각된
다. 필자가 數年 이래 조사와 관심을 집중시켜왔던 斷石山 神仙寺 石窟
은 그 대표적인 初期石窟의 適例라고 생각하고 있다.

이 神仙寺는 참으로 중요하다. 경주에서 西南方으로 약 40里 斷石山
頂밑에 자리잡은 것은 吐含山 石佛寺가 이와 正反의 東方으로 거의 等
距離에서 吐含山頂 가까이 경영된 것과 거의 같다. 필자는 서쪽의 斷石
山石窟이 앞으로 더욱 주목을 받아야 마땅하다고 생각하면서 전문학도
뿐 아니라 많은 사람이 그곳을 찾아주기를 바라고 있다. 이 斷石山石窟
은 ㄷ字形을 이루는 몇개의 巨石이 屹立하므로서 天成의 石室을 이루었
으며 西方만을 향하여 開口하였다. 그리고 天蓋는 巨岩사이를 건너서
木造瓦葺의 屋蓋가 덮여 있던 사실이 확인되었다. 人工을 加한 이같은
新羅의 石窟은 통일후인 8세기에 조성된 吐含山 石窟 또한 동일하다.
이곳에 한국 石窟寺院의 초기의 성격이 규정지어졌다고 생각한다. 다행
히 斷石山 석굴에는 內壁에 銘文이 남아 있다. 그리하여 필자는 1968~
9 兩年에 걸쳐서 그 내용을 판독하였던 바 寺名은 神仙寺라 하였으며
석굴에 봉안된 佛名은 彌勒三尊임을 알 수가 있었다. 석굴은 내외로 구
분되는 바 내부의 北壁에는 높이 23척의 如來立像(圖1)이 새겨졌으며
東壁과 南壁에는 각 一軀의 菩薩立像이 새겨져 있어 비록 風化를 입었
으나 그 윤곽을 짐작할 수는 있다. 이같은 彌勒三尊에 대하여 外室의
北壁上에는 합계 四軀의 佛菩薩의 立像과 그 밑에 人物立像 二軀가 있
다. 그리고 현존하는 新羅唯一의 半跏思惟形 菩薩像(圖2)이 이 北壁에
서 他佛像菩薩과 나란히 원위치를 지키고 南面하고 있으며 古代의
徵笑와 그 양식을 오늘에 보여주고 있다. 이 석굴이야말로 이른바 三國

시대 古新羅(6~7世紀)의 彌勒窟인바 寺名 神仙은 동시에 國仙을 가리
킨다. 國仙은 곧 彌勒의 화신이라고 믿어왔으며 花郞을 가리킨다. 따라
서 神仙寺는 곧 彌勒寺요 또 花郞寺이기도 하다. 그런데 이 石窟을
三國史記가 기록한 金庚信 將軍이 入山修道한「中岳石崛」로 추정할 수
있었던 것은 그 造形과 內實에서 推論된 것이라 하겠다. 이에 대하여
吐含山 石窟이 近年의 연구에 따라서 新羅統一의 英主이신 文武大王의
海中陵과 관계되어서 그보다 후대에 이르러 營造된 사실이 추정되기도
하였다. 이들 君臣 二人은 合力하여 三國의 통일을 이룩하였으며 그들
의 死後에도 二人은 힘을 모아서 東海를 지키고 있다고 믿어왔다. 신라
의 國都 東西에서의 신앙과 역사와 인물의 妙好한 三者契合이야말로 신
라 조각의 걸작을 낳았으며 그 같은 믿음이 또한 수호의 힘이 되어서 양
자가 오늘에 전래함에 이르렀다고 필자는 생각하고 있다.

 그러나, 三國期 古新羅의 石佛은 그것만에 그치는 것이 아니다. 그들
은 또하나의 集中區域을 형성하고 있으니 그것이 바로 서울인 慶州南山
의 北峰이라고 생각하며 그 동서 양계곡과 北麓에 남아 있는 石像이 바
로 그것이다. 그들은 오늘 寺址에 있던지 또는 일찌기 옮겨져서 博物館
으로 자리를 바꾸기도 하였다. 그 중에서도 으뜸을 삼을 수 있는 것은
南山北峰(長倉谷)에 자리잡았던 이름높던 三花嶺 彌勒 世尊[註2]이라고 하
겠다. 필자는 이 三尊에 대한 연구를 통하여 오늘 경주박물관에 옮겨진
그들 三像의 尊名과 그 봉안의 장소와 방식 등을 알수가 있었다. 이 三
花嶺三尊(圖3)에 이어서 南山拜里의 三尊(圖4)이 나타난다. 이들 三尊
은 원래 禪房寺址에 있던 것을 그자리에 복원한 것으로서 三花嶺 三尊
보다도 더욱 年代는 降下하나 그보다 크며 모두 立像이다. 그리고 南山
佛谷의 坐像(圖5)은 이들보다 年代가 앞서는 것으로 추정되는 獨尊으로
서 裳懸座의 古式을 보이며 작은 石龕안에 奉安되어 있다. 경주市 仁旺
里서옮긴 石造如來坐像(경주 박물관)이나 原場所가 불분명한 如來立像
(경주 박물관)등은 비록 작으나 또한 古式을 지니고 있어 初期石像으로
추정할 수가 있겠다.

이와같은 三尊形式 또는 獨尊으로서의 佛菩薩像과 더부러 彌勒半跏思惟菩薩像은 古新羅 석상중의 유익한 양식중의 으뜸이 될 것이다. 그중에서도 1909년 松花山 東麓인 오늘의 金山齋에서 발견된 머리가 없는 石像(註3)은 그중의 대표작품으로서 그 전래장소가 古代寺址인 松花房으로 추정된 사실과 더부러 주목할만하다. 이에 비하면 상기한 神仙寺石像은 이보다 앞서는 작품이며 또 近年에 새롭게 조사된 奉化北枝里寺址의 石像은 松花房像보다도 더 늦은 작품으로서 7세기 중엽의 거작으로 추정한다. 이같은 石像은 금동상의 遺例와 더부러 주목되어야 할 것인 바 특히 古新羅에서 이같은 半跏思惟像의 유행은 그 배경이 다시금 추구되어야할 것이다. 해방후의 조사에서 우리는 고구려의 金銅像(註4)一例(圖6)(平壤出土)의 現存함을 알 수 있었으며 또 百濟에서는 扶餘出土의 蠟石小像의 遺例나 그보다도 瑞山 伽倻峽 磨崖三尊像5)(圖7)의 脇侍인 半跏思惟像에서 삼국을 통하여 이같은 양식상의 유행을 알 수가 있었다. 그러나, 三國중에서도 특히 古新羅에서의 이같은 半跏思惟樣式像의 유행은 他二國에 비할때 보다 강력한 믿음의 배경을 생각하지 않을 수가 없다. 그 같은 배경은 같은 彌勒信仰이 중국을 비롯하여 韓半島의 삼국에서 모두 유행되었다하더라도 國情을 따르던 殊異相이 각기 있었으며 그 같은 內實의 차이가 이 형식상의 造形에도 그대로 반영되었다고 할 수 있을 것이다. 오늘 우리는 二軀의 높이 약 3尺의 金銅半跏像(圖8, 9)을 국내에 보호하고 있으며 또 같은 크기의 磨崖像 二軀(註6)를 새로 조사할 수가 있었다. 이에 따라서 東洋三國중에서도 6, 7 두세기에 걸쳐서 韓半島에서의 이 양식상의 유행과 그에 따르던 걸작들의 오늘의 전래를 이해할 수가 있을 것이다. 半跏樣式像은 다시 일본으로 전달되었는데 일본 書紀 敏達天皇 13年(584)條에 보이는 鹿深臣에 의하여 일본에 將來된 彌勒石像이 바로 半跏石像으로 추정된 사실은 주목할 만 하다(註7). 동시에 上記한 三花嶺彌勒世尊의 兩菩薩立像이 일본 白鳳期의 작품들과 매우 닮고 있는 사실 또한 일본과 신라와의 깊었던 交流相을 보이고 있다. 일본에 전래하는 48體佛은 매우 유명하거니와 그중의 數例만을 제

외하고 모두 일본에서의 조성인 사실은 그대로 일본에서의 신속한 受容
相을 보이고 있다. 그같은 사실은 반대로 古新羅에서의 石像 彫刻에서
도 지적할 수 있을 것이다. 花崗岩을 주재로 삼아 圓刻 또는 磨崖로 조
성된 작품의 古拙한 양식과 그 彫法은 시대에 따르던 중국과의 交流相
이 濃淡하게 반영되어있다 하더라도 신라의 석상은 또한 新羅人의 손에
의하여 그들이 습득하고 그들의 信仰內實이 技工의 練磨를 통하여 구현
된 것임은 다시 말할 것도 없다. 이같은 物心兩面에서의 고찰만이 신라
의 古代石像을 고찰하는 길이 될 것이다.

3. 統一初期의 彫刻

　三國의 오랜 對立抗爭이 終幕을 내리고 새로운 질서의 확립을 따르던
것은 왕성한 佛敎伽籃의 건립이었다. 이미 三國末에 있어서 「寺寺星張
塔塔雁行」이라고 표현되었던 王京 경주의 장엄은 다시금 평화와 안정의
새시대를 맞아서 가속되었던 것이다. 文武大王에 의한 四天王寺의 창립
은 護國의 염원이며 동해안에 그 자신이 창립한 感恩寺 또한 그가 死後
까지 東方을 몸소 지키려는 聖慮의 具顯化이었다. 望德寺 등 통일초에
신설된 寺院의 수효도 많거니와 또 한편에 있어서는 기존 사원에 대한
장엄도 한층 加하여졌을 것이다. 그리하여 마침내 新羅王國의 一大佛國
化의 길이 마련되기 시작하였던 것이다. 이같은 國利이외에도 국왕이나
귀족에 의한 大小伽籃의 창립은 國都 경주의 여러곳을 차지하였는데 그
중에서도 신라의 三山의 하나인 狼山 北麓을 차지하였던 皇福寺는 그
으뜸이 되었을 것이다. 이같은 祈福寺院은 더욱 유행되어서 마침내 8세
기 중엽에 이르러 예술의 王者 景德王의 治世에 있어서는 화려하게 꽃
이 피어 문자 그대로 신라 미술의 황금시대를 이룩하였으며 경주의 繁
榮은 아마도 오늘의 상상을 허락하지는 않을 것이다. 중국의 長安 新羅
의 金城 일 본의 奈良은 그당시 세계의 이름난 大都市로서 이들 사이는
서로의 교류에 그쳤을 뿐 아니라 멀리 海陸을 통한 인도와 沿道 각국과

의 교통은 마침내 불교로 하여금 동양전체를 묶은 유일의 連鎖로의 역할을 다하였을 것이다. 조각의 융성 또한 예배대상의 으뜸인 佛教造成에서 거작을 남겼으며 그중에서도 石像의 優品을 가장 많이 들 수 있을 것이다. 이같은 평화와 풍성을 배경으로 신라 石像彫刻의 걸작들이 만들어졌다고 생각된다.

三國에서 統一期로 넘어가는 과도기에 있어서는 처음보는 碑像(圖10)의 優品이 忠南燕岐를 중심으로 새로 수습된 것은 또한 큰 성과(註8)라고 할 수 있을 것이다. 1960年부터 약 3년 사이에 조산된 七石중 四石에는 銘文이 있어서 尊名과 더부러 그들의 發願者가 모두 百濟王國의 遺民들임을 알 수 있었다. 그들은 阿彌陀信仰을 따르던 造形인바 모두 蠟石에다 細刻되었으며 그중 二個石에는 半伽思惟像이 조각되어 있어 특히 주목되었다. 이것은 阿彌陀 · 彌勒 兩像에 대한 당대 신앙의 구현인바 이같은 컴비네이숀은 統一期에 있어서도 계속되어서 예컨대 甘山寺 立像 二軀를 8세기 초두에서 들 수 있을 것이다. 이같이 7세기 중엽을 막 지나서 지방에서 조성된 碑像을 제외하고는 신라의 石彫는 또한 國都 경주와 그 주변지역에서의 寺院建立을 따르는 것이었다. 경주 西岳 정상에 조각된 거대한 磨崖三尊은 오늘 몹시 손상되었으나 거작이 될 만하다. 그리고 신라 五岳의 하나인 中岳 八公山北麓 深谷에서 1962년 처음 조사한 軍威三尊像(註9)은 또한 當代 阿彌陀三尊像의 유행을 보이고 있다. 그중 중앙을 차지하는 方座의 本尊은 裳懸座의 古式을 전하고 있으며 左石의 觀音 · 勢至의 兩菩薩 立像 또한 百濟의 金銑像과의 樣式의 親緣을 잘 표현하고 있다. 이 軍威三尊은「第二의 石窟庵」이라고 俗稱되어서 발견당시 크게 국민의 주목을 받기도 하였었다. 이같은 거작이 그사이 深山幽谷에 埋沒되어서 국민의 주목을 받지 못하였던 사실은 앞으로도 이같은 새로운 작품에 着眼할 수 있는 가능성을 시사하기도 하였다. 奉化 榮州는 古新羅 版圖의 北境으로서 그곳에서 전래하는 석상, 예컨대 奉化 北枝里의 如來坐像 또한 7세기 후반의 최대의 거작이라고 할 수 있을 것이다. 이 석상과 이웃하여서는 文武大王의 勅建인 義湘大

師의 浮石寺가 자리잡고 오늘에 法燈을 이어오고 있다.

　다음 8세기에 들어서는 聖德王代를 맞이한다. 때는 통일후 이미 반세기를 지났으며 三國各別의 불교미술의 精華는 새로운 국토를 무대로 종합되어 堂塔伽籃의 건립이 절정에 오른다. 경주 南山에 있어서는 三國時代의 北峰中心이 다시 남으로 확대되어서 滿山佛利의 盛觀을 이룬다. 石彫에 적합한 岩面이 있으면 그대로 간과하지는 않았으며 廣狹의 땅을 가리지 않고 寺庵建立이 유행하였다. 실로 경주에서의 石彫美術의 성행은 尊像을 堂宇안에 봉안하였던지 또는 자연의 巖面을 깎았던지 8세기 전반기의 작품을 優作으로 꼽을 수가 있을 것이다. 石像으로서는 위에서 들은 甘山寺 阿彌陀如來立像(圖12)과 同彌勒菩薩立像(圖13)을 그 대표로 삼을 수 있을 것이다. 이들은 신라의 귀족인 金志誠에 의하여 先亡父母의 資福을 위하여 조성되었는데 모두 背面에 造像銘記가 있어서 聖德王 18년(719)에 彫像된 사실을 알 수 있다. 이 兩像을 통하여 신라 佛菩薩의 전형을 볼 수 있는데 각기 높이 약 二米의 거작으로 석상으로서 대표를 삼을 수 있을 것이다. 그리고 이들 阿彌陀·彌勒의 奉安은 또한 상기한 바 碑岩寺碑像 이래의 신라의 믿음을 보여주고 있다.

　이어서 8세기 중엽에 이르러 造營되기 비롯한 吐含山 石佛寺의 彫像(圖14)을 들어야 할 것이다. 이 石窟寺院은 상기한 바와같이 三國에서 비롯한 石窟寺院의 頂點의 자리를 차지한다. 멀리 인도에서 비롯한 불교 石窟寺院의 系脈은 마침내 우리 국토의 東南隅에 이르러 동해를 굽어보는 新羅의 靈岳에다 最優最美의 작품을 남겼다. 비록 그 규모는 적다고 하더라도 前方後圓의 평면에서 主室과 前室을 연결시켰으며 前室로서 禮拜供養을 위한 장소를 삼았다. 신라의 大相 金大城은 景德王의 뜻을 받들어 吐含山을 무대로 그 西麓에는 佛國寺를 이룩하였으며 그 東面山頂 가까이 勝地를 택하여서는 石窟을 경영하였다. 전자는 現世父母를 위한 곳이요 후자는 前世父母를 위한 동시의 造營이라고 하였으니 前世父母란 東海에 葬事지낸 王族金氏의 先代를 가리키며 그중에서는 먼저 통일의 英主이신 文武大王을 들어야 할 것이다. 그러므로 石窟中

央에 鎭坐하시는 大佛의 視覺은 오늘도 東東南을 향하여 大王의 東海海中陵과 일치되고 있는 까닭이다. 이같은 우리 석굴은 大小石材로서 구성된 인공의 石龕形式인데 인도나 중국의 것은 자연의 암벽을 뚫어서 만들었으므로 서로 크게 다르다. 비록 우리의 것이 규모가 매우 작다하더라도 東洋石窟寺院중의 金剛石 같이 빛나는 주옥임에는 아무도 이론이 없을 것이다. 더우기 중앙인 蓮花座위에 結跏趺座한 如來坐像은 크기에 있어, 優作임에 있어, 8세기 石佛로서 동양제일의 칭찬을 받는 것도 또한 마땅하다.

　　前室의 南北兩壁에는 八部神將이 각 四구석 대립하였는데 이 조각이 다소 치졸하고 硬直되고 형식화된 것은 수십년을 소요하여 종말에는 「國家畢成」되었다는 이 石窟工事의 順位를 따르는 것으로 보겠다. 그리고 圓形石窟에서는 方形通路의 入口에는 각 1구의 仁王立像이 岩座위에 있고 이어서 四天王이 2구석 對立되어 있는데 通式을 보이는 甲衣의 조각보다는 이 작품의 변화와 配案이 도리어 兩足下 惡鬼像에 표현되고 있다. 그들의 자세도 그러하려니와 얼굴의 표정이 더욱 재미있다. 窟內에서는 중심보다 약간 뒤로 大佛이 안치되었으며 周壁을 돌아서는 天部 菩薩 十大弟子가 左右對稱의 방식을 따라서 배치되었으며 奧壁중앙에는 十一面觀音立像이 자리잡고 있다. 이 立像은 일본 또는 중국의 木石像과 비교할 때 時代樣式의 유사함을 지적할 수 있으나 이 石窟像으로 으뜸을 삼을 수 있을 것이다. 菩薩立像 중에서도 向右像은 窟內를 향하여 動的표현을 하였으며 긴 體軀에 흐르는 天衣와 영락의 장식이 한층 流麗하다. 十大弟子의 근엄한 표정속에 큰 코와같은 異國人의 표현을 잊지 않았으며 各人各態의 몸가짐이 또한 주목된다. 前室에서 本尊에 대한 예배가 끝나면서 佛徒들은 인도의 繞塔樣式과같이 向右에서 비롯하여 窟內各像에 대한 拜禮가 또한 따랐을 것이다. 그를 위하여 各像의 자리와 그 얼굴과 몸의 방향이 또한 配慮되었을 것이다. 이같은 諸像의 윗면에는 합계 8軀의 龕佛坐像이 있어 모두 정면하였는데 그들의 우아한 표정과 단정한 자세 그리고 화려한 장엄 등이 또한 우수한 작품임을 깨

닫게 한다. 다만 애석한 것은 龕佛 二軀와 窟內에 奉安되었던 石塔이
일본으로 搬出되었는데 장차 그들이 반환되어서 原位置에 안치될 날이
와야할 것이다. 穹窿의 천정에는 枓栱石이 突出되어 天井石을 지탱하였
으며 이들 計 108石은 정상의 一大蓮花盤石으로서 마감되고 있다. 이
蓮花大石은 3分되어 있는데 그에 대한 三國遺事의 설화 또한 이 석굴건
설의 고심과 정성을 오늘에 전한다고 하겠다. 근년의 보수로 前室에 瓦
屋이 얹혀졌는데 이것은 창건이래의 수법일 뿐 아니라 三國이래 우리나
라 石窟寺院의 傳統方案임은 다시 말할 것도 없을 것이다. 이 前室架構
로서 석굴은 비로소 내부의 안정을 얻고 풍화 또한 小康에 이른 것은
다행이나 앞으로 더욱 조심스런 연구와 정성을 다한 관리가 따라야만 할
것이다. 그리고 상기한 바와 같이 이 石窟經營의 發願이 동해에 장사지
낸 文武大王 이하 신라의 국왕과 왕족의 祈福에 있었던 사실은 중국 唐
代에서의 황실에 의한 같은 경영사실을 연상케함이 있다. 신라의 石彫
는 이 石窟에 이르러 마침내 수세기에 걸친 오랜 전통과 工技 연마의
결정을 얻었으니 우리의 주옥같은 至寶일뿐 아니라 동양불교조각의 精
華라 할 것이다. 8세기의 圓刻像으로서는 상기한 작품 이외에 南山에서
전래한 석상이나 박물관으로 移管된 석상 등이 있다.

8세기의 석상은 위와같은 석굴암像이나 박물관 소장품 이외에 경주
南山을 비롯하여 그 부근의 寺址에서 전래하는 것을 들 수 있을 것이
다. 南山은 8, 9세기에 걸쳐서 大小寺庵이 건립되었으며 그 全數는 알
려진 것이 약 70에 이르고 있다. 그중 塔像을 남기고 있는 것이 다수인
데 優作으로서는 또한 8세기의 것을 들 수 있을 것이다. 三陵溪 上禪庵
磨崖 如來坐像 같은 것은 巨像에 속하며, 오늘 서울 국립중앙박물관으
로 옮긴 여래좌상은 원래 南山 三陵溪에 있던 것으로 臺座와 光背를 구
비하고 있는 優品이다. 기타 南山의 東西面에는 적지않은 유품이 남아
있는데 塔谷의 마애불상은 巨岩의 各面을 이용하였으며 彌勒谷의 여래
좌상은 석굴암 본존을 이어서 造形된 優作이다. 七佛庵의 三尊과 四面佛
그리고 그 위에 자리잡은 神仙庵 觀音坐像(圖15)은 당당한 작품들이며

長溪의 마애 여래좌상은 彫線이 우아하고 相好의 단아함에서 일찍부터 알려져 있다. 또 月城郡 陽北面 骨窟庵의 본존은 風化가 심하나 이시대의 초기를 넘지 않는 작품으로 추정된다. 그리고 석상 이외에 경주박물관에 옮겨진 거대한 石燈臺石의 坐像이나 月城郡 陽北面 奬項里의 八角臺座, 周圍의 彫像과 그 光背片 등은 또한 8세기의 優作이라 하겠다.

4. 新羅末期의 彫刻

석굴암 彫像은 8세기의 으뜸으로 아마도 그 후반에 이르러 완성되었을 것이다. 신라의 역사는 이 佛國·石佛 兩寺의 경영을 지나서 신라 왕권의 동요에 따라 國內不安의 싹이 트고 한편 地方豪族의 대두가 나타난다. 신라 불교미술의 쇠퇴는 동시에 동양각국에서의 추세를 따르는 것이었으며 조각 또한 그 예외일 수는 없었다. 이같은 추세에 상기한 바와같은 국내불안이 加重되어서 8세기를 지나면서 신라의 조각은 쇠퇴의 길을 걷기 시작하였다. 그것은 국력이나 民力을 가릴 것 없이 佛寺建設에 결집되는 힘의 약화에 따르는 것이며 그에 따라 마침내 傳統地盤의 약화를 초래하였던 것이다. 그러나 이같은 경향에도 불구하고 한편 도리어 그같은 불안을 반영하여서 國刹같은 大刹의 경영은 없어지고 국왕 또는 귀족들의 작은 願刹이 京鄕各地에 건립되었는바 그것도 서로 대립하는 왕족사이에 있어서는 각기 따로 各自의 願刹을 세우게되었다. 이같은 힘의 분산 또한 필연코 寺刹規模의 縮少와 그에 따르는 石像彫刻의 鈍化를 초래하였다. 이것은 9세기에 들어서 더욱 주목되었는데 그것은 동시에 신라 불교가 지방으로 傳播됨을 따라서 나타나기도 하였다. 9세기부터 창립된 지방사찰중에서도 慶州에서 근거리에 있는 桐華寺(註10)나 法廣寺(註11) 海印寺 등은 모두 이같은 시대의 배경에서 이룩되었으며 그곳에 造形된 塔像의 규모 또한 그같은 추세를 정확하게 따랐던 것이다. 다만 이곳에 말하여둘 것은 석상의 규모와 彫塑의 힘이 약화됨을 따라서 纖弱한 氣風이 나타났다 하더라도 臺座나 光背에서의 화려한 장식은 도리어 加增된 사실이 주목되었다. 예를 들어본다면 桐華寺 毘盧庵의 毘盧舍那佛坐像(圖16)은 규모는 매우 작으나 衣紋의 조각에서 密集段狀의 양식을 보였으며 그 臺坐나 光背같은 佛身以外의 部品에서 한층 화려하고 섬세한 彫紋을 표현하고 있다. 이같은 특색은　또한 경주에서 멀어진　太白 智異 八公같은 신라五岳에　占定한 大小寺院에서도　지적할 수 있다. 동시에 本尊如來坐像이 7～8세기의 阿彌陀·彌勒像 보다는 智拳印을 結하는 毘盧舍那佛로 바꾸어가는 곳에 또한 시대에 따르던 신앙의 變遷相을 보이고 있다. 이같은 毘盧舍那佛은 한편　거대한 鐵像으로도 鑄造되어서 신라 9세기 彫像史의 특색을 크게 보이기도 하였다.

　다음에 이시기에도 또한 적지 않은 磨崖像이 만들어졌다.　특히 넓은 岩面에 대담한 線刻으로 마련된 三尊 또는 如來像은　이 시기의 것으로 들 수 있는데 南山 三陵溪의 三尊佛 또는 如來坐像(圖17)등을 들 수 있을 것이다. 線刻像이 아니라도 南山의 大小磨崖佛菩薩像과 지방에 있어서는 桐華寺入口 磨崖如來坐像 등을 들 수 있을 것이다. 또 南山以外의 경주부근에서도 그같은 세기의 遺例를 적지않게 찾을 수가 있을 것이다. 大邱市 慶北大博物館 如來坐像, 月城郡 斗垈里 磨崖三尊,　月城郡　影池의 如來坐像 경주박물관안에 진열된 十大弟子像이나　開善寺藥師如來立像 그리고 塔身이나 基壇面石에 새겨진 八部神將像이나　天部像등은 모두 9세기의 작품으로서 경주 또는 그 부근에서 傳來한 작품들이다.

　끝으로 新羅의 佛像彫刻 이외에 陵墓를 비롯하여 石塔 石燈등 石造物에 이르기까지 혹은 護石周邊을 돌아서 혹은 臺座에 조각된 十二支生肖像의 유행을 이 시기에서 보아야 하겠다.　十二支生肖는 원래 藥師如來의 眷屬으로서 그 守護神으로 信仰되었는데 그것이 古來의 方位와 시간을 표시하는 사상과도 결부되어서 특히 신라 통일시대에 들면서 造形되었다고 생각된다. 중국의 오랜 墳墓에는 十二支生肖의 土偶같은 것이 副葬되기도 하였으나 그들이 외부에 노출되어서　그들의 거대한 彫像石板이 각기 方位를 따라 王陵등에 배치되는 것은　신라의 창안이라고 말할 수 있을 것이다. 이 신라에서의　十二支生肖의 조각은 맨처음 8세기

에 들어서서 신라 聖德王陵에서 初見되었는바 그것은 方座위의 圓刻
된 立像으로서 각기 방위에따라 독립되어 배치되어 있었는데 그중의 一
軀(申像)는 오늘 경주 박물관에 진열되어있다. 이같은 圓像은 얼마아니
되어서 護石板에 高肉彫되어 陵基를 周回케 되었다. 景德王陵을 비롯
하여 元聖 興德 憲德의 各王陵 그리고 金庾信墓 같은 것을 오늘에 전
래하는 작품으로 들 수 있겠다. 또 이같은 圓墳 이외에 方形墳에 돌린
유례가 있는데 狼山 陵只塔은 최근에 새로 조사되어서 復原을 기다리고
있는 것이며 旣知의 것으로서는 佛國寺 가까이 자리잡은 九政洞의 그것
을 들 수 있을 것이다. 이들 十二支生肖像의 양식에는 크게 두가지가
있어서 武裝像과 平服像의 구별이 있는데 대부분은 전자에 속하고 있
다. 十二支生肖의 조각 또한 8, 9 兩세기의 조각양식의 변천을 따르고
있는데 특히 9세기에 들어서는 형식화에 흐르고 있다. 이같은 十二支生
肖像은 石造物에도 加用되고 있어서 月城郡, 遠願寺東西三層石塔을
대표 예로 삼을 수 있을 것이다. 이 탑에는 上層基壇을 各面三分하여서
平服坐像을 배치하였는데 衣紋의 표현이 또한 流麗하다. 기타 月城 五
柳里에서 경주 博物館에 이관된 小品 또는 경주시 金庾信墓 外周에서
출토된 蠟石製品같은 것은 또한 9세기의 작품들이다.

5. 結 言

9세기 후반에 이르러 신라의 왕권은 한층 약화되어가는 동시에 지방
에서는 豪族이 대두되어서 완연히 後三國을 이룬다. 고려의 건국은 10세
기에 들어서서의 일이나 後百濟 또한 西南部를 차지하고 稱王함에 이르
렀다. 그리하여 마침내 이 양자 사이의 決戰이 連山에서 王建의 승리
로 끝이 나고 신라 왕국이 평화속에 고려에 항복함에 이르렀다. 그리하
여 「合三韓爲一家」의 건국이념을 내건 고려 太祖의 통치로 바뀌게 되
었다. 그리하여 신라의 王都는 慶州라는 새로운 이름을 얻고 舊都의 면
목을 간직하였으며 귀족들은 새로운 왕조에 참여하므로써 한국의 정치

문화의 중심은 오랫만에 韓半島의 중앙으로 옮아갔다. 그리하여 새로운 고려왕조시대의 조각의 기반과 그 양식이 형성되어 갔다.

이상을 通觀하면서 신라는 비록 韓半島 東南隅에 偏在하여왔다 하더라도 一千年의 社稷을 지켜왔으며 남달리 외래 문화의 섭취와 고유문화와의 종합을 이루므로써 그 자신의 뚜렷한 미술문화의 발전을 이룩하였던 것이다. 그리하여 三國 중 가장 늦기는 하였으나 6세기에 들어 비로소 불교를 受容하므로써 他二國과는 다른 비약과 內實의 계기를 잡았던 것이다. 三國의 통일이 신라에 의하여 완수된 것에는 그만한 까닭이 있어서의 일인데 그것은 비단 정치적 군사적인 면에서 뿐만은 아니다. 그같은 偉業에의 불교의 기여는 그 敎化的인 면에서 뿐 아니라 그 彫像史를 통하여서도 말할 수 있을 것이다. 삼국시대의 유행한 彌勒信仰의 구현인 如來·菩薩 두가지 양식으로서의 造形 특히 半跏思惟菩薩形式은 또한 신라 初期造像史의 가장 두드러진 특징이라 하겠으며 그에 따라 오늘에 전래한 우리의 걸작이 있는 것이다. 그것이 통일기에 들어서서는 彌勒像과 병행하여서 阿彌陀佛이 유행되었으며 그것은 나아가 王室과 귀족들의 願堂建立에서 主尊의 자리를 잡게되었으니 佛國 石佛 兩寺의 창립은 그 절정이 될 것이다. 그리고 한편 藥師如來像의 造成이 또한 동시에 유행하였다. 그런데 이곳에서 지적할 것은 이들 여래 坐像들의 手印이 모두 降魔印을 나타내고 있다는 사실이다. 그러므로 신라의 如來像이 이같은 手印을 보인다고 하여서 그들을 모두 釋迦如來像으로 볼 수 없다는 것이다. 바꾸어 말한다면 降魔印은 신라 석상의 통일기에서의 通印이라 하겠다.

다시 9세기에 들어서면서 믿음의 변천은 紛亂의 세태를 반영하여서 毘盧舍那佛의 등장과 그 유행을 보이게되었던 것이다. 동시에 국가세력의 盛衰와도 정비례하면서 그 규모와 彫法에도 差別相을 나타냈으며 불상의 莊嚴에도 변화가 있었다. 三國의 상징적 표현에서 8세기에 이르러 사실적 특색을 보이던 신라조각은 9세기에 들어 위축과 纖弱에의 길로 접어들었다. 이것은 동시에 인도 중국이 모두 彫塑作品에서 衰運을

보이기 시작한 이시대의 추세를 따르기도 하였다. 그러나 신라의 석상
은 그 국토에서의 생산적 조건, 바꾸어 말하면 花崗岩을 主材로 삼아 圓
刻 또는 磨崖한 곳에서 신라 古代石像의 큰 특징을 나타내었으며 그에
따라 오랜 전통의 작품으로서 新羅石佛은 그 존재가치와 그 아름다움을
오늘에 지니고 있는 것이다.

註

1) 皇龍寺塔단에서 조사한 刹柱本記를 따랐다.
   拙稿 新羅皇龍寺九層木塔 刹柱本記와 그 舍利具 (東洋學報 第3輯 檀國大學校 刊)
2) 拙稿 新羅南山三花嶺彌勒世尊 (「韓國佛像의 研究」 所收 1973年 三和出版社 刊)
3) 拙稿 新羅半跏思惟石像 (同上 註 2)
4) 拙稿 高句麗金銅佛像의 新例二座(同上)
5) 拙稿 百濟半跏思惟石像小考 (同上)
6) 拙稿 斷石山神仙寺石窟磨崖像 (同上)
7) 藤澤一夫 鹿深臣百濟將來彌勒石像說 (「史跡と美術」 177호 1947年 3月 刊)
8) 拙稿 忠南燕岐石像調査 (同上 註 2)
9) 拙稿 軍威三尊石窟 (同上)
10) 桐華寺 毘盧庵은 閔哀王의 祈福을 위하여 建立되었다.
    拙稿 新羅閔哀大王石塔記 (「史學志」 第3輯 1969年 7月)
11) 拙稿 新羅法廣寺石塔記 (「白山學報」 第8號 1970年 6月)

新羅佛教と 飛鳥・白鳳佛教
—半跏思惟像と聖徳太子信仰—

田 村 圓 澄

1. 飛鳥・白鳳仏教史の三段階

　日本に仏教が伝来して以降，平城遷都までの飛鳥・白鳳時代の仏教史を大観すると，およそ三つの段階を画している。第一段階は，百済から日本に仏教が伝えられた538年(欽明戊午，法興王25)から，聖徳太子がなくなった622年(推古30，真平王44)までの85年間である。この時期の前半は，仏教の受容をめぐる豪族層の対立がつづき，反仏派の勢力が一掃された587年(用明2，真平王9)を境として，仏法興隆の時勢を迎える。日本最初の本格的な伽藍である法興寺(飛鳥寺)が，飛鳥の地に姿をあらわし，ついで，大和・河内・山城を中心に，豪族による私寺の建立がつづくが，この時期の仏教界の指導者は，百済と高句麗から来日した僧によって占められていた。そのなかには，新装なった法興寺に迎えられた慧慈(高句麗)や慧聡(百済)をはじめ，観勒(百済)・恵灌(高句麗)などがあった。

　第2段階は，622年(聖徳太子の死)より，斑鳩の法隆寺が焼亡した670年(天智9，文武王10)までの約半世紀間である。この時期には，聖徳太子の時代に隋に留学した学問僧が，あい前後して帰国し，また唐におもむく

201

学問僧もあった。すなわち，これまでの日本—百済，日本—高句麗のルートのほかに，日本—唐の新しいルートが開かれ，その往来が可能となった。日本は，仏教の源流にあたる唐と，直接の交渉をもつことになったのである。在唐24年の経歴をもつ僧旻や，同じく31年の恵隠のほか，摂論宗を将来した道昭も，この時期の僧であった。

　第3段階は，670年(法隆寺焼亡)より平城遷都の710年(和銅3，聖徳王9)までの40年間である。この時期に，新羅は朝鮮半島を統一し，そして日本との関係が親密になった。双方の使者が往来し，新羅学問僧が海を渡った。明聡・観智・弁通・神叡などの新羅学問僧の名が伝えられている。

　第1段階では，百済・高句麗から来日した僧が，日本の仏教界で指導的役割を果たした。第2段階では，第1段階の継続がみられるが，それに加えて，唐に学んだ学問僧の帰国があり，また唐におもむく学問僧もあった。注意されるのは，第1・第2段階において，新羅の僧の来日や，また日本の学問僧の新羅留学がみられないことであった。第3段階では，すでに百済・高句麗が滅亡しており，新羅が朝鮮半島の唯一の国家であった事実も考えなければならないが，いっぽう日本と唐との外交関係は疎遠であった。すなわちこの時期の日本の仏教は，新羅の直接の影響をうけていたのである。

　日本美術史の時代区分にしたがい，670年(天智9)をもって，飛鳥時代と白鳳時代とにわけるならば，飛鳥時代は，第1・第2段階の時期にあたり，白鳳時代は，第3段階の時期にあたる。

　さて日本の飛鳥・白鳳時代に相当する朝鮮の来教史を概観すると，多くの著名な学僧ないし高僧の名を伝えるのは，新羅である。三国時代の高句麗・百済では仏教が盛んであり，かなりの数の僧の学問や行状については，あきらかでない点が多い。それに較べると，新羅は朝鮮の統一をなしとげた主役でもあり，仏教史の面でも，多くの史実が伝えられている。三国時代から統一時代にかけての新羅の代表的な僧をあげると，次のとおりである。

円光 （532〜630）　　　　　慈蔵 （608〜677）

元暁 （617〜686）　　　　　義湘 （620〜702）

道証 （640〜710頃）　　　　璟興 （道証と同時代）

　このなかで，円光・慈蔵は飛鳥時代に，また元暁・義湘・道証・璟興は白鳳時代に活躍している。これらの僧の多くは，唐(隋)に留学しており，したがって7・8世紀の新羅仏教は，唐(隋)の直接の影響をうけていた。入唐僧は他にもあるが，ともあれ学僧が連続して輩出しているのは，新羅仏教の学問的基礎がかたく，また学問僧の層があつかったからであろう。

　ところで高度の水準を保ち，それが伝統ともなっていた新羅仏教が，第1・第2の段階にあたる飛鳥時代に，日本の仏教界になんらの影響をも与えなかったとは考えられない。新羅僧の来日は，史料の上でみることはできないが，しかし仏像つにいては，伝来の事実がある。

　『日本書紀』について，仏教の日本伝来以降670年（天智9）までの間，朝鮮半島から仏像が日本に伝えられた記事を示そう（第1表「朝鮮半島仏像伝来一覧」参照）。これによれば，飛鳥時代の130余年間に，百済から仏像がわたってきた記事が2回，新羅は3回である。なお高句麗からの仏像伝来の記事はない。

　第2表の記載について，史実としての信憑性に疑問がもたれるものもある。また朝鮮半島からの仏像の伝来が，1世紀あまりの間に，わずか5回であったとすることはできないであろう。半島から渡来僧が，仏像をもたらした場合があったことも，充分に考えられるからである。ところで第1表で知られるように，百済から伝来した仏像については，釈迦または弥勒

第1表　朝鮮半島仏像傳来一覧

百　　済			
西　紀	日 本 年 紀	朝 鮮 年 紀	事　　　　　項
552	欽明13	聖王30	釈迦仏金銅像一軀
584	敏達13	威徳王31	弥勒石像一軀

新　羅			
579	敏達 8	真平王 1	仏像
616	推古26	真平王40	仏像
623	推古31	真平王45	仏像一具
高句麗			
な　し			

と明記してあるのに対し，新羅の場合，3回とも仏像の種類は，不明である。しかし，新羅僧の来日がみられなかったにもかかわらず，新羅から仏像が送られていること，しかもその回数が，百済からの仏像伝来の回数を上まわっていることは，注目しなければならない。

　百済や高句麗の場合，本国からの渡来僧が仏像をたずさえてきており，したがって，とくに仏像伝来の記事にならず，いっぽう新羅の場合は，新羅僧の来日がなく，ただ仏像のみが送られてきたので，記事になった場合があったことも考えられる。しかし新羅伝来の仏像が，百済や高句麗の仏像と異なっており，そのため日本側ではこれを求め，新羅側ではこれに応じて仏像を送ってきた場合があったことも，考えられるであろう。

　すでに述べたように，第1段階の時期では，百済・高句麗仏教の直接の指導・影響をうけ，第2段階の時期では，これに加えて，隋・唐の影響をうけた。しかし飛鳥仏教が，新羅仏教の影響を全く排除した形で成立したのではなく，仏像をとおして，なんらかの関連をもっていたことは，認めなければならない。とくに第3段階の時期の白鳳仏教は，第1・第2段階で，制限された形でしか影響を及ぼさなかった新羅仏教が，直接の指導・影響を与えることにより，成立した点を重視すべきであると思う。

2. 悉達太子像と半跏思惟像

欽明13年紀10月条に，有名な仏教伝来の記事がある。すなわち，

> 冬十月，百済聖明王名王明遣西部姫氏達率怒唎斯致契等，献釈迦仏金銅像一軀，幡蓋若干，経論若干巻，別表讃流通礼拝助徳云，是法於諸法中最為殊勝，難解難入，周公孔子尚不能知，此法能生無量無辺福徳果報，乃至成弁無上菩提，譬如人懐随意宝，逐所須用尽依情，此妙法宝亦復然，祈願依情無所乏，且夫遠自天竺，爰泊三韓，依教奉持，無不尊敬，由是百済王臣明謹遣陪臣怒唎斯致契，奉伝帝国，流通畿内，果仏所記我法東流。

右の百済王の上表文は，唐の則天武后の長安3年(703，大宝3)に，義浄によって訳出された『金光明最勝王経』の文句をつかっている。したがって『日本書紀』の仏教伝来条は，703年以降に修文されたことはあきらかである。[1] また『日本書紀』が，仏教伝来の年次として南都に伝えられていた欽明戊午年(538，聖王16)説をしりぞけ，欽明13年(552，聖王30)説をとったのは，この年が，唐の仏教界において唱えられていた末法第1年にあたることと，関連をもつように思われる。[2]

さて『日本書紀』の仏教伝来の記事の粉本になったのは，『元興寺伽藍縁起并流記資財帳』である。すなわち，そこでは仏教伝来の記事が，「露盤銘」→「丈六光銘」→縁起文と発展しており，やがて『日本書紀』の仏教伝来の記事にうけつがれていることが知られる。[3] 縁起文は次のとおりであろ。

> 大倭国，仏法，創自斯帰嶋宮治天下天国案春岐広庭，天皇，御世蘇我大臣稲目宿禰仕奉時，治天下七年歳次戊午十二月度来，百済国聖明王時，太子像并灌仏之器一具及説仏起書巻一篋度而言，当聞，仏法既是

世間無上之法，其国亦応修行也。

　これによれば，百済の聖明王が送ってきたのは，「釈迦仏金銅像一軀」で
はなく，(1)「太子像」と，(2)「灌仏之器一具」および，(3)「説仏起書
巻一筐」であった。「灌仏之器一具」は，釈迦の誕生仏に，盤などの付属
器一揃であろう。「説仏起書巻一筐」は，『太子瑞応本起経』『修行本起
経』などの本生経の類と考えられる。「太子像」は，半跏思惟像であるか
ら，したがって(1)は，出家入山前の悉達太子像，(2)は釈迦の誕生の像，
(3)は釈迦の前生の物語であり，すなわち，伝来当初の仏教では，成道以
前の釈迦の比重の大きかったことが知られる。本生経も，いわば太子の物
語であった。

　敏達紀13年(584，威徳王31)条によると，百済からきた鹿深臣は，「弥勒
石像一軀」をもっていた。蘇我馬子は宅の東に仏殿をいとなみ，この石像
を安置したというが，この石像も，半跏像とみるべきであろう。

　百済から，はじめて大和朝廷に送られた仏像は，釈迦の像ではあった
が，成道した釈迦像ではなく，成道前の悉達太子像であり，そして誕生仏
であった。印度におこり，中国・朝鮮を経て伝えられた仏教は，日本人に
とって異国的であり，このことは，仏像の表情や服装においてもいちじる
しかったが，しかし太子像には，一般の仏像に見られぬ，或る種の親しみ
やすさが感じられたのであろう。また太子伝である本生経にも，特別の関
心がもたれたと思われる。

　日本に伝えられた仏教が，釈迦中心であったことは，当初の寺院の伽藍
配置が，塔に比重をおいていたことによっても知られる。中門を入ると，
まず仏舎利を奉安した塔がある。日本最初の伽藍である飛鳥の法興寺（飛
鳥寺）も，また，いわゆる四天王寺式伽藍配置である大阪の四天王寺も，
ともに中門(仏門)は塔の正面におかれていた。

　釈迦に対する崇拝，また釈迦の生涯についての関心が，飛鳥時代を通じ
てつづいた。『仏所行讃』や『太子瑞応本起紀』などの本生経により，釈

迦の伝記が知られるようになり，こうして半跏思惟像は，仏・菩薩像のな
かでも，とくに親しみ深いものになったと思われる。

　さて太子像は，古代中国では半跏思惟像であった。これについては，水
野精一氏の研究があるので，[4] 以下，これによって述べよう。

　片手を頬にあて，片脚を膝にのせた中宮寺や広隆寺の半跏思惟像は，親
しみぶかい仏像であるが，仏像の歴史のなかで，この様式の像が最初にあ
らわれるのは，中国山西省雲岡の石窟においてである。たとえば，第六洞
明窓の右方像には，重畳とした山岳を背景に，馬のひざまずいている姿が
あるが，これは成道前の釈迦，すなわち悉達太子が，愛馬カンタカに別れ
を告げる情景であり，仏伝中の一節をあらわしている。太和16年(492)在
銘の陰密県郭元慶等の碑像には，白馬カンタカのほか，従者チャンダカも
あらわされており，刻文には「太子思惟像」と明記されている。

　北朝における半跏思惟像，および背後の情景は，『仏所行讃』の所説にも
とづくと考えられるが，いっぽう日本の現存する『過去現在因果経』にも
悉達太子の行歴として，病者をみては思惟し，死者をみては思惟し，比丘
をみては思惟し，出家に際して出惟する太子の姿が語られ，そしてこれに
対応する絵の部分に，太子思惟像が描かれている。悉達太子たる所以は，
苦悩し，思惟するところにあるといえるから，太子をあらわすのに，半跏
思惟像をもってしたのであろう。

　半跏思惟像は，この像式が最初にあらわれる北魏の時代から，その流行
が終る隋の時代にいたるまで，もっぱら太子思惟像とみられていた。これ
に対して弥勒像は，北魏では交脚像として，北斉末以降は倚坐像としてあ
らわされていた。半跏思惟像が弥勒とみられるようになるのは，北斉(559
〜575)に限られており，多少ゆとりをみても，東魏か竜門末期である。こ
うして半跏思惟像は弥勒像として，まず河北にちかい高句麗に入り，つい
で百済にひろがり，新羅に伝えられた。

　以上が，水野清一氏の論旨の要点である。ところで仏教の朝鮮半島の伝
流を考えると，まず高句麗は小獣林王2年(372)に後秦から伝えられた。[5]

百済は枕流王元年（384）に東晋から、[6] また新羅は，法興王14年(527)に高句麗から伝えられた。[7] 半跏思惟像の朝鮮伝流は，したがって，仏教が朝鮮半島三国に定着した後に行われたのであり，また弥勒信仰をともなっていたことが推定される。

韓国の慶州南山（慶尚北道慶州郡内東面南山里）の神仙庵磨崖菩薩半跏像は，十数丈の断崖絶壁の上の巨岩に刻まれている。像の高さは約1・4メートルあり，左手は大指と中指・無名指とを捻じ，右手は一枝の宝相華を捧げている。左足は裳台に跏し，右足は伸ばして小蓮華を踏んでいる。新羅中代の盛期，すなわち八世紀中葉の造像と考えられ，南山磨崖仏中では稀有の半跏像である。[8]

忠清南道瑞山郡雲山竜賢里の磨崖の三尊仏像は，高さ2.05メートルの如来の立像を中央に，左右に菩薩を配しているが，向って右方にあるのは，半跏思惟像である。高さ1.09メートルあり，上半身は裸形で，細腰には下裳をつけ，膝頭におかれた右手の指先は軽く頬にふれ，左手の指は右膝の上におかれている。右足は半跏で，左足は下にのばしているが，衣文の褶は足指の上まで達している。三尊像は一つの巨岩に彫刻されており，製作年代は600年頃，すなわち三国時代の末葉と考えられる。 なお如来像を中心とし，立像の菩薩像と半跏像とを左右に配する三尊形式は，他に類例がなく，したがって三尊の名称について明確にすることは困難である。[9]

瑞山磨崖の半跏像は， 7世紀前半の百済の石仏であるのに対し，神仙庵の磨崖半跏像は， 8世紀中葉の新羅の石仏である。 前者は三尊形式であり，後者は単独の半跏像であるが，なお私は，両者の図像上の相違に注目したい。片手を頬にあて，片脚を膝にのせる瑞山の磨崖像は，典型的な半跏思惟像であるが， 神仙庵の磨崖像は， すでに思惟する形を逸脱している。すなわち前者はあきらかに「太子像」であるのにたいし，後者は「思惟」の形態をうしなっており， したがって「菩薩像」ではあるが，「太子像」の名に価しない。法隆寺金堂の壁画の第2号壁と第5号壁の菩薩の名称については，弥勒説や日光・月光説などがあるが，[10] 半跏像とみるべきで

あろう。第2号壁と第5号壁は，同形を裏返しにした像であるが，右手を
あげて第1指と第3・4指を捻じ，左手を下げて蓮華の茎をつまむ姿は，
すでに「思惟」の形をなくした神仙庵磨崖菩薩半跏像と，共通している。
　中吉功氏は，主として韓国に現存している半跏像について解説されてい
る。[11]これにもとづいて作製したのが，第二表「朝鮮三国半跏像一覧」で
ある。この表によって知られることは，第一に，半跏像は高句麗・百済・

第2表　朝鮮三国半跏像一覧

番号	像　　名	像　高	製作年代	製作場所
1	金銅菩薩半跏像	17.5センチ	6世紀	高句麗
2	銅造菩薩半跏像	28.5センチ	6世紀後半	(不明)
3	銅造菩薩半跏像	80.2センチ	6世紀末葉	新羅
4	銅造菩薩半跏像	94.0センチ	7世紀初頭	百済
5	金銅菩薩半跏像	21.0センチ	6世紀後半	新羅
6	金銅菩薩半跏像	14.2センチ	7世紀初頭	新羅
7	金銅菩薩半跏像	16.6センチ	7世紀初頭	(不明)
8	銅造菩薩半跏像	16.4センチ	7世紀前半	百済
9	銅造菩薩半跏像	9.4センチ	7世紀前半	(不明)
10	銅造菩薩半跏像	10.0センチ	6世紀末葉	(不明)
11	銅造菩薩半跏像	10.0センチ	7世紀初葉	(不明)
12	金銅菩薩半跏像	15.1センチ	7世紀前半	(不明)
13	銅造菩薩半跏像	14.2センチ	6世紀後半	(不明)
14	銅造菩薩半跏像	12.2センチ	7世紀初葉	新羅
15	銅造菩薩半跏像	12.4センチ	7世紀初葉	(不明)
16	銅造菩薩半跏像	23.5センチ	6世紀末葉	百済
17	石造菩薩半跏像	1.26メートル	7世紀中葉	新羅
18	石造菩薩半跏像	41.0センチ	7世紀後半	新羅
19	断石山神仙庵磨崖菩薩半跏像	1.1メートル	7世紀初葉	百済

番号	像　　　　名	像　　高	製作年代	製作場所
20	瑞山磨崖菩薩半跏像	2.8メートル	7世紀中葉	百　　済
21	慶州南山神仙庵磨崖菩薩半跏像	1.4メートル	8世紀中葉	新　　羅

新羅の朝鮮半島三国から発見されている。すなわち半跏像をともなう弥勒信仰は，三国に流布していたことが知られる。第二に，(17)(18)の石造菩薩半跏像，および(19)(20)(21)の磨崖菩薩半跏像をのぞき，(1)〜(16)の銅造または金銅造の菩薩半跏像は，おおむね小形である。(3)の08.2センチ，(4)の94.0センチは，むしろ例外であり，いずれも30センチ未満の小像であるが，これは一個人の信仰の対象としてつくられたことをうかがわせる。また，このような小形の半跏思惟像は，「太子像」と呼ぶのにふさわしいであろう。第三に，製作年代であるが，半跏像の造顕は，6世紀後半から7世紀前半，すなわち日本の欽明朝から孝徳朝にいたる一世紀に集中している。つまり三国時代の高句麗・百済・新羅でつくられており，統一新羅時代の半跏像は，(21)のほかにはない。ただし厳密に一線をひくことはできないが，統一新羅時代にはいり，半跏像の製作が急におとろえたことは推察できるであろう。[12] そして半跏像の製作の急激な減少は，弥勒信仰の変化と関連をもっているように思われる。

3. 新羅の花郎と弥勒信仰

高句麗・百済の弥勒信仰については，資料的制約があり，明確にすることは困難であるが，いっぽう新羅の場合は，ある程度の考察が可能である。新羅の弥勒信仰は，花郎および花郎集団とかかわりあっているが，先行の業績に導かれ，[13] まず花郎の制度について述べよう。

新羅において，貴族の青少年の集団組織があり，その集団の首領は花郎と呼ばれた。花郎集団は，歌舞遊娯を行なう社交クラブであり，国家有事の際には国難におもむく戦士団であり，また国家的社会的訓練をうける教

育組織であった。

　花郎には美貌の男子がえらばれた。花郎の前身である原花は女性であったが，真興王(540〜575)の時代に，女性の原花が廃され，男性の花郎の制度が始まった。

　　　取美貌男子，粧飾之，名花郎以奉之，徒衆雲集。[14]

　花郎は美しく装われ，そしてそれを奉ずる集団ができたのである。

花郎制度の実質的な成立が，真興王の時代であったとすると，新羅に仏教が伝来した法興王の時代に接している。新羅の仏教も，日本の場合と同様，まず貴族層にうけいれられるが，法興王[15]および真興王[16]は，仏教の受容に積極的であった。

　新羅の国家的発展は，法興王および真興王の時代にいちじるしかった。すなわち，法興王は律令制度の基礎をさだめ，仏教を公認したが，また金海の本加耶をおさえ，洛東江流域に進出した。真興王は，高句麗が領有する漢江上流地域にまで領土を拡大した。[17]　花郎集国が，新羅の国家的発展の中核となったことは，『花郎世記』の，

　　　賢佐忠臣，従此而秀，良将勇卒，由是而生。[18]

の言葉によってもうかがわれるであろう。

　花郎集団は弥勒信仰によって結ばれていた。花郎は弥勒の下生であり，そして花郎集団には，弥勒の加護があると信じられていた。

　　　及真智王代，有興輪寺僧真慈一作真慈也，毎就堂主弥勒像前，発原誓言，願我大聖化作，花郎，出現於世，我常親近晬容，奉以周施。[19]

　国都慶州の興輪寺の真慈は，つねに弥勒像を拝し，我が大聖，すなわち

弥勒が，花郎となって下生するよう願っていたが，ついに霊妙寺の近く
で，「断紅斉具，眉彩秀麗」なる一小郎子を見出した。この小児は，やがて
「国仙」として国王の敬愛をうけたという。

弥勒は，兜率天で説法をつづけているが，56億万歳の後，人間世界に下
生し，竜華樹の下で成道する。そして三会の説法によって衆生を済度する
のであるが，弥勒が下生する国土について，

> 時世安楽，無有怨賊劫竊之患，城邑聚落無閉門者，亦無衰悩水火刀兵
> 及諸饑饉毒害之難，人常慈心恭敬和順，調伏諸根，語言謙遜。[20]

すなわち，弥勒下生の世界は，豊楽安穏であり，怨賊，兵火，饑饉な
ど，人びとの最もおそれる災害から解放された理想界であった。花郎は，
このような憧れの国土の実現を目指す弥勒そのものであり，そして花郎集
団は，弥勒の化生である花郎を奉じ，弥勒信仰によって結合していたので
ある。[21]

> 初述宗公為朔州都督使，将帰理所，時三韓兵乱，以騎兵三千護送之，
> 行至竹旨嶺，有一居士，平理其嶺路，公見之歎美，居士亦善公之威勢
> 赫甚，相感於心，公赴州理，隔一朔，夢見居士入于房中，室家同夢，
> 驚怪尤甚，翌日使人問其居士安否，人曰，居士死有日矣，使来還告，
> 其死与夢同日矣，公曰，殆居士誕於吾家爾，更発卒修葬於嶺上北峯，
> 造石弥勒一軀，安於塚前，妻氏自夢之日有娠，既誕，因名竹旨，托而
> 出仕，与庾信公為副帥，統三韓，真徳，太宗，文武，神文，四代為家
> 宰，安定厥邦。[22]

『弥勒下生経』によれば，弥勒は翅頭末城の波羅門の妙梵を父とし，梵摩
波提を母として生まれた。出家学道して竜華樹の下で成道するが，竹旨郎
を弥勒の化生とする右の記事は，『弥勒下生経』による信仰を示してい
る。[23]

統一新羅の英雄の金庾信は，15歳で花郎となった。

　　公年十五歳為花郎，時人洽然服従，号竜華香徒。[24]

　金庾信にひきいられた花郎集団は，「竜華の香徒」であり，すなわち弥勒信仰によって結ばれた同信者であることを，表榜していたのである。

　それぞれの花郎集団は，独自の歌曲，すなわち郷歌をもっており，遊娯集会して歌儛を行なったが，これらの歌の多くは，僧の手によって作られている。「兜率歌」を作った月明や，郷歌集「三代目」を編修した大炬は有明，[25]「彗星歌」を作った融天[26]の名なども伝えられているが，ともあれ花郎集団では，僧が指導的役割を果たしていたことが知られる。

　新羅の花郎集団は，弥勒の同信者であったが，では，その弥勒は，どのような姿であらわされたか。私は，半跏思惟像がそれであったと思う。花郎が美貌の男子であり，また花郎集団が青少年の集まりであったことは，半跏思惟像との関連を推察させるからである。半跏思惟像，すなわち太子像は，出家入山前の悉達太子をあらわしており，数多い仏・菩薩像のなかでも，実在の人物像であった。花郎集団の人びとは，半跏思惟像に，かれら首領の花郎を見たのであった。

　金庾信の修錬道場として知られる断石山神仙庵石窟（慶尚北道月城郡西面）の石壁には，大小10軀の仏・菩薩像が彫刻されているが，そのなかに半跏思惟像があり，この像は他の像と異なって正面向きに刻まれている。[27] すでにのべたように金庾信は弥勒の下生と仰がれ，その集団は弥勒の加護があると信じられていたのあった。

　第3表にみられる新羅関係の半跏思惟像が，すべて花郎の弥勒信仰に結びつくとは断定できないが，しかし半跏像の造顕は，花郎の制度が確立された真興王の時代から，新羅が三国を統一した金庾信の時代までの間，すなわち，6世紀後半から7世紀前半までの約一世紀間に集中している。統一新羅時代に入ると，半跏思惟像の造顕は衰退するが，この事事は，半跏

思惟像と花郎制度とが，不可分の関係にあったことを示しているのである。

4. 広隆寺と四天王寺

推古紀11年(603，真平王25)条に，蜂岡寺，すなわち太秦の広隆寺の造立にかかわる記事がある。すなわち，

> 十一月己亥朔，皇太子謂諸太夫曰，我有尊仏像，誰得是像以恭拝，時秦造河勝進曰，臣拝之，便受仏像，因以造蜂岡寺。

聖徳太子は，秦河勝に「尊仏像」を与えたが，広隆寺は，この仏像を本尊として建てられたという。これによれば広隆寺の創建は，630年(推古11)になる。

推古紀24年(616，真平王38)条にも，次の記事がある。

> 秋七月，新羅遣奈末竹世士，貢仏像。

ただし，このとき新羅から送られてきた仏像の種類は，あきらかでない。

いっぽう，承和3年(836)につくられた『広隆寺縁起』によれば，広隆寺は，聖徳太子の追善のため，秦河勝によって建てられた。

> 謹撿日本書紀云，推古天皇十一年冬十一月己亥朔，皇太子上宮王謂諸大夫曰，我有尊仏像，誰得此像，将以恭敬，時秦造河勝進曰，臣拝之，便受仏像，因以造峯岡寺者，謹撿案内，十一年冬，受仏像，小墾田宮〔治〕天下御宇，推古天皇即位壬午之蔵，奉為聖徳太子，大花上秦造河勝，所建立広隆寺者。

『日本書紀』は，聖徳太子の死去を，推古29年2月条にかけているが，し

かし，『上宮聖徳法王帝説』の記事により，壬午年，すなわち推古30年(622)とすべきであろう。そうすると秦河勝は，太子がなくなった年に広隆寺の建立をはじめ，その本尊として，太子より賜った「尊仏像」を安置したことになる。

　寛平2年(890)の『広隆寺資財校替実録帳』によれば，「檜皮葺五間金堂壱宇」の条下に，

　　金色弥勒菩薩像壱軀 居高二尺八寸 所謂太子本願御形

とある。いわゆる「宝冠弥勒」は，実測像高2尺7寸6分あり，[28] 右の「太子の本願の御形」の金色弥勒像に該当すると考えられる。[29]「宝冠弥勒」は木造であるが，金箔の痕跡がのこっていることからも，この像が「金色」であったことが知られる。秦河勝が聖徳太子より賜った「尊仏像」は，すなわち「宝冠弥勒」であり，そしてこの半跏思惟像こそ，創建以来の広隆寺金堂の本尊であった。

　『扶桑略記』の推古天皇24年条に，

　　七月，新羅王貢金仏像，高二尺，置蜂岡寺，此像放光，時々有異

とあるのは，前掲の推古紀24年条の記事をうけたものであるが，1499年(明応8)の成立になる『山城州葛野郡楓野大堰郷広隆寺来由記』には，「安置応広隆寺三尊」として，

　(1)　金銅弥勒菩薩像 坐像高二尺八寸.
　(2)　金銅救世観音像 坐像高二尺二寸, 如意輪也.
　(3)　檀仏薬師如来 立像高三尺

をあげている。(1)(2)(3)の 三像は，「一厨子」に安置されているのであるが，さて，(1)金銅弥勒菩薩像は，「宝冠弥勒」であろう。「金銅」としたのは，木像に金箔をおしたのを誤認したからであると思われる。

ところで広隆寺には,「泣き弥勒」の名称で知られる半跏像がある。実測像高は2尺2寸1分である[30]が, ⑵金銅救世観音像は,「泣き弥勒」に相当すると考えられる。ただし「泣き弥勒」も木造であり,「金銅」とあるのは,誤認とすべきである。なお『来由記』は, ⑵金銅救世観音像について,

> 推古天皇廿四年,丙子,秋七月,自新羅国遣使,奉献,此像放光時々有怪

と記している。すなわち『扶桑略記』の記述をうけ,新羅伝来としているのである。

1314年(正和3)に橘寺の法空が撰した『聖徳太子平氏伝雑勘文』に,

> 新羅王献金仏像事
> 准広隆寺記,此像是弥勒像也,即金堂中尊也,
> 彼寺古記云
> 弥勒中尊金仏高二尺.
> 如意輪東安置金銅居高二尺八寸
> 薬師西安置長一撰手半或記云,三尺
> 已上御帳内文

と記している。「広隆寺古記」を引き,厨子の帳内に安置された三像をあげているが,『来由記』の記載と異なり,ここでは高さ2尺の⑵金銅救世観音,すなわち「泣き弥勒」が,金堂の中尊となっている。また東に安置された2尺8寸の如意輪観音が, ⑴金銅弥勒菩薩,すなわち「宝冠弥勒」を指すことはあきらかである。

創建以来,広隆寺金堂の本尊は,弥勒—薬師—三尊と変動しているが,[31]ともあれ創建当初の金堂の本尊は,秦河勝が聖徳太子から与えられた弥勒半跏像であり, また新羅伝来の由来をもつ他の半跏像も, 安置されてい

た。

秦氏は，新羅系の渡来氏族であった。[32] 広隆寺の宝冠弥勒の素材が，ア
カマツであることから，この木像の朝鮮渡来説を裏づける鍵とも見なされ
ている。クスノキやヒノキは日本の特産であるが，アカマツは朝鮮にもあ
るからである。[33]

広隆寺は，その創建において，新羅—半跏像—聖徳太子の三位一体の関
係をもっていたがこれと似た歴史をもっているのが，難波の四天王寺であ
る。

崇峻天皇即位前紀によれば，大臣蘇我馬子の呼びかけに応じ，聖徳太子
は諸皇子や諸群臣とともに，大連物部守屋の討伐に参加し，河内の渋河の
守屋の家に迫った。しかし守屋側の激しい抵抗にあい，馬子側は苦戦した。

是時，厩戸皇子束髪於額，古俗年少児年十五六間，束髪於 而随軍後，自斫
額十七八間，為角子 今亦然之，
度曰，将無見敗，非願難成，斫取白膠木疾作四天王像，置於頂髪，而
発誓言，白膠木此 今若使我勝敵，必当奉為護世四王起立寺塔。
　　　　云農利望，

ついに物部守屋は殺され，守屋の軍は崩壊した。

（1）平乱之後，於摂津国造四天王寺，分大連奴半与宅，為大寺奴田　荘

四天王寺は，仏敵ともいうべき物部守屋の滅亡を契機とし，そして守屋
の没収資財によって創建されたが，『御手印縁起』により，その場所を玉造
とする説がある。[34] すなわち，

（2）以丁未歳始建玉造岸上，改点此地鎮祭青竜，癸丑歳，壊移荒陵東。

丁未歳(587)は，物部守屋が滅亡した年にあたる。
推古紀元年条に，次の記事がある。

（3）是蔵，始造四天王寺於難波荒陵。

　四天王寺は，（1）（2）によれば，587年(用明2，真平王9)に聖徳太子により創建されたことになるが，しかし(3)によれば，593年(推古1，真平王15)の創建となり，創建者はあきらかでない。

　(2)の荒陵移建説は，(1)と(3)との不統一を解消するようであるが，しかしこれに史実性を認めず，四天王寺の創建を623年(推古31，真平王45)頃に求める見解がある。[35] この見解は，推古紀31年条の次の記事にもとづく。

　　　秋七月，新羅遣大使奈末智洗爾，任那遣達率奈末智，並来朝，仍貢仏像一具，及金塔并舎利，且大灌頂幡一具，小幡十二条，即仏像居於葛野秦寺，以余舎利金塔灌頂幡等皆納于四天王寺，是時，大唐学問者僧恵済，恵光，及医恵日，福因等並従智洗爾等来之。

　聖徳太子の死去は，壬午年，すなわち622年(推古30，真平王44)にあたるから，このときの新羅の遣使の目的は，直接には，聖徳太子の死去を喪うことにあったとみるべであろう。新羅の使者がもたらした仏像・仏具のうち，仏像は葛野の秦寺，すなわちた秦の広隆寺に納められ，舎利・金塔・灌頂幡などは四天王寺に納められた。いずれも聖徳太子の追善の意味があったと考えられる。

　四天王寺の創建の年次については，諸説があるが，[36] もし推古31年創建説[37]が支持されるならば，四天王寺は，聖徳太子が建てたのではなく，聖徳太子のために建てられたことになる。つまり太子追善の寺であり，この点でも，秦氏の広隆寺と創建の動機を同じくするといえよう。

　孝徳紀大化4年条に，四天王寺の記事がある。

　　二月，己未，阿倍大臣，請四衆於四天王寺，迎仏像四軀，使坐于塔
　　内，造霊鷲山像，累積鼓為之。

　福山敏男氏は，右の記事よりも時代的に遡つて，四天王寺の存在を示す
確実な記録は存在しないとし，現在の位置に，現在の規模をもって，四天
王寺が建立され，あるいは完成されたのは，大化の初め頃とされる。すな
わち右の記事は，四天王寺の塔の構立が終わり，内部の仏像の供養が行わ
れた時期を示しているのである。[38]
　では，創建当初の四天王寺の金堂の本尊は何であったか。
　『太子伝古今目録抄』に，「大同縁起云」として，次の文をかかげている。

（a）二重金堂一基，阿弥陀三尊，右恵光法師従大唐請坐者，弥勒菩薩一
　　　軀蓮華坐，右近江朝庭御宇天皇御世請坐。

　この引用の終りに，「延暦22年，三綱寺主云云」とあることから，803年
（延暦22）に勘録された四天王寺の資財帳の遺文と考えられる。「大同縁起」
と名づけられた理由はあきらかでないが，あるいはその奥に，大同初年の
僧綱所の検判があったからであろうか。[39]「大同縁起」は史料としての信憑
性が高いと考えられるが，そこでは金堂の本尊が，阿弥陀三尊となってい
る。その三尊が，恵光により唐から将来されたとあるのは，推古紀31年条
に対応するのであろう。
　『御朱印縁起』によれば，

　　　金堂壱宇二重瓦葺，
　　　金銅救世観音像一体，
　　　四大天王像四体，
　　　金塗六重宝塔壱基，

　　　　金銅舎利塔形壱基壱,

　　　　納入舎利拾参粒檐婆羅門六体,

　　講法当〔堂〕壱宇瓦葺八間,

　　　　夏堂四間, 金色阿弥陀仏像一軀, 丈六,

　　　　冬堂四間, 塞観音像一軀, 丈六,

とあり, 平安朝中期において, 四天王寺の金堂の本尊は, 金銅救世観音であったことが知られる。この救世観音は, 前掲 (a) の「弥勒菩薩」とみてさしつかえないであろう。(a) の「大同縁起」の引用につづいて,

　　　案本願縁起云, 救世観音菩薩像, 従百済国渡請坐者, 今案, 此文注前帳弥勒像也, 若誤歟

と記すように, 「本願縁起」, すなわち『御手印縁起』の救世観音は, 弥勒とされていたものであった。聖徳太子を, 救世観音の化身とする信仰によって, 弥勒像が観音像に変えられたと考えられる。

　ところで, (a)「大同縁起」の恵光将来の阿弥陀三尊は, 創建当初からの金堂の本尊であったか。阿弥陀三尊につづいて, 「弥勒菩薩一軀蓮華坐」とあるのは, この弥勒像が, 半跏像であったことを示している。仏像は一般に, 蓮華座に坐すのであるが, とくにこの場合, 「蓮華に坐す」と記すのは, 蓮華座が殊勝であったからであろう。すなわち, 高い蓮華座に腰をかけ, 一方の脚をたれ下げる形の半跏思惟像であったと思われる。[40]

　さて「大同縁起」は, 右の弥勒像が, 「近江朝庭御宇天皇御世」, すなわち天智天皇の時に安置されたと記している。しかし, 四天王寺の金堂造立の下限を, 孝徳朝に求められる福山敏男氏はこの弥勒像を, 四天王寺の創立当時からの本尊ではなかったと解されている。[41] しかしこの解釈は,「近江朝庭御宇天皇御世」の文字にこだわっているように思う。天智天皇, すなわち中大兄皇子は, 645年(大化１)に20歳で孝徳天皇の皇太子となり, ま

た斉明天皇の時代も，皇太子として執政の座にとどまった。それだけでは
ない，斉明天皇の死後もただちに即位せず，称制すること6年間におよび，
668年（天智7）にようやく近江大津宮で即位したのである。[42] そして671年
（天智10）に死んでいるから，正確にいえば，「近江朝庭御宇天皇御世」は，
わずか4年間にすぎない。では，弥勒像が四天王寺の金堂に安置されたの
は，天智天皇が在位した4ヶ年のことであろうか。はやく本居宣長が指摘
したように，大化改新の典法を，「孝徳天皇といはずして，天智天皇の立給
へりとするよしは，此事孝徳天皇の御世ながらも，皇太子中，皇子の御心
より出て，物し給へる御しわざなるが故」であった。[43] 「天下の政は，いよ
いよ中大兄の御心にぞ有けむ」というのは，斉明の治世においても同様で
あった。

　「近江朝庭御宇天皇御世」は，中大兄皇子が皇太子であった時期をふく
め，天智末年までの27年間を指していると解すべきである。したがって四
天王寺金堂の弥勒像は，この間に安置されことになるが，私は，四天王寺
の金堂が完成した最下限である孝徳朝から，金堂の本尊は，半跏思惟像で
あったと思う。『太子伝古今目録抄』には，

　　　天皇寺金堂中尊，大同縁起弥勒注

とあり，四天王寺金堂の中尊が，「大同縁起」によって，弥勒とされてい
た。そしてその弥勒像は，聖徳太子の姿に似ているとの伝承があった。す
なわち『御手印縁起』に，

　　　金堂内安置金銅救世観音像，百済国王，吾〔告〕入滅後，恋慕渇仰，
　　　攸造顕〔贈〕之像也。

　百済王が，聖徳太子の入滅の後，太子を恋慕渇仰して造顕したのが，金
堂安置の救世観音像，すなわち弥勒像であるという。百済の国王が造った

との所伝は，にわかに首肯できないが，四天王寺金堂の半跏思惟像が，太子を「恋慕渇仰」してつくられたとする伝承に注目しなければならない。四天王寺が，聖徳太子の追善のための寺であるとすれば，その金堂の半跏像に，生前の太子の姿を見，思慕をささげたと考えられるからである。

　四天王寺金堂の本尊であった半跏思惟像が，どこでつくられたか，ないし，どこから将来されたかはあきらかでない。その弥勒像は，すでになくなっており，もはや探求する手がかりをもたないのである，しかし，新羅―半跏像―聖徳太子の，三位一体の関係が，四天王寺においても見出されることは重要である。

　聖徳太子の追善の意味をもこめて創建された広隆寺金堂の本尊，また聖徳太子にゆかりある四天王寺の金堂本尊は，いずれも半跏思惟像であった。聖徳太子を思慕する人々は，眼前の半跏像に，なき太子の面影を求めたのである。聖徳太子にたいする思慕・追善と，半跏思惟像との結びつきは，太秦の広隆寺にはじまったと考えられるが，その半跏思惟像が新羅仏教の系譜を引いている事実に注目したい。

5. 聖徳太子と新羅

　大和朝廷は，朝鮮半島の三国のなかで，百済との親近政策の維持をはかってきたが，その反面，新羅にたいしては，おおむね敵視策をとってきた。しかし，そのなかにあって聖徳太子は，百済，高句麗との友好関係の維持につとめるとともに，とくに新羅との親近政策をおしすすめた異例の人物であった。

　聖徳太子には，二人の師があった。慧慈は仏教の師であり，また博士の覚哿は，儒教の師であったという。また秦河勝は太子の側近であった。

　慧慈は高句麗僧であり，595年(推古3，嬰陽王6)に来日し，615年(推古23，嬰陽王26)に帰国した。聖徳太子が内政・外交面で多彩な活動をした時期に，慧慈は太子の傍にいたことになる。

　覚哿の本国はあきらかでない。「博士」といわれているので，百済の人で
あったようにも思われる。百済では，375年（近肖古王30）に，博士の高興
によって記録が始まったといい，[44] また541年（聖徳19，欽明２）に百済の
使者が梁におもむき，毛詩博士を招請している。[45] 博士の制度は，百済で
は６世紀にととのっていたと考えられる。

　秦氏は新羅系の渡来氏族であった。610年（推古18，真平王32）に新羅の
使者が来日したとき，秦河勝は土部連蒐とともに「新羅導者」を命ぜられて
いる。

　ともあれ聖徳太子は，高句麗の慧慈，百済の覚哿，そして新羅系の秦河
勝の三人を側近とした。偶然にこのようになったとも考えられるが，当時
の朝鮮半島では，これら三国がたがいに抗争・対立していただけに，太子
が独自の立場からバランスをとっていたことに注目される。執政者として
の太子の政策の立案や，また外国の情報の入手などに，この三人の側近が
関係していたとみるべきであろう。

　聖徳太子は，はじめて隋と外交関係をもったが，いっぽう朝鮮半島の三
国のなかで，とくに新羅にたいして親近政策をとった

　571年（欽明32，真興王 32）に，新羅は任那を滅ぼした。任那の再興を意
図する大和朝廷と新羅との関係は，その後いっそう悪化するが，591年（崇
峻４，真平王33）に，任那再建のため，二万余の軍隊が筑紫に集められた。
こうして軍事的威圧を背景とし，新羅との交渉が始まったが，しかし崇
峻天皇の暗殺，推古女帝の即位という異常な事態を迎え，595年（推古３，
真平王17）には，将軍たちは筑紫を引きあげた。新羅にたいする軍事的政
策は放棄されたかに見えたが，大和朝廷の方針は一貫していた。600年（推
古８，真平王 22）には，新羅攻撃の軍勢が海を渡った。新羅から攻撃され
た任那を救援するという名目であったが，日本の軍勢が引きあげると，新
羅はまた任那を攻めた。602年には，聖徳太子の異母弟の来目皇子を撃新
羅将軍に任じ，２万５千人の軍勢を指揮させた。しかし来目皇子が筑紫で
死んだので，来目皇子の兄の当麻皇子を征新羅将軍に任じたが，同行の当

麻皇子の妻が病死し，新羅征討は中止された。

　このように聖徳太子の執政のはじめには，新羅との対立が深まり，戦火をまじえるまでになったが，しかし605年の斑鳩宮移住の頃から，日本と新羅は親密になっていく。608年(推古16，真平王30)に多数の新羅人が日本に移ってきたが，この年に高句麗が南下して新羅を攻略したことと関係があるであろう。610年には，新羅の使者が来日したが，大和朝廷では，入京の日には荘馬をならべ，「新羅導者」や「新羅共食者」を任命し，使者を歓迎した。

　611年にも，新羅の使者が来日した。616年には新羅から仏像が送られ，621年にも，新羅の使者が来日している。そしてこの間，日本は新羅にたいして軍事的行動をおこすことはなかった。622年(推古30，真平王44)に聖徳太子が死ぬと，翌623年には，新羅の使者が仏像，仏具などをもって来日した。聖徳太子の死をとむらうためのものと考えられるが，同年，任那の問題が再燃し，数万の軍兵が海を渡って新羅を攻めている。もっとも任那の措置をめぐって，大和朝廷の内部で意見の対立があり，まず交渉派の立張にしたがい，新羅と任那に使者を派遣したが，その間に武断派がのり出し，使者の帰国を待たずに，新羅攻撃の軍勢が出発した。蘇我馬子が，武断派をおさえることができなかったとも解されるが，ともあれ聖徳太子の死を契機として，親新羅路線はくずれ，強硬路線が表面に出てきたのである。

　いっぽう百済についていうと，新羅との親近政策があらわになった608年以降，聖徳太子が死ぬ622年までの間に，百済の使者が来日したのは，615年(推古23，武王16)だけであった。そしてこの場合も，遣唐使の犬上君御田鍬の帰国に際し，百済の使者はこれに随行して来日したのであった。新羅との親密関係とはうらはらに，百済と日本との疎外関係がうかがわれる。

　当時の新羅は，真平王の時代であった。父の銅輪王は，『仁王般若波羅蜜経』などに説く転輪聖王の輪宝にちなんで命名されており，また妃の金

氏は摩耶夫人と呼ばれたように，真平王の宮廷の仏教信仰はさかんであっ
た。真平王の在位は，579年（敏達8）から631年（舒明3）までの53年間に及
んだが，その間に，隋（陳）にたいする接近をはかるとともに，智明・円光
・曇育などの学問僧の入隋がつづき，新羅の文化は高まった。聖徳太子は，
大和朝廷内部の新羅強硬派をおさえ，新羅との友好関係の維持をはかっ
たが，そこには新羅の文化にたいする評価があったからであろう。

　聖徳太子の時代には，百済や高句麗の僧の来日はあったが，新羅の僧の
来日はなかった。太子の時代以前から，新羅僧の来日または移住はなく，
また本国の仏教界の事情もあり，太子の時代を迎えたとはいえ，にわかに
新羅僧の来日をみることはなかったのであろう。飛鳥仏教は，新羅仏教を
疎外した形で形づくられたといえる。したがって，聖徳太子が，飛鳥仏教
の主流である百済仏教と異なるところの，新羅仏教をうけいれていたとす
るのは困難である。

　にもかかわらず，聖徳太子が従来の大和朝廷の外交路線を転換し，独自
の新羅親近策をうち出したことは否定できない。そしてこれにこたえるよ
うに，太子の死をいたむ使者が新羅から派遣されている。使者がもたらし
た仏像や仏具の類は，広隆寺と四天王寺に納められたが，この二つの寺の
金堂の半跏思惟像は，なき聖徳太子の追慕の対象となり，やがて広汎に展
開する太子信仰の中心となったのである。

6.　白鳳時代の日本と新羅——外交と仏教

　660年（斉明6，武烈王7）に，唐の高宗は新羅の要請をうけいれ蘇定方
に命じて百済を討たせた。これに応じて新羅の金庾信らも百済を攻め，ま
ず泗沘（扶余）が陥ち，同年7月に熊津（公州）に逃がれた義慈王は降伏して，
百済は滅んだ。

　百済側の要請にこたえ，大和朝廷は百済援助を決定した。斉明天皇・皇
太子中大兄らの大和朝廷の首脳は筑紫に移り，軍事援助の指揮をした。日

本から百済に送りこまれた兵士は万をこえ，食糧や兵器の数もおびただしいものがあった。百済復興の活動も活潑となり，日本に滞在していた百済王子の余豊が百済に迎えられ，王位についた。しかし663年の白村江の戦で，日本の水軍は壊滅し，百済復興軍も決定的な敗北をうけた。4カ年にわたる百済側の抵抗と，それを支援していた大和朝廷の介入に終止符がうたれた。

白村江の敗戦により，日本は一転して，唐・新羅の連合軍の進攻の危機にさらされることとなった。大和朝廷では，対馬・壱岐・筑紫に沿岸警備の防人や，信号用の烽を配置し，また筑紫には水城(福岡県筑紫郡太宰府町)・大野城市(福岡市大野城市)・椽城(佐賀県三養基郡基山町)を築造して大宰府の防衛の措置をとり，長門(山口県下関市付近)・屋嶋(香川県高松市)にも築城し，瀬戸内海の防備をかためた。さらに河内と大和との境の高安(大阪府八尾市)にも城をおき，大和進攻の敵にそなえた。

百済の滅亡の前後から，多数の百済人が日本に亡命したが，なかには兵法・医薬・陰陽・儒教・法制などの専門の分野において，大和朝廷の要職につくものもあった。同じ韓民族ではあるが，日本に定住した百済系氏族と，いっぽう日本に対立し，そして朝鮮半島の国家統一を実現した新羅の人々とのあいだには，無視しえぬ溝があったとも考えられ，このことも，新羅にたいする日本の国家意識の形成に，影響を与えたであろう。667年(天智6，文武王7)以降，新羅の使者は連年のように来日するが，しかし大和朝廷の警戒はきびしく，かれらは，筑紫で饗応をうけ，そのまま帰国するのが常であった。新羅の使者が難波に遡られるようになるのは，690年(持統4，神文王10)以降である。

大和朝廷がとったこのような措置は，主として軍事的配慮によるものであり，そして，亡命百済人の意見が反映しているようにも思われる。しかし，新羅にたいする警戒がつづく反面，新羅との和親関係が生まれてきたことも事実であった。朝鮮半島では，新羅の対日接近をうながす新情勢が展開しつつあったからである。

　668年(文武王8，天智7)に，唐と新羅の連合軍が，高句麗を滅ぼした。しかしその直後から，唐と新羅とのあいだに，新たな抗争が始まった。朝鮮半島の政治統一を目ざす新羅は，唐の軍事援助を求め，唐もこれに応じて水陸の兵力をさしむけたが，しかし唐は当初から，朝鮮半島の属領化を意図していた。百済・高句麗の滅亡後も，唐は朝鮮半島から撤退せず，新羅と唐との戦闘がくりひろげられたが，676年(文武王16，天武4)に，新羅は漢江流域一帯から唐軍を撃退することに成功し，朝鮮半島における支配権を確立した。

　ひとたびは対決の事態になった日本と新羅との関係も，新羅と唐との軍事的な緊迫化にうながされ，和解の方向をたどることとなった。その転換の時期は，668年(天智7)であった。同年9月に，唐・新羅の連合軍の前に高句麗の宝蔵王は降伏し，高句麗はその歴史を閉じたが，同じ月に新羅の使者の金東厳らが来日した。内臣中臣鎌足は，新羅の使者に托し，新羅統一の英雄の金庾信に船一隻を贈り，天智天皇も船一隻の調を文武王に贈った。同年11月に金東厳らが日本を離れるに際し，大和朝廷は道守臣麻呂・吉士小鮪の2人に命じ，金東厳らを新羅に送りとどけた。

　668年の新羅の使者の来日を契機として，日本と新羅との関係は，対立から親和へ転換することとなった。そして以後は，ほとんど連年のように新羅の使者は日本を訪ねており，日本の使者も新羅に向っている。676年(天武5，文武王16)には，はじめて遣新羅大使と同小使が任命された。

　709年(和銅2，聖徳王8)に，右大臣藤原不比等は，来日中の新羅の使者の金信福らを藤原京の弁官の庁内に引見し，これまでも新羅の使者は日本に来ているが，かつて執政の大臣と談話したことがない，いまこうしてうちとけて話すのは，二国の修好をすすめ，往来の親密をなすためである，と語ったという。

　668年の新羅使者の来日の際，中臣鎌足が金庾信に贈物をし，そして709年には，藤原不比等が先例をやぶって親しく新羅使者を引見したことは，象徴的である。すなわち669年(天智9)に法隆寺が炎上し，また710年(和

銅3)に平城遷都が行われるが，この間の白鳳時代は，藤原鎌足，および
その子の不比等の主導により，日本と新羅との間は親密であり，そして安
定していたことが暗示されているからである。

　白鳳時代における日本と新羅との友好関係の持続は，その前後の時代に
見ることができないが，いっぽうこの時期の日本の仏教界は，新羅に学ぶ
ことについて積極的であった。

　この事実を暗示するのは，大唐学問僧・新羅学問僧の動向である。 670
年より710年までの間に，出国または帰国した大唐学問僧・新羅学問僧は
第3表「大唐学問僧・新羅学問僧一覧」のとおりであるが，これによると，
すべて24名の学問僧のうち，類別の不明な道久と勝暁の2名をのぞき，大
唐学問僧は8名，新羅学問僧は14名である。さらに大唐学問僧のなかで，
平城遷都以後に帰国した道慈と行善，おとび資料的に信憑性が低い智鳳・
智鸞・智雄，また新羅仏教に接したと考えれる智宗・義徳・浄願，さらに客
死した弁正を除くと，大唐学問僧はいなくなるのである。いっぽう観常に
はじまる新羅学問僧14名のうち，還俗した山田史御形一人をのぞき，13名
のすべてが学問僧として終始しており，史実としての確実性をもってい
る。そしてこれらの学問僧により，仏教を含む高度の新羅文化が，日本に
伝えられたのである。

　689年（持統3，神文王9）に，天武天皇の喪を弔う新羅の使者が来日した
が，明聴，観智らの新羅学問僧もこれに同行して帰国した。大和朝廷は筑
紫大宰の粟田真人らに詔を下し，明聴・観智らに綿各140斤を与えたが，
これらの学問僧が新羅に留学中，世話になった「新羅の師友」に送るための
ものであった。

　この頃の新羅の仏教界は，元暁・義湘・道証・勝荘・遁倫・恵通・明朗
・勝詮などが活躍し，興隆の時期を迎えていた。[46) 新羅の王都の慶州に
は，多くの寺が建てられており，そのなかで，寺名・遺蹟の明白なもの
31，遺蹟に擬定されるもの30，計61の寺名があげられている。[47)

　左右に各基の塔を配するいわゆる双塔式伽藍配置様式も，当時の新羅で

第3表 大唐学問僧・新羅学問僧一覧（天智朝より文武朝までの帰国者）

	僧名	出発年次	船便	帰国年次	船便	類 別	典 拠
1	定恵	653（白雉4）		665 （天智4）	唐船	大唐学問僧	貞慧伝
2	好位			668 （王智7）		大唐学問僧	日本書紀
3	法勝			668 （天智7）		大唐学問僧	日本書紀
4	道久			671 （天智10）	唐船		日本書紀
5	観常			685年（天武14）		新羅学問僧	日本書紀
6	雲観			685年（天武14）		新羅学問僧	日本書紀
7	智隆			687年（持統元）		新羅学問僧	日本書紀
8	明聴			689年（持統3）		新羅学問僧	日本書紀
9	観智			689年（持統3）			日本書紀
10	智宗	653年（白雉4）		690年（持統4）	新羅船	大唐学問僧	日本書紀
11	義徳	653年（白雉4）		690年（持統4）	新羅船	大唐学問僧	日本書紀
12	浄願			690年（持統4）	新羅船	大唐学問僧	日本書紀
13	山田史御形					新羅学問僧	日本書紀
14	弁通	693年（持統7）		696年（持統10）以前に帰国か		新羅学問僧	日本書紀
15	神叡	693年（持統7）				新羅学問僧	日本書紀
16	道慈	701年（大宝元）		718年（養老2）		大唐学問僧	続日本紀
17	行善			718年（養老2）		新羅学問僧	続日本紀日本霊異記
18	智鳳	703年（大宝3）				新羅僧大唐学問僧	三国仏法伝通縁起
19	智鸞	703年（大宝3）				大唐学問僧	三国仏伝通縁起
20	智雄	703年（大宝3）				大唐学問僧	三国仏伝通縁起
21	弁正	701～3年（大宝年中）		（客死）		大唐学問僧	懐風藻
22	義活			707年（慶雲4）		新羅学問僧	続日本紀
23	義基			707年（慶雲4）		新羅学問僧	続日本紀
24	惣集			707年（慶雲4）		新羅学問僧	続日本紀
25	慈定			707年（慶雲4）		新羅学問僧	続日本紀
26	浄達			707年（慶雲4）		新羅学問僧	続日本紀
27	勝暁					学問僧	続日本紀

考案されたものである。すなわち，唐の来寇を攘う目的で，慶州狼山に建てられた四天王寺は，679年(文武王 19，天武 8)に竣功し，また文武王の霊廟寺である感恩寺は， 682年(神文王 2，天武11)に完成している。前者は木造の双塔を，また後者は石造の双塔を東西に配した様式であるが，飛鳥の薬師寺の伽藍配置は，直接これらの寺にならったと考えられる。

　白鳳時代の日本の仏教界は，新羅の仏教界の動向に敏感であり，そして早い反応を示した。新訳経典の受容，とりわけ『大般若経』や『金光明勝王経』の重用の傾向は， 新羅からうけついだものであった。[48] 法相宗も新羅から伝えられたが，[49] その他，寺院建築や仏像彫刻の様式も，新羅から移されたものがすくなくなかったと思われる。いわゆる白鳳美術の源流を，初唐に求めるこれまでの見解にたいし，私は，むしろ新羅との関係を重視すべきであると考える。たとえば，白鳳時代の日本と唐との外交関係をみると， 702年(大宝 2)に 1度だけ遣唐使が派遣されているにすぎない。[50] 大和朝廷は，新羅との修好に積極的であった反面，唐にたいして消極的であった。

　日本美術史の時代区分として，法隆寺焼亡の年を境とし，飛鳥時代と白鳳時代とにわけることは，正当な理由があると思う。ともあれ，白鳳仏教に与えた唐仏教または新羅仏教の評価について，改めて検討すべきであろう。

註

1)　辻善之助『日本仏教史』上世篇（東京，1944年），35頁
2)　田村円澄『飛鳥仏教史研究』（東京，1969年），166頁
3)　福山敏男「豊浦寺の創立」（『日本建築史研究』所収，東京，1968年）
4)　水野精一「半跏思惟像について」（『中国の仏教美術』所収，東京，1968年）・同上「飛鳥白鳳仏の系譜」（『仏教芸術』4号，東京 1949年
5)　『三国史記』18，小獣林王 2年条
6)　同上 24，枕流王元年条
7)　『三国遺事』3，原宗興法，獣髑滅身条

8)　中吉功『新羅・高麗の仏像』(東京 1971年)，117頁

9)　黄寿永「瑞山磨崖の三尊仏像に就いて〔抄訳〕」(『朝鮮研究年報』2号，京都，1960年)

10)　町田甲一『法隆寺』(東京，1972年)，154頁・『奈良六大寺大観』5巻 (東京，1971年)，
　　　解説 98頁

11)　中吉，上掲書，および同『海東の仏教』(東京，1973年)による

12)　松原三郎「飛鳥白鳳仏と朝鮮三国期の仏像」(『美術史』17巻4号．東京，1968年)

13)　三品彰英「新羅花郎の源流とその発展」(『史学雑誌』45編 10.11.12号，東京 1934年)

14)　『三国史記』4，真興王 37年条

15)　江田俊雄「新羅の仏教受容に関する諸問題」(『文化』2巻 8号 東京，1935年)

16)　忽滑谷快天『朝鮮禅教史』(東京，1930年)，39頁

17)　李基白『韓国史新論』(東京，1972年)，65頁

18)　註 14)に同じ

19)　『三国遺事』2，「弥勒仙花，末尸郎，真慈師」条

20)　『弥勒下生成仏経』(大正蔵経，14巻)

21)　八百谷孝保「新羅社会と浄土教」(『史潮』7年 4号，東京，1937年)

22)　『三国遺事』2，「孝昭王代，竹旨郎」条

23)　註 21)に同じ

24)　『三国史記』41，列伝第一

25)　『三国遺事』5，「月明師兜率歌」条

26)　同 上，5，「融天師彗星歌」条

27)　中吉功『海東の仏教』(東京，1973年)，51頁

28)　小林剛「太秦広隆寺弥勒菩薩像について」(『史迹と美術』176号，京都，1947年)

29)　毛利久「広隆寺の本尊と移建の問題」(『史迹と美術』189号，京都 1948年)

30)　註 28)に同じ

31)　註 29)に同じ

32)　平野邦雄「秦氏の研究」(1) (2) (『史学雑誌』70編 3号・4号．東京，1961年)

33)　上原昭一『飛鳥・白鳳彫刻』(東京，1968年)，54頁

34)　今井啓一「四天王寺玉造創始考」(同『秦河勝』所収，京都，1968年)

35)　藪田嘉一郎「四天王寺の創立に関する研究」(『大谷史学』1号，京都，1951年)

36)　村田治郎「四天王寺創立の研究史」(『史迹と美術』216・217・218号，京都，1951年)
　　　福山敏男「初期の四天王寺史」(『仏教芸術』56号，東京，1965年)

37)　註 35)に同じ

38)　福山敏男「四天王寺の建立年代」(同『日本建築史研究』所収，東京，1968年)

39)　註 28)に同じ

40)　註 35)に同じ

41)　註 28)に同じ

42)　田村円澄『飛鳥仏教史研究』(東京，1968年)，298頁

43)　「続紀歴朝詔詞解」(『増補 本居宣長全集』第5 所収)

44)　『三国史記』24，近肖古王30年条

45）　同上，26，聖王 19年条

46）　李能和『朝鮮仏教通史』上・中篇（ソウル，1968年）による

47）　斉藤忠『朝鮮古代文化の研究』（東京，1943年），173頁

48）　田村円澄「三論宗・法相宗伝来考」（『森克己博士古稀記念論文集・対外関係史』
　　　所収，東京，1973年）

49）　田村円澄「日本古代仏教における旧訳経典と新訳経典」（『古代学』 18巻 1 号，京都，
　　　1972年）

50）　森克己『遣唐使』（東京，1955年），26頁

高麗時代 佛書刊行과 印刷文化

安 啓 賢

인쇄는 陶磁와 더불어 高麗의 문화를 대표하는 것이다. 고려 때 인쇄
문화가 발달되었던 것은 불교와 유교의 경전을 비롯한 각종의 서적을
보급하고 또 이를 보존하려고 하였기 때문이었지만 여기에는 외국으로
부터 수입된 板本으로부터 받은 자극과 영향이 또한 컸다. 前期의 인
쇄는 순전히 木板印刷에 지나지 않았으나 후기에는 金屬活字를 만들어
쓰기에 이르러 高麗의 인쇄 문화는 실로 세계 인쇄사상 중요한 위치를
차지하였다. 그런데 高麗 때의 여러 서적인쇄 가운데서도 그 대부분을 차
지하고 또 가장 대표적인 것은 불교에 관한 것이다. 이는 高麗 사람들
이 대개 불교의 관념세계에 사상적 기반을 두고 생활하고 있었던 당시
의 사회에 있어서 지극히 당연한 일이었다고 하겠다. 이미 초기의 定宗
1년(946)에 국가에서 佛名經을 널리 펴기 위해 米穀 7만석을 기금으로
하여 전국 각 대 사찰에 佛名經寶라는 재단을 두어 佛名經을 인쇄 간행
하고 이를 받들게 하였던 것이다. 그리하여 후기에 갈수록 고려 때에는
사원경제의 발전과 국가정세의 움직임이 佛書간행에 더욱 박차를 가하
게 했으니, 혹은 국가적인 대사업으로서 혹은 여러 사원 자체내에서 수
많은 불교관계 서적들이 간행되었다.

1. 高麗大藏經

佛法을 일정한 규준아래 集成해놓은 佛教聖典을 大藏經이라 한다. 大

藏經을 뜻하는 梵語 Tripitaka는 3개 (tri)의 광주리 (pitaka)라는 말이
니, 대장경은 經·律·論등 붇다의 가르침이 광범하게 담뿍 담겨져 있
는 큰 광주리라는 뜻이다. 중국에 불교가 전래되면서부터 수많은 경전이
梵語로부터 한문으로 번역되어져 갔는데, 東晉의 道安(314—385)이 漢
代 이래의 각종 경전의 총목록을 작성한 것이 계기가 되어 그후 여러
사람들에 의해서 계속 목록이 만들어졌다. 그 가운데서도 編次나 체재
에 있어서 보다 더 짜임새 있는 것은 唐 開元18년(730) 智昇이 총 5,048
권을 계통적으로 배열 분류하되 480함으로 묶고 그 차례를 千字文에 따
라 天函(No. 1)으로부터 英函(No. 480)까지 매겨놓은 開元釋敎目錄이
바로 그것이다. 그리하여 天函(No. 1)에서 奈函(No. 60)에 이르는 앞
의 60函 안에는 大般若波羅蜜經 600卷이 수록되었다. 이어서 唐 貞元16
年(800)에는 圓照가 다시 앞서 開元釋敎目錄에 수록하지 않았던 259卷
의 佛典을 추가한 貞元釋敎目錄을 또 만들어 開元釋敎目錄을 보충하
였다.

중국에서 대장경이 인쇄간행된 것은 宋나라 때부터다. 宋朝 불교문
화의 精華로서 또한 漢譯大藏經의 모체로서 후세에 높이 받들어졌던 開
寶版藏經 일명 蜀版藏經은 이 開元釋敎目錄에 수록된 5048卷 480函의
佛典을 하나도 빠짐없이 모두 雕造한 大藏經으로서 宋 太祖 開寶4년
(971)에 착수하여 다음 宋 太宗 太平興國8년(983)에 그 완성을 보게 될
때까지 전후 12개년이 걸렸던 것이다. 그후 宋 眞宗 咸平年間(998—
1003)에는 貞元釋敎目錄에 수록된 경전이 宋朝 때 새로 漢譯된 경전과
아울러 雕造되었다.

가. 高麗初雕藏經(高麗舊藏經)

우리나라에 불교가 전래된 이후 수많은 경전이 여러 차례에 걸쳐 들
어오기는 하였으나, 그 방대한 양으로 보나 또는 계통적으로 정리된
체재로 보나 成宗 10년(991)에 韓彦恭이 宋으로부터 귀국하여 올 때
함께 가지고 온 開寶版大藏經은 고려사람들로 하여금 경탄케 하는데 남

음이 있었다. 顯宗 13년(1022)에는 또 韓祚가 宋으로부터 538권의 佛典
을 가지고 왔으니, 이 佛典은 開寶版藏經을 보완한 것이다.

顯宗 13년이라 하면, 즉위 당초부터 있어 왔던 契丹의 침입이 일단 가
시게 되어 비록 小康狀態로 접어들었다고는 하나 언제 또 再侵이 있을
런지 예기치 못할 때였다. 또 不義의 씨를 낳았다는 죄명으로 일찌기
세상을 떠나야 했었던 자기 부모의 명복을 빌고자 현종이 국력을 기울
여 玄化寺라는 국가적 대사원을 세운지 4년 째 되던 해다. 바로 이 玄化
寺가 창건된 반년후 제3차로 침입해온 契丹軍은 姜邯瓚에게 패배당하여
두 나라사이에는 和約이 맺어지기도 했었다. 王位繼承爭奪의 무대에서
어려서부터 희생되다시피 고배를 마셔야 했을 뿐만 아니라, 즉위 후에
도 끊임없는 契丹의 침입으로 계속 시달리어야 했던 孤兒 顯宗에 있어
서 玄化寺의 건립과 契丹軍의 격퇴 그리고 先考와 先妣에 대한 명복은
서로 떼어놓을 수 없는 하나의 이념이었다.

顯宗은 다시 나아가서 20여년 전에 전래된 바 있었던 開寶版藏經을 모
체로 하여 우리도 대장경을 만들어 놓음으로써 대외적으로 文化尺度를
자랑하는 한편 그대장경이 하나씩 이루어져가는대로 玄化寺에 봉안하
여 玄化寺를 더욱 장엄하려고 했다. 玄化寺가 창건되자 곧 이어서 그
玄化寺에 般若經寶가 설치되고 大般若經・華嚴經・金光明經・妙法蓮華
經 등이 차례차례 만들어진 것은 이 때문이다. 실로 玄化寺 낙성과 대
장경 봉안은 佛力에 의해서 대외적으로는 외적의 침략으로부터 나라를
지키려는 염원과 또 자주적인 문화국으로서의 긍지를 표시하려는 데 있
었던 것이지만, 그것은 또한 안으로는 佛의 위력에 그 뒷받침을 둔 정
치 체제와 왕권강화 확립의 성공을 뜻하는 것이기도 한 것이다.

이렇게 해서 고려에서 처음 顯宗 10년경부터 시작된 大藏經雕造는 꾸준
히 계속되어 宣宗 4년(1087)에 가서 그 끝을 맺었으니, 이를 가리키어
高麗初雕藏經이라 한다. 총 6,000卷에 이르는 이 高麗初雕藏經의 經板
은 그후 대구 符仁寺에 옮겨졌다가 마침내 高宗 19년(1232) 몽고의 兵
火로 高麗續藏經의 經板과 더불어 불에 타서 없어져버렸다.

나. 高麗續藏經

高麗續藏經은 大覺國師 義天(1055—1101)에 의해서 만들어졌다. 이는 經·律·論등 三藏에 대한 註釋書인 章疏들만을 하나로 모아서 간행한 것이니, 續藏經의 간행은 불교문화권에서 처음으로 義天에 의해서 비로소 시도되었던 것이다.

高麗初雕藏經이 거의 그 완성단계에 접어들었던 文宗27년(1073)서부터 義天은 宣宗7년(1090)에 이르는 25년간에 걸쳐 국내는 물론 宋·遼등 멀리 외국에까지 최대한으로 註釋書를 수집하는데 힘을 기울였다. 經·律·論 三藏은 이미 정리되고 開板까지 되었음에 대해 章疏는 아직 하로 묶어 정리되어 간행되어지지 않았을 뿐만 아니라 장차 없어지게 될 우려도 있기 때문에 이를 널리 수집하고 간행하여 후세에 오래 남기고자 한 것이 義天의 생각이었던 것이다. 그가 入宋求法한 그 목적의 하나도 기실은 여기에 있었다. 宣宗7년 그가 작성한 新編諸宗教藏總錄은 일명 義天錄이라고도 일컫는데, 이것은 바로 그가 수집한 章疏의 총목록이다. 3권으로 편찬한 이 목록에는 그 上卷에 華嚴經·涅槃經·法華經·楞伽經·維摩經·金光明經·般若經 등 여러 경에 대한 章疏 561종 2,586권이, 그리고 中卷에는 梵網經·遺教經·四分律·十誦律 등 戒律에 관한 章疏 142종, 467권이, 또 下卷에 大乘起信論·釋摩訶衍論·成唯識論·瑜伽師地論·因明論 등 論에 대한 章疏 307종 1,687권이 수록되어 있다. 이 新編諸宗教藏總錄 가운데 수록된 총 1,010종, 4,740권의 書目은 자연 거의 다 宋僧을 중심으로 한 中國僧의 撰述이지만, 元曉·義湘·太賢·憬興·義寂·圓測 등 新羅僧의 저술 119종 355권과 또 鮮演·覺苑·非濁·法悟·志延 등 12명의 契丹僧의 著述 39종 190권이 아울러 들어 있음은 이 목록을 더욱 빛내는 것이다. 오늘날 義天의 목록이 귀중한 것으로 되어 있는 그 까닭은 편파성없이 章疏가 널리 고루 수집되어 정확하게 수록되어있기 때문만이아니라 당시까지만해도 남아오고 있었던 新羅僧이나 契丹僧의 註釋書를 그 書目이나마 이에 의

해서 알게 되기 때문이다.

義天은 이어서 興王寺에 敎藏都監을 두고 이 목록에 담아놓은 章疏를
하나하나 간행하였다. 續藏經이 간행된 후 이것이 국내 방방곡곡에 보
급되었음은 물론이요 멀리 宋과 遼 및 일본에까지 전하여져 실로 東
洋文化史上의 精華를 이루었다. 그러나 이 모든 典籍이 우리나라에는
오늘날까지 온전하게 전하여 오지 않았음은 義天 당시로부터 약 130년
후인 高宗 19년(1232) 몽고군의 침략으로 강화도로 遷都할 때 兵火에
興王寺가 불타고 4,000권이 넘는 板木도 아울러 전부 잿더미로 되었기
때문이다. 그 일부분이 朝鮮時代 世祖 전반기(1456—1464) 때까지만해
도 남아 있어서 이를 重修한 일이 있었으므로 이것에 의해서 그 편모나
마 엿보게 됨은 여간 다행한 일이 아닐 수 없다. 지금 順天 松廣寺에
소장되고 있는 唐僧 法寶의 撰述인 大般涅槃經과 역시 唐僧 慧淨이 선
술한 妙法蓮華經續述 그리고 契丹僧 思孝의 撰述인 妙法蓮華經觀世音菩
薩普門品三玄圓贊科文은 다같이 그 刊行場所가 興王寺로 되어 있고 또
그 간행연대도 大安이라든가 혹은 壽昌이라든가 당시 사용되었던 契丹
의 年號로 되어 있어서 그 체재가 얼핏 보아 義天 당시의 續藏經 원본
인 듯 하지만 자세히 조사하면 원본을 모체로 하여 重刊된 것임을 알 것
이다. 한편 原刊記는 없으나 世祖 때 刊經都監에서 간행된 다음 章疏등
은 모두 다 義天의 續藏經을 모체로 하여 重刊한 것이다.

○ 瑜伽師地論疏 卷35 (唐僧 智周撰)

○ 華嚴論 卷10 (唐 李通玄撰)

○ 起信論疏筆削記 卷3 (宋僧 子璿撰)

○ 四分律鈔詳集記 卷6 (契丹僧 澄淵撰)

○ 大毗盧遮那成佛神變加持經義釋演密鈔 卷7 (契丹僧 覺苑撰)

이와같이 쉽게 續藏經 原刊本을 찾아보기가 어려운 가운데 일본 東大
寺에 소장되어 오는 唐 華嚴僧 澄觀의 華嚴經隨疏演義鈔 40권은 宣宗11

년(1094)에 간행된 당시의 원본 그대로이니 內外 無雙의 것이다. 또 같은 일본의 名古屋 眞福寺에도 소장되어 있는 契丹僧 志福의 釋摩訶衍論通玄鈔 4권은 그것이 義天에 의해서 간행되던 그 6년 후인 肅宗 10年(1105)에 일본으로 전해진 것이다.

義天의 續藏經 간행에 있어서 契丹佛敎의 영향은 매우 컸다. 高麗와 契丹 양국간의 무역이 정치적인 제약으로 지극히 기형적인 형태로 진행되고 있었음에 비하여 불교문화의 교류는 양국의 문화사상에 독특하고도 찬란한 위치를 차지하고 있었다. 契丹에서도 開寶版藏經에 자극되어 興宗의 發願으로 시작된 契丹大藏經이 다음 道宗 때에는 완성되어 流布되었는데 579함으로 된 이 契丹大藏經은 그 函號의 배열에 있어서 開元釋敎目錄에 의거한 開寶版藏經과는 달리 石晋의 可洪이 택한 新集藏經音義隨函錄에 의거했다. 宋의 불교와는 전혀 그 계통을 달리하는 중국 지방의 불교에 기초를 두고서 정확하고 견실한 학풍을 쌓아 올린 契丹 學僧들이 고심을 기울여 만든 이 契丹大藏經에는 중국에서는 일찍 산질되어 오는 釋摩訶衍論과 一切經音意 등이 수록되었다. 一切經音義는 唐僧 慧琳이 엮은 것으로 開元釋敎目錄에 수록된 佛書를 총망라한 字典이다. 그리하여 이 契丹大藏經이 완성된 약 10년 후인 文宗 17년(1063)에는 이것이 고려에 전래되었던 것이다. 이밖에 고려에 전래되었던 契丹의 佛書 가운데에는 契丹學僧들의 저술도 많았으니, 非濁의 首楞嚴經玄贊科와 希麟의 續一切經音義 그리고 일반 字典으로서도 널리 애용되어 朝鮮時代에 간행된 바도 있어 우리나라 문화에 한층 이채를 띠고 있는 行均의 龍龕手鏡 등은 그 한 예에 지나지 않는다. 이같은 契丹僧의 撰述 가운데서 義天은 39종 190권 이상을 골라서 續藏經의 일부로 간행한 것이다. 이리하여 契丹僧 志福의 釋摩訶衍論通玄鈔가 직접 고려로부터 일본으로 전하여지게 되었을 뿐만아니라 遼에 대한 서적수출을 엄금하고 있었던 그 宋에 契丹僧 鮮演의 저술인 華嚴經談玄決擇 6卷이 고려로부터 도입되어지기도 했다. 또 契丹大藏經 가운데 釋摩訶衍論이 義天을 통해서 다시 宋으로 逆傳되기도 했었으니 이러한 일 등은 당시 불교문화 내지 文獻交流史上에 있어서 차지하는 고려의 위치를 알기에 남음이 있게 하여 주는 것이다. 특히 慧琳이 엮은 一切經音義의 속편으로서 契丹僧 希麟이 貞元釋敎目錄에 의하여 엮은 續一切經音義 10권은 義天의 新編諸宗敎藏總錄에 수록되었을 뿐만 아니라 그 후 高麗再雕藏經에도 入藏되어 契丹佛敎가 남긴 찬란한 업적의 하나로 평가되고 있다.

다. 高麗再雕藏經

高宗 19년(1232)에 初雕藏經과 續藏經의 板木이 몽고군의 침략으로 모두 불에 타서 없어지게 되자, 그 4년 후인 高宗24년(1236) 大藏都監과 分司大藏都監을 각각 江華와 晋州에 두고서 大藏經을 다시 雕造하기 시작했다 그 이듬해 李奎報가 지은 大藏刻板君臣祈告文에도 밝혀져 있듯이 大藏經의 再雕는 佛力에 의해서 침략군을 격퇴하려는 高麗人들의 절실한 염원에서 시작된 것이다. 그리하여 무자비한 몽고 침략군에 국토가 유린된 민족적 수난을 극복하고 평화의 悲願을 오직 佛에의 믿음에 걸어 온갖 정성을 쏟아 16년이라는 긴 세월을 거쳐 마침내 高宗38년(1251)에 그 완성을 보게 되자 江華府 西門 밖에 大藏經板堂을 지어 그 곳에 경판을 봉안하였다. 지금 海印寺에 있는 高麗大藏經은 바로 이 再雕藏經인 것이다. 이 경판이 언제 江華로부터 해인사로 옮겨졌는지는 자상치 않다. 다만 분명한 것은 朝鮮時代 초기의 太祖 7년(1398) 江華에서 서울의 支天寺로 옮겨졌으며, 또 定宗 1년(1399)에는 高麗再雕藏經이 해인사에서 印經되었다는 사실이다.

高麗再雕藏經 속칭 高麗大藏經은 1915년의 경판 조사 때 약간의 분실이 있었기 때문에 당대의 명필 金敦熙의 글씨로 새로이 刻板하여 보충한 일이 있기는 하였으나 고려 高宗이래 오늘에 이르기까지 腐蝕됨이 없이 고스란히 81,137장의 경판이 전부 온전하게 전해 내려오고 있다. 高麗再雕藏經에 入藏된 佛書는 총 1,511종 6,805권이다. 宋代에 전후 5회에 걸쳐 雕造된 대장경 가운데 현재 완전히 남아 있는 것은 5,740권으로 된 思溪版藏經과 6,362권으로 된 磧砂版藏經 뿐이다. 그러

므로 高麗再雕藏經은 元版藏經의 하나인 弘法奢版 7,182권 다음으로 가는 방대한 佛典의 全集이 되는 셈이다. 이 방대한 6,805권을 639함으로 나누고 그 函號의 배열을 千字文에 의했으니 天函(No. 1)으로부터 洞函(No. 639)에 이르고 있다. 이제 그 내용을 좀더 자상하게 말하면 다음과 같다.

① 天函(No. 1)——英函(No. 480)…… 開元釋敎目錄에 수록된 佛典
② 杜函(No. 481)——穀函(No. 510)……宋代에 새로 漢譯된 經典
③ 振函(No. 511)——侈函(No. 515)……契丹本인 新集藏經音義隨函錄
④ 富函(No. 516)——輕函(No. 520)…… 宋 太宗이 撰한 蓮華心輪廻文偈頌 등 宋室의 御製
⑤ 策函(No. 521)——丁函(No. 560)…… 貞元釋敎目錄 가운데 佛典
⑥ 俊函(No. 561)——密函(No. 563)…… 高麗再雕大藏經校正別錄
⑦ 勿函(No. 564)——寔函(No. 567)…… 大般涅槃經
⑧ 寧函(No. 568)——楚函(No. 570)…… 佛名經
⑨ 更函(No. 571)……高麗再雕大藏目錄
⑩ 覇函(No. 572)——何函(No. 585)……法苑珠林傳
⑪ 遵函(No. 586)——塞函(No. 628)…… 宋代에 새로 漢譯된 經典
⑫ 雞函(No. 629)……續一切經音義
⑬ 田函(No. 630)——洞函(No. 639)……一切經音義

그런데 貞元釋敎目錄에 소수된 佛典을 策函(No. 521)서부터 丁函(No. 560)에 까지 入藏시키는데있어 佛名經은 따로 寧函(No. 568)·晋函(No. 569)·楚函(No. 570)등 3函에 入藏하고 대신 契丹本인 大宗地玄文論과 釋摩訶衍論을 간간 回函(No.554)과 漢函(No. 555)에 入藏하였다.

高麗再雕藏經은 守其에 의해서 정확한 校合을 거쳤다. 守其는 初雕藏

經의 高麗本과 開寶版藏經의 宋本 그리고 契丹大藏經의 契丹本 등 셋을
서로 면밀히 對校하여 그 잘못된 곳을 바로 잡아 놓았던 것이다. 그러
므로 高麗再雕藏經 가운데 天函(No. 1)으로부터 英函(No. 480)에 이르는
앞의 부분은 그 체제가 初雕藏經이나 開寶版藏經과 같으면서도 내용은
달리 새롭게 잘 다듬어졌다. 守其가 그 얼마나 정확하게 校合을 보았던
것인가는 星函(No. 464)에 入藏된 集古今佛道論衡 4권의 경우를 보아도
알 수 있다. 唐僧 道宣이 撰한 이 集古今佛道論衡은 後漢 明帝 때부터
唐 高宗때에 이르기까지의 佛敎政策과 道敎政策에 대하여 논평한 것으로
高麗本과 宋本 그리고 契丹本 등 셋이 서로 다르게 그 체제와 내용이
전해 내려 왔던 것이다. 즉, 高麗本과 宋本은 다같이 唐 高宗 때의 7개
사항이 제3권에 실려있고 唐 太宗 때의 10개 사항과 道士 郭行眞의 捨
道歸佛文은 함께 8張으로 된 제4권에 실려 있음에 대해 契丹本은 이와
달리 唐 太宗 때의 10개 사항이 제3권에 실렸으며 唐 高宗 때의 7개 사
항과 捨道歸佛文은 34張으로 된 제4권에 실려 있는 것이다. 그러나 郭
行眞이 捨道歸佛文을 발표한 것이 唐 高宗 때의 일이었을 뿐만 아니라
시대순으로 서술되고 있는 이 集古今佛道論衡의 서술방식으로 보아 高
麗本과 宋本이 다같이 앞뒤가 바뀌어진 것은 분명하다. 그래서 守其
는 高麗本과 宋本을 契丹本에 의해서 바로 잡고 아울러 脫漏된 부분도
이를 보완하였다. 더우기 松函(No. 270)의 雜阿含經 같은 것은 아예 高
麗本과 宋本을 전면적으로 버리고 契丹本을 그대로 채택하였다.

　이처럼 守其가 契丹本을 위주로 하였던 까닭은 契丹大藏經이 지니고
있는 그 내용의 우수성 때문이었음은 물론이다. 이렇게 해서 契丹大藏
經은 高麗再雕藏經에 있어서 큰 구실을 했던 것이다. 守其가 여러 經마
다 면밀히 校合한 그 과정을 자상히 적어놓은 高麗再雕大藏校正別錄 30
권은 다른 佛典 등과 함께 이 再雕藏經에 入藏되어 오늘날 高麗 初雕藏
經과 再雕藏經과의 관계를 알려 주는 동시에 지금은 없어진 契丹大藏經
의 윤곽도 어느 정도나마 짐작케 하여 주고 있다.

　해인사에 전해 내려오고 있는 高麗大藏經이 현존하는 여러 漢譯大藏

經 중에서도 가장 학술상 우수한 것으로 공인되고 있는 것은 그 校合에
있어서 정확한 契丹大藏經을 중심으로 했었다는 것 뿐만에서가 아니라
刻板에 있어서 誤字와 脫字가 없는 철저한 교정이 있었기 때문이다. 또
한 진작 없어졌거나 혹은 아직 널리 퍼지지를 못해서 알려지지 않았었
던 新集藏經音義隨函錄・大宗地玄文論・摩訶衍論・一切經音義・續一切經
音義 등이 契丹本에 의해서 高麗再雕藏經에 入藏됨으로써 그후 불교문
화권에 널리 알려지게 된 일도 이 高麗藏經의 가치를 더욱 높이는 것이
다. 契丹大藏經이 없어진 오늘날, 그 契丹大藏經의 가치가 高麗再雕藏
經에 의해서 재인식되고 있는 것은 高麗와 契丹 두 나라 사이에 전개된
장기간의 세속적인 利害鬪爭 가운데서도 이를 초월하여 꾸준히 이루어
지고 있었던 종교적 접촉의 아름다운 열매라 하겠다.

해인사에는 고려 高宗 때 分司大藏都監에서 雕造된 宗鏡錄・祖堂集・
金剛三昧經論・禪門拈頌 등 15종의 補板이 보존되어 온다. 이들은 비록
高麗再雕藏經에 정식으로 入藏되지는 않았으나 모두 다 주옥같이 귀한
것들이다. 이 가운데 특히 高宗 32년(1245)에 이룩된 祖堂集 20권은 唐
靜修禪師가 엮은 것인데 寶林傳의 完本이 전하지 않는 오늘날 傳燈에
관한 史籍 중에서 完本으로서는 이것이 가장 오래된 것이라 보아 좋을
것이다. 祖堂集이 다시금 세상에 알려지게 된 것은 오직 이 해인사의
補板에 의한다.

고려 말기에서 朝鮮 초기에 걸쳐 일본은 倭寇의 소탕과 그 倭寇들에
게 납치당한 남녀노소를 돌려 보내는데 적극 주선하겠다는 것을 미끼로
하여 우리나라에 전후 80회에 걸친 大藏經 청구가 있었다. 世宗 5년
(1423)에는 해인사의 大藏經板의 청구까지 했던 일이 있었다. 世宗도
처음에는 無用之物이라 하여 고려대장경판을 주어버리려고까지 하였었
으나 朝臣들의 반대로 飜意하게 되었던 것은 다행한 일이었다. 그래서
뜻을 이루지 못한 일본使臣 梵齡은 단식투쟁을 하여 소란을 피우기까지
하였었다.

이렇듯 우리 民族精神史의 일면을 장식하여 문화유산의 주류를 이루

고 온 高麗再雕藏經은 大藏經雕造史로 보거나 佛敎學術史로 보거나 세계적인 의의를 지니는 것이다. 1896년 James Legge 가 法顯의 撰인 佛國記의 英譯本 *A Record of Buddhistic Kingdoms*를 간행함에 있어서 사용했던 그 텍스트가 바로 高麗雕再藏經本이었다는 것은 결코 우연한 일이 아니다.

2. 寺刊本

국가에서 출판된 高麗大藏經 이외에 또 施主들이 희사하는 비용으로 각 寺刹에서 출판한 寺刊本이 널리 퍼졌다. 우리는 이같은 寺刊本을 통해서 당시 일반 국민들의 신앙생활과 아울러 불교교리에 대한 그들의 이해를 엿보게 되는 것이지만 寺刊本에는 대개 그 간행 시기와 간행장소 및 간행자가 표시되어 있기 때문에 寺刊本은 書誌 연구에 좋은 자료가 되고 있을 뿐만 아니라 그 卷首마다 變相圖라고 일컫는 일종의 揷圖가 있는 것이 보통이므로 사상적으로나 圖像學的으로나 불교미술 연구에도 여간 도움이 되는 것이 아니다.

가. 海印寺本

해인사에는 高麗大藏經과 補板에 관계가 없는 寺刊本의 板木이 도합 11,139張 보존되고 있다. 이것들은 대부분이 朝鮮時代에 刻板한 것이지만 고려 때의 것도 적지않게 들어 있다. 이 가운데 元曉가 撰한 十門和諍論은 肅宗 3년(1098)에 海印寺僧 成軒에 의해서 이룩된 것이고, 義湘이 撰한 白花道場發願文은 忠肅王 15년(1328)에 같은 해인사의 僧 體元이 이룩해 놓은 것이다. 體元은 또 華嚴經觀自在菩薩所設法門別行疏幷集略解를 엮고 이를 忠惠王 1년(1331)에 刻板케 하기도 하였다.

이 밖에도 해인사에서는 佛說長壽滅罪護諸童子陀羅尼經과 人天寶鑑의 간행이 각각 忠烈王 4년(1278)과 同王 16년(1290)에 있었다. 大覺國師集은 그 刻板年代를 정확히 알 수는 없으나 仁宗 10(년1132) 이후의 것임이 틀림없다. 한편 澄觀이 撰한 華嚴經隨疏演義鈔는 宣宗 11년(1094)

에 간행되었던 續藏經의 원본을 그대로 따서 후일 다시 刻板한 것이다. 그런데 해인사의 寺刊板 가운데 忠烈王21년(1295)에 刻板된 또 하나의 小字楞嚴經은 그 末尾에 붙어있는 跋文 속에 宋僧 戒環과 그의 저술인 楞嚴經要解에 대하여 언급한 것이 있어 우리의 주목을 끌게 하여 준 다. 왜냐하면 楞嚴經에 대한 註釋書가 이것 하나만이 아닌데 戒環의 楞 嚴經要解에만 언급하고 있음은 분명히 이것만이 널리 통용되고 있었음 을 알게 하기 때문이다. 이는 고려때서부터 줄곧 우리나라에서 妙法蓮 華經의 註釋書로서 같은 戒環의 妙法蓮華經要解가 유독 널리 애용되어 온 것과 더불어 우리나라 불교를 이해하는데 유의하여야 할 하나의 문 제가 아닐 수 없다.

나. 其他 寺刊本

宋僧 戒環이 妙法蓮華經要解를 선술한 때는 1119년서부터 1126년에 이르는 전후 8년간의 사이다. 禪과 華嚴의 입장에서 여러 경전에 주석 을 붙인 그는 華嚴과 天台에 대해서도 이를 서로 하나로 묶어서 이해하 였다. 이같은 그의 불교이해가 總和佛教를 지향하고 있었던 한국불교의 체질에도 맞았을 뿐만 아니라 주석서로서도 그 요점이 간결하게 조리가 서있어 따라서 이해하기도 수월하였기 때문에 그의 주석서인 妙法蓮華經 要解와 楞嚴經解要解 등이 고려사회에서 널리 환영되었던 모양이다. 高 宗 27년(1240) 아마 黃海道 成佛寺에서 간행되었으리라고 믿어지는 妙 法蓮華經도 그 내용은 바로 이 妙法蓮華經要解인 것이다. 恭愍王 10년 (1361)에는 全州 圓岩寺에서 佛祖三經의 간행이 있었으니, 이것은 四十 二章經과 遺教經 및 潙山禪師의 가르침을 한책으로 묶은 것이다. 이 恭 愍王때 萬日寺에서 般舟三昧經이 간행되기도 했다. 또 陀羅尼를 모아놓 은 梵書摠持集이 開泰寺에서 高宗 5년(1218) 간행되었는데 陀羅尼에 관 한 경전으로서는 이보다 훨씬 앞서서 穆宗 10년(1007) 摠持寺에서 간행 된 寶篋印陀羅尼經이 있는. 陀羅尼經을 舍利와 함께 탑 속에 모시기는 新羅 때부터 있어 오는 것이지만 無垢淨光大陀尼經 대신으로 이 寶篋印

陀羅尼經을 高麗에서 탑 안에 모시게 되어진 데에는 아마 吳越의 王인 錢弘俶(940—978)이 인도의 阿育王을 본따서 널리 전국에 걸쳐 小塔 84,000을 세우고 각각 그 속에 寶篋印陀尼經을 넣어 모셨던 일로부터 영향을 입었던 것이 아닐까 한다. 또한 法華信仰을 널리 펴기 위해 忠肅王 무렵(1314—1330)에는 法華靈驗傳이 萬義寺에서 간행되었다. 다시 나아가서 禑王 8년(1379)에는 宋나라 張商英이 韓退之의 排佛論을 논박하기 위하여 1110년에 저술한 護法論이 간행되기도 하였다. 이때 李穡이 이 護法論에다가 서슴치않고 跋文을 붙였음은 말기의 적극적인 排佛論者 鄭道傳과는 매우 대조적이다.

그러나, 고려 때 많이 간행되었고 또 그 중 가장 많이 남아 오고 있는 것은 禪宗 관계의 佛書와 禪僧들의 語錄이다. 景閑(1299—1375)의 語錄인 白雲和尙語錄이 禑王 4년(1378) 鷲岩寺에서 간행되어졌으며, 慧勤(1320—1376)의 語錄인 懶翁和尙集이 또한 禑王 5년(1379)에 간행되었다. 禪籍으로서는 禪門拈頌集과 禪門寶藏錄의 간행이 각각 高宗 30년(1243)과 忠烈王 19년(1293)에 있었다. 둘 다 모두 우리나라의 대표적인 禪籍이다. 전자는 曹溪山 제2世 慧諶의 것이고, 후자는 萬德山 白蓮社 제4世 天頙의 것이다. 宋僧 宗杲의 禪林寶訓과 書狀도 각각 禑王 4년(1378)과 同王 13년(1387)에 간행되었었는데, 그 禪林寶訓은 忠州 靑龍寺에서 간행되었다. 智賢이 1313년에 엮은 緇門警訓이 처음으로 우리나라에 전래되기는 忠穆王 4년(1348)의 일이었지만 이로부터 30년후인 禑王 4년(1378)에는 이것이 비로소 출판되었다. 六祖法寶壇經이 熙宗 3년(1207)에 高麗에서도 간행되었을 때 知訥이 湛默의 간청으로 이에 跋文을 붙인 일이 있었거니와 그후 六祖法寶壇經은 忠烈王 26년(1300)과 忠肅王 3년(1316)년에도 각각 간행된 바 있었다. 모두 다 元나라에서 전래되어진 것을 모체로하여 본떠 간행한 것으로 忠肅王 3년(1316)에 간행된 것을 1290년 元나라에서 간행된 것과 서로 맞대어보면 篇章의 배열과 명칭 뿐만 아니라 그 내용에 있어서도 서로 다른 점이 상당히 많다. 이는 六祖法寶壇經이 애초 중국에서부터 여러 板本이 있어 온 것이기 때문이니, 우리나라 禪宗의 系脈을 생각하는데 있어서도 하나의 실마리를 풀게 하여주는 것이라 하겠다.

한편 慧定이 엮은 金剛般若經疏論纂要助顯錄이 元나라로부터 전래됨을 계기로 말기에는 金剛般若經에 대한 연구에 생기를 부어넣었다. 그리하여 高麗에서도 이 金剛般若經疏論纂要助顯錄이 禑王 4년(1378)에는 忠州 宴晦庵에서 간행을 보게 되었는데, 그 간행연대가 宣光8년(1378)으로 되어 있다. 宣光은 北元의 年號이다. 이때 고려에서 계속 北元의 연호를 쓰고 있었음은 신흥국가 明에게 패배당하여 멀리 외몽고지방으로 쫓겨 간 昭宗 愛獻識理達臘와 그의 生母 高麗人 奇氏皇后에 대한 측은한 마음에서 였을까.

다. 靈驗說話集의 刊行

고려 때 간행된 佛書 가운데 靈驗說話集 또는 이에 준하는 것이 더러 있음은 주목할 만한 일이다. 심오한 철학적인 내용과는 달리 일반 상식으로는 생각할 수 없는 줄거리로 엮어진 靈驗說話集은 종교로서의 실천적인 입장을 오직 관철하여 불교신앙을 진지하게 체험하여간 하나의 事例集이라는데서 가볍게 넘겨버릴 수는 없는 佛書이다. 고려사회에서 행해지고 있었던 불교신앙이 어떤 것이었는가를 알게 하는 유력한 史料가 되는 것이기도 한 것이다.

忠肅王 때 萬德寺에서 간행된 法華靈驗傳은 法華信仰을 널리 펴기 위해 편찬한 것이다. 妙法蓮華經에 설된 가르침을 굳게 믿고 이를 진실하게 실천에 옮겨 생활화하여가는 것이 다름아닌 法華信仰이다. 이 法華靈驗傳에 실려진 약 90편의 설화는 거의 중국의 자료에 의해서 추려낸 것인 만큼 자연 中國人의 생활체험기록이기는 하지만 新羅를 비롯한 우리나라 사람들이 얻은 靈驗도 아울러 적지않게 수록하여 놓았다. 이 法華靈驗傳은 우리 사회에서 널리 진지하게 요구되어져 朝鮮時代에도 中宗 29년(1534)과 同王 39년(1544)에 각각 高敞 文殊寺와 安邊 釋王寺에서 再版되었다. 이같이 法華靈驗傳이 요구된 것은 이속에 觀音菩薩에

관한 靈驗說話가 비교적 많이 실려 있기 때문이었을 것이다. 觀音菩薩의 자비는 妙法蓮華經 가운데 설된 중요한 대목의 하나이지만, 華嚴經에도 觀音菩薩의 자비에 대하여 설된 부분이 있다. 忠惠王 1년(1331) 해인사의 體元이 唐 澄觀의 行願品別行疏 가운데서 觀音菩薩에 관한 부분만을 추려내어 華嚴經觀自在菩薩所說法門別行疏并集略解를 편찬하고 이를 간행한 것도 觀音信仰을 널리 펴기 위해서 였다. 이 속에 體元이 그 자신의 주석과 아울러 실린 20편의 靈驗說話는 法華靈驗傳에 있는 觀音菩薩의 靈驗說話와는 거의 중복되지 않은 새로운 것을 소개하여 놓은 것이다. 한편 禑王 4년(1378)에 간행된 金剛般若經疏論纂要助顯錄 가운데 실려진 5편의 靈驗說話가 또한 亡者에 대한 명복을 비는 金剛經信仰에 도움을 주었음은 물론이다.

3. 金屬活字本

고려말기에 이르러 금속활자가 발명된 일은 종래의 木版印刷技術에 일대 혁명을 가져오는 것이 되었다. 고려에서 금속활자가 이미 高宗 26년(1239) 이전에 만들어지고 있었음은 바로 이 高宗 26년에 간행된 南明泉頌證道歌의 刊行辭에 의해서도 알 수 있다.

고려 때 금속활자로 인쇄된 佛書 가운데 현존하여 오는 것으로는 白雲和尙抄錄佛祖直指心體要節과 淸凉荅順宗心要法門이 있다. 일명 直指心經이라고도 불리우는 이 白雲和尙抄錄佛祖直指心體要節은 白雲和尙 景閑이 엮은 것으로 禑王 3년(1377)에 인쇄되었다. 淸凉荅順宗心要法門도 대체로 이 무렵에 인쇄되었는데, 이것은 元나라 高官 別不花가 자기나라 사람들에게 나누어 주려고 高麗의 선진적인 기술을 동원하여 인쇄된 것이라는데서 당시 고려와 元나라 兩國 간에 이루어지고 있었던 불교문화교류의 일면을 보여 주는 것이라 하겠다. 忠烈王 31년(1305)에도 元나라의 요청으로 고려의 寫經僧이 100명이나 파견되었던 일이 있었던 것을 보면 高麗의 寫經이나 인쇄술은 元나라에서 술곧 관심의 대상이 되어 온 것을 알 것이다.

　이렇게 해서 元나라로 들어간 고려의 금속활자 인쇄기술은 그후 아라
비아를 거쳐 유럽으로 소개가 되어 1453년에는 구텐베르그가 高麗의 금
속활자 鑄造術을 보다 발전시킨 새로운 금속활자를 만들어 내게 되는
것이다.

萬海 韓龍雲論

廉 武 雄

　萬海 韓龍雲 선생은 3.1독립선언에 참가한 민족대표의 한 분으로서, 「님의 沈默」을 노래한 뛰어난 시인으로서, 그리고 근대한국에 있어 가장 위대한 승려로서 이미 우리에게 그 이름이 익히 알려져 있다. 그의 생애와 업적에 대한 관심 역시 대단히 깊어져 60년대 이후에는 저서와 논문의 형태로 상당한 분량의 연구가 이루어졌으며, 최근에는 그의 全集이 발간된 바 있다. 그러나 萬海의 인간적 크기나 사상적 깊이에 비추어 그에 대한 연구는 이제 겨우 시작되었다고 할 수 있는 정도에 지나지 않으며, 그에 대한 연구가 필연적으로 제기하는 문제 즉 오늘의 사회와 문학 속에서 그를 실천적으로 계승하는 문제는 뜻있는 몇 사람의 손을 벗어나 있지 못한 것으로 생각된다. 이 글은 지금까지 이루어진 研究와 論議들을 토대로 萬海의 인간적·사상적·문학적 발전과정을 살펴 보고, 그렇게 함으로써 오늘의 이 현실 속에서 그를 옳게 알고 그에게서 옳게 배우는 길이 어떤 것일까 함께 모색하는 하나의 기회로서 씌어졌다.

1

　韓龍雲 선생은 1879년 8월 29일 충청남도 洪州郡(지금의 洪城郡)에서 韓應俊의 둘째 아들로 태어났다. 잘 알려진 바와 같이 이 시대는 조선왕조의 관료적 봉건체제가 그 체제의 이상인 유교적 王道政治의 실현을

추구하던 초기의 활력을 오래전에 잃어버리고, 집권계층인 관료귀족들의 부패와 타락 및 체제 자체의 모순으로 말미암아 심각한 老衰現象을 드러내고 있었다. 李朝政權은 한편으로 18세기 전후한 實學派 지식인들의 진보적 개혁안을 받아들이지 못했고 다른 한편 洪景來亂에서 시작된 여러 차례의 민중봉기로 더욱 허약해진 상태에서 강력한 서양 독점자본주의의 침략을 받게 되었다. 萬海가 출생하기 3년전의 江華島條約은 세계사적 규모의 西勢東漸 과정에 있어서 바로 그 서양 제국주의의 침략에 대한 봉건적 후진왕국의 굴복을 기록하는 또 하나의 사건이었다. 그리하여 얼빠진 봉건지배자들은 밀려드는 外勢의 어느 한 가닥을 붙잡고 그것에 의지하여 민중의 항거를 억누르는 동시에 개인적 안전과 영달을 계속 누리고자 꾀하였다.

이러한 시대적 배경 속에서 태어난 萬海는 6살때 고향의 書堂에 들어가 당시의 정규적인 한문 교육을 받았다. 「小學」「通鑑」에서 시작하여 18세까지 소위 四書三經을 모두 배웠고, 한편으로 틈틈이 「西廂記」「三國誌」 등의 희극·소설·기타 잡서들을 읽었다고 하며, 이런 면에서도 그는 어려서부터 특출한 재능을 보였다고 한다. 그러다가 18세 되던 1896년 집을 떠나 설악산 五歲庵으로 들어가 수년간 불교서적을 중심으로 독서에 정진했다. 이 무렵의 萬海와 관련하여 그의 가문 및 입산 동기를 지금까지의 자료들은 대체로 다음과 같이 기록하고 있다. 즉, 첫째 그의 가문은 여러 대에 걸친 士族으로서 증조 光厚는 知中樞府事, 조부 永祐는 訓練院僉正, 부친 應俊은 忠勳府都事를 지냈다. 둘째, 그의 부친과 형 允敬은 창의대장 閔宗植과 함께 定山(지금의 靑陽)에서 義兵을 일으켜 藍浦와 洪州를 점령했으나 마침내 패배하여 죽음을 당했다. 세째, 萬海는 18세 때에 그 동안의 학업을 팽개치고 감연히 東學에 가담하여 투쟁에 참가하였으나, 실패하여 몸을 피하기 위해 설악산 오세암으로 들어가게 되었다. 자료에 따라서는 연대가 틀리는 것이 있기도 하지만 대강 이상과 같다.

그러나, 우리는 단순히 萬海의 경력을 따지자는 관점에서가 아니라 그의 인간 형성과정을 바르게 알자는 입장에서 위의 몇 가지 사실에 대해 의심을 품게 된다. 첫째, 그의 가문이 정말 累代士族이었느냐 하는 점이다. 이 점에 대해서는 이미 安秉直씨가 올바른 의문과 추측을 던진 바 있다. (「萬海 韓龍雲의 獨立思想」 참조) 여러 가지 점으로 미루어 萬海의 가문은 관료귀족이나 선비의 집안이 아니라 경제적 실력과 얼마간의 교양을 갖춘 衙前 정도의 중인이었던 것 같다. 후일 부친에 대하여 萬海가 『고향에 있을 때 나는 선친에게 조석으로 좋은 말씀을 들었으니, 선친은 서책을 보시다가 가끔 어린 나를 불러 세우시고, 역사상에 빛나는 의인·걸사의 언행을 가르쳐 주시며, 또한 세상 형편, 국가사회의 모든 일을 알아듣도록 타일러 주시었다』(수필「西伯利亞 거쳐 서울로」 참조)라고 술회한 것으로 보나 그 자신의 후일의 行蹟으로 보아, 그의 부친은 전통적인 봉건유교적 세계관에 자기를 얽매둘 필요가 없었던 中人 출신의 농촌 지식인이 아니었던가 짐작된다. 18세기 이후에 있어 沒落兩班이 농민으로 전락하기도 하고 농민이 새로운 진보적 지식인으로 성장하기도 하는 상황 속에서 양반과 농민의 계급적 경계가 부분적으로 허물어지고 있었던 점을 생각할 때 萬海의 부친은 士族과 농민의 어느쪽이든 이 경계선 가까운 자리에 위치한 인물이었을 것이다. 뒷날에 있었던 萬海의 활동은 물론 이러한 그의 가문과 결코 무관한 것이 아니었다.

다음으로 그의 부친과 형이 창의대장 閔宗植과 함께 의병에 참가했다가 죽었다는 문제이다. 일반적으로 구한말의 의병운동은 1895년의 閔妃살해사건, 斷髮令, 1905년의 을사보호조약, 1907년의 高宗 양위와 군대해산 등을 각각 계기로 하는 세 차례의 거센 파도가 있었던 바, 閔宗植의 起兵은 이중 두번째로서 1906년 3월 초순부터 5월 말까지 활동한 것으로 되어 있다. 그런데, 萬海의 부친과 형이 작고한 것이 통설대로 1896년 경이라면 그들이 閔宗植의 의병부대에 참가했다는 기록은 잘못일 것이다. 1896년 초 洪州에서 의병을 일으킨 것은 金福漢·安炳瓚·李世永 등으로서, 이들도 체포된 후에 國母의 시해를 원통히 여겨 병사를 일으켰다는 정상이 참작되어 그다지 무거운 형벌을 받지 않았다. 따라서 이런 점들을 감안하여 추론해 본다면 萬海의 父兄이 죽음을 당한 것은 1894년의 東學軍 제 2 차 봉기에서나 혹은 1906년의 閔宗植 의병 전투에서 일것이다.

세째로 萬海의 입산동기와 직접 관련하여 그가 18세 때 (1896년) 동학란에 가담, 洪州戶房을 습격하여 천 냥이란 거액의 군자금을 탈취하는 등 눈부신 활약을 하다가 결국 실패하고서 몸을 숨기기 위해 설악산 오세암으로 들어가 절에서 불목한이 노릇을 하게 되었다는 점이다. 이 역시 대단히 의심스러운 사실이다. 민비 살해사건과 단발령을 계기로 1895년 겨울부터 전국 각처에서 의병이 일어났던 것은 史料가 증명해 주는 바이고 특히 洪州에서는 1896년 2월경 대단한 기세를 올렸다고 한다. 당시 우리 나라 각지에서 일어났던 저항 투쟁은 그 성격이 대단히 복잡하여 정부에서도 <東學인지 義兵인지>판별할 수 없다고 고백하고 있지만(國史編纂委員會편 「高宗時代史」 卷四, p.152 참조), 적어도 이 무렵의 무장봉기가 이미 단일한 역사적 운동단위로서의 東學농민전쟁의 성격을 일단 벗어나 있었던 것만은 분명하다. 더구나 1896년의 金福漢 등의 의병활동은 봉건적 억압에 반대하고 그것을 철폐하려는 싸움이 아니라 오히려 봉건유교적 理想을 고집하려는 싸움이었던 만큼, 같은 해에 萬海가 동학에 가담하여 주동적 역할을 했다는 사실은 당연히 의심스러운 것이다. 오히려 그가 이 金福漢 등의 의병활동에 참가했을 가능성이 인정되는 터이다. 그렇다면 洪州府 관찰사 李勝宇에 의해 의병 주모자인 金福漢・安炳瓚 등이 체포된 것이 4월 초순이므로 萬海가 설악산으로 피신한 것은 역시 이 무렵일 것으로 추측된다.

5,6년간 설악산 오세암에 머무는 동안 그는 佛經에 대해 공부를 하는 한편 기타의 근대적인 교양서적과 접촉하게 되었던 것 같다. 「瀛環地略」을 읽고 세계사정에 눈을 떴다고 하며, 특히 중국의 선각자인 梁啓超의 「飮氷室文集」을 통해 칸트와 베이컨 등의 서양 근대사상을 알게 되었다. 이 무렵 그는 세계여행을 계획하고 설악산을 내려와 블라디보

스톡(海蔘威)으로 건너갔으나, 박해를 받고 곧 귀국하여 이곳저곳 돌아다니다가 고향으로 돌아왔다. (1904년 초) 그러나 1904년 여름 그는 다시 고향을 떠났다. 14살 때 부모의 뜻에 따라 결혼을 했던 그의 아내 金氏는 남편이 다시 떠난지 몇달 뒤인 1904년말에 아들(保國)을 낳았다. 이후 그는 다시 고향을 찾은 적이 없으며, 뒷날 아들이 찾아왔을 때에도 지극히 냉랭하게 대했다고 한다. 승려의 娶妻자유를 주장했고 만년에 스스로 재혼을 했던 萬海로서, 그가 왜 본부인과 아들에 대해서는 그처럼 끝까지 냉담했는지 분명히 알 수 없는 노릇이다. 아뭏든 그는 이듬해 1월 26일 강원도 인제군에 있는 百潭寺에서 그곳의 金連谷 스님에 의해서 奉琓이란 계명을 받고 승려가 되었다. 후에 乾鳳寺의 萬化禪師로부터 법을 이어받아 법명을 龍雲, 법호를 萬海라 하였다.

2

봉건체제의 모순과 제국주의 外勢의 침략으로 인하여 조선왕조의 몰락이 결정적인 것으로 되어가던 시기에 있어서 정의감이 강한 농촌 지식인의 아들로 태어난 萬海는 십수년간의 漢學교육을 받고 짤막한 현실 참여의 격동을 거친 다음 마침내 佛僧으로서의 자기를 정착시켰다. 1905년 이후에 있어 萬海의 모든 행동적·사상적 발전은 이처럼 불교의 승려로서 테두리지어진 한계 내에서 이루어졌다. 따라서 우리가 萬海를 제대로 알자면 불교를 알아야 되고 특히 한국불교의 역사적 전개과정을 알아야 된다.

승려가 된 다음 그는 佛經공부와 參禪에 전념하는 한편, 1908년에는 5월부터 약 반년 동안 일본으로 건너가 東京과 京都를 비롯한 각지의 사찰과 새로운 문물들을 구경하였고, 東京의 曹洞宗大學(駒澤大學)에서 약 석달 동안 불교와 서양철학을 청강하였다. 당시 일본에 유학중이던 崔麟과 사귄 것은 이때였다. 1911년 가을에는 다시 滿洲로 건너갔으나 이 때에도 한국인 청년들에게 의심을 사서 불의의 총격을 받고 죽을 번

한 고초를 겪은 끝에 되돌아 왔다. 어쨌든 萬海는 이러한 넓은 견문을
통해서 변화하는 세계를 알았고 근대적인 지식을 흡수하였으며 인류가
문명을 향해 전진하는 존재임을 깨달았다. 이러한 인식을 토대로 하여
그는 당시 한국 불교의 침체와 낙후성과 은둔주의를 대담하고 통렬하게
분석·비판한 일대논설「朝鮮佛敎維新論」을 집필했던 것이다.

1913년에 출판된 이 「朝鮮佛敎維新論」은 학구적인 입장에서 불교의
진리를 해설한 이론서가 아니라 한국불교의 현상을 타개하려는 열렬한
實踐論이다. 그러나, 바로 그러한 실천적 의도로 인하여 이 논문은 한
국불교의 현실을 올바르게 보았을 뿐더러 불교 자체의 진리를 올바르게
본 불후의 저작이 되었다. 여기에는 지금까지의 萬海의 모든 교육과 사
색과 견문이 한국불교의 현상에 대한 비판의 형태로 집약되어 있으며
또한 이미 앞으로 전개될 萬海의 모든 행동과 사상과 문학의 윤곽이 뚜
렷하게 부각되어 있다.

모두 17章으로 되어 있는 이 論著에서 第5章부터 第16章까지는 당시
의 한국불교가 직접 당하고 있고 또 해결하지 않으면 안될 문제들에 대
해서 구체적인 자기의 의견들을 피력한 것이고, 第1章부터 第4章까지
는 그러한 구체적 해결방안들의 근거가 되는 萬海의 佛敎觀을 전개한
것이다. 따라서 먼저 우리의 흥미를 끄는 것은 앞부분이라 하겠다. 불
교에 대해 문외한인 필자로서는 그가 불교의 진리와 한국불교의 현실을
얼마나 정확하게 이해했는지 판가름할 수는 없으나 불교의 형태로 표현
된 그의 세계관이 탁월한 것임을 단언할 수는 있다. 이 논문에 제시된
그의 사상은 대체로 다음의 세 가지로 요약될 수 있다.

첫째, 萬海는『금후의 세계는 진보를 그치지 않아서, 진정한 문명의
의상에 도달하지 않고는 그 걸음을 멈추지 않을 것이므로 우선 불교가
장차의 인류문명에 적합할 것인가 하는 문제를 제기한다. 만약 불교가
장래의 문명에 적합지 않을 경우에는 마르틴 루터 같은 宗敎改革家를
불러오더라도 불교는 지탱할 수 없을 것이다. 이 점 불교야말로 문명의

이상에 합치되는 종교이며, 깨달음과 지혜의 종교라고 萬海는 말한다. 그런데 우리가 종교를 믿는 것은 무엇 때문인가. 그것은 다름아니라 인간에게 미래에 대한 희망을 주기 때문이다. 이러한 희망이 없다면 사람은 누구나 게으르고 편하게 그날그날을 사는 데 만족할 것이고 구태여 애써 노력하지 않을 것이며, 따라서 세상은 필시 지옥 같은 생활과 야만적인 행위로 가득차게 될 것이다. 이런 점을 염려한 나머지 『예수교의 天堂, 유태교가 받드는 神, 마호멧교의 永生 따위』가 나오게 된 것이지만, 그러나 이것들은 어디까지나 일종의 속임수로서 말하자면 미신이라고 아니할 수 없으며, 이러한 미신으로써 어찌 사람을 깨달음의 경지로 이끌 수 있겠는가. 불교는 이처럼 『민중의 지혜에 부당한 제약을 주는』미신과 미혹에서 떠나 깨달음에 이르도록 하는 종교라는 것이다. 그러면 천당이니 영생이니 하는 超人間的 實在에 의하지 않고서 중생에게 지혜를 가르치고 희망을 갖게 하는 길은 무엇인가. 불교에서는 바로 각 개인의 마음 속에 진리에 이르는 최종적 근거(佛性, 眞如)가 있다고 가르친다. 『중생이 이런 더없는 보배를 마음 속에 간직하고 있으면서도 스스로 미혹하여 알지 못하는 까닭에 우리 부처님께서 대자대비한 마음으로 이들을 위하여 설법하시었다』그리하여 불교는 불생불멸의 경지를 영원한 참된 自我에서 구하도록 가르쳤고, 미신에 의해서가 아니라 미신을 버림으로써 올바른 희망을 가지고 진리에 이르는 길을 보여 준다고 한다.

둘째 萬海는 불교의 가르침이 平等主義에 입각하고 있음을 역설하였다. 평등이란 곧 불평등의 반대인 바, 우리가 이 불평등이란 견지에서 세상을 바라본다면 무엇 하나 불평등하지 않은 것이 없다. 같은 현인이건만 顔淵은 요절했고 仲由는 형벌을 받았으며, 같은 영웅이건만 워싱톤은 성공했고 나폴레옹은 귀양살이로 막을 내렸으며, 어떤 것은 강하고 어떤 것은 약하고 어떤 것은 착하며 어떤 것은 악하다. 평등의 견지에서 바라본다는 것은 이런 현상적 불평등에 얽매이지 않고 진리의 눈으로 보는 것이다. 현상이 필연의 법칙에 지배받음에 반하여 진리는 시

간과 공간을 초월한 참된 존재의 세계이다. 萬海는 근대의 자유주의 및
세계주의 속에서 이러한 불교적 평등의 역사적 실현과정을 보았다. 그
는 이 세계가 평등의 완전한 실현에 이르기까지 발전하고야 말 것임을
확신하였다. 이 평등의 역사적 실현과정에서 나타나는 자유라고 하는
것은, 내가 남의 자유를 침범하지 않는 것으로 한계는 삼는 바, 각자의
자유가 모두 수평선처럼 가지런하게 되어 조금의 차이도 없게 되고 보
면, 이것이 곧 평등의 이상이 실현된 상태인 것이다. 萬海는 부처님의
평등정신이 다만 개인과 개인, 인종과 인종, 나라와 나라 사이의 관계
에만 미치는 것이 아니라 하나하나의 물건과 하나 하나의 일들도 빠뜨
림이 없는 철저한 것이라고 말한다.

세쩨로 萬海는 불교의 또 하나의 특징이 救世主義에 있다고 설명한
다. 그러면 구세주의란 무엇인가. 그것은 자기 한 몸만 이득을 취하고
자기 혼자만 행복을 얻으려는 주의(獨利主義)에 반대되는 개념이다. 흔
히 불교를 참선과 고행에 의해 자기 혼자만의 깨달음을 얻으려는 종교
로 잘못 알고 있으나, 불교야말로 이러한 종류의 이기주의와 정히 반대
되는 것이다. 부처님의 모든 설법은 衆生濟度의 자비심으로 가득차 있
다고 萬海는 역설한다. 이상과 같은 그의 불교이해가 「般若經」이나 「維
摩經」 같은 大乘佛教에 입각해 있음은 문외한의 눈으로서도 짐작할 수
있을 듯하다. 아뭏든 그는 불교의 새로운 해석을 통해서 진보적인 계몽
주의자가 되었고, 근대적인 자유주의와 합리주의를 불교적 평등의 개념
속에 흡수하였으며, 그러면서도 자유주의에 결부되기 쉬운 이기주의를
배격하였다. 그런데 여기서 우리가 간과해서 안될 사실은 萬海의 이러
한 불교사상이 19세기말·20세기초의 우리 나라 불교가 빠져 있는 침체
와 몽매를 깨뜨리고자 하는 실천적 의욕 속에서 나타났다는 점이다. 처
음부터 그는 불교침체의 원인을 하늘이니 운명이니 하는 초월적 실재에
돌리는 데 반대하고 우리 인간 자신이 바로 일을 꾀하는 자일 뿐더러
일을 성공시키는 자임을 강조하고, 따라서 우리 불교가 올바르게 발전
하기 위해서는 시대에 맞지 않는 舊習들을 과감하게 파괴해야 한다고

주장하였다. 그리하여 그는 염불당을 폐지하라. 산중에 틀어박힌 절간을 대폭 없애고 사람들이 많이 사는 곳에 절을 세워라, 승려들의 결혼 금지를 해제하라는 등의 대담한 개혁론을 주창하는 것이다. 이러한 구체적 개혁론의 근거는 다름아니라 진보주의·평등주의·구세주의로 요약되는 그의 佛敎觀이다. 예컨대 參禪에 대해 그가 개탄한 한 대목을 옮겨 보겠다.

요즘의 참선하는 사람들은 참 이상하다. 옛 사람들은 그 마음을 고요하게 가졌는데, 요즘 사람들은 그 처소를 고요하게 가지고 있다. 옛 사람들은 그 마음을 움직이지 않았는데, 요즘 사람들은 그 몸을 움직이지 않고 있다. 그 처소를 고요하게 가지면 厭世가 되는 것뿐이며 그 몸을 움직이지 않으면 獨善이 안되려야 안 될 수 없다. 불교는 救世의 가르침이요, 衆生濟度의 가르침인 터에 부처님의 제자된 사람으로서 염세와 독선에 빠져 있을 따름이라면 잘못된 것이 아니겠는가.

萬海는 또한 승려라고 해서 절간에 앉아 참선과 독경하는 것만으로 지낼 수는 없고 마땅이 자기 먹을 것을 자기의 노동으로 생산해야 한다고 주장하였다. 이 문제와 관련된 다음의 글에서 우리는 그가 勞動價値說 및 이와 결부된 사회적 불평등의 경제적 기초에 대해 상당한 지식을 가지고 있었음을 확인하게 된다.

수백년 이래 승려들은 대단한 압박을 받아 사람이면서 사람 취급을 못 받았는데, 놀면서 입고 놀면서 먹은 것도 그 一大原因이 되었음을 부정할 길 없다. 놀면서 입고 놀면서 먹는 것은 요즘의 경제학자가 말하는 分利(남이 올린 이익을 나누어 가짐)의 개념에 해당한다. 이런 分利者가 남에게 해롭고 나라에 해롭고 세계에 해로운 존재임은 말할 나위도 없는 일이다. 사람이 옷을 입을 수 있는 이유는 길쌈질하는 데 있고, 먹을 수 있는 이유는 밭가는 데 있다. 따라서 길쌈질하지 않고 옷을 입는다면 반드시 남이 길쌈질한 것을 입는 것일 터이며, 밭갈지 않고 먹는다면 반드시 남이 밭간 것을 먹는 것이 될 것이다. 이같이 길쌈질도 밭갈기도 않고 남의 것으로 입고 먹는 경우, 나도 한 물건의 가치가 내가 입고 먹는 것을 갚기에 족한 것을 갖추어 보답해야 할 것이며, 그런 다음에야 피차에 원한이 없어지고 전체의 경제도 결함이 없게 될 것이다. 만약 한 사람이 있어서 徒衣徒食할 뿐 조금도 갚는 것이 없다고 가정하면, 이는 공연히 농사짓고 길쌈질하는 이의 노력의 몇분지일을 소비하는 것이며, 전체 경제의 입장에서 본대도 한 명의 역량이 감소하는 결과가 된다. 대중 노동력의 增減과 경제의 발달·위축이 반드시 分利人의 多寡에 비례를 이루는 터이니, 分利者는 생산의 도둑인 셈이다. 그러므로 부득불 생산자에 의해 압박을 받을 수 밖에 없고, 그래도 한 마디 변명할 말조차 없을 것은 이론상 당연한 일이다. 내가 상당한 가치를 내어놓지 않은 채 남에게 부양을 받는다면, 이는 내 생존의 권한이 나에게 있지 않고 남에게 있다는 뜻이 되는 것이다.

여기서 우리는 사상가로서의 萬海의 모든 윤곽이 이「朝鮮佛教維新論」속에 완전하게 그려져 있음을 뚜렷이 보게 된다. 이러한 불교 사상가 萬海로부터 전투적인 민족독립지사 萬海까지에 이르는 발전은 단순한 직선적 확대에 의해서 이루어졌다고 할 수 있다. 그리고 이렇게 될 수 있었던 것은 그가 고요한 가운데 독서와 사색을 쌓았기 때문이 아니라 당시 조선불교의 은둔주의와 몽매주의를 타파하려는 열렬한 意志에 따라 불굴의 행동을 펴나갔기 때문이다. 우리는 萬海의 불교해석과 조선불교개혁론 속에서 實學思想이나 開化思想의 새로운 계승을 읽을 수도 있고, 중국과 일본을 통해 접촉한 서구적 近代思想의 영향을 찾을 수도 있을 것이다. (실제로「朝鮮佛教維新論」에서 플라톤·데카르트·베이콘·칸트·루쏘·헤겔 등이 인용 또는 검토되어 있다) 그러나, 무엇보다도 萬海는 元曉와 知訥의 전통을 이어받은 불교 그것에서 자라난

인물이며, 봉건양반의 오랜 착취와 제국주의 外勢의 침략에 의해 산산
조각으로 허물어져 가던 조선왕조 그것이 낳은 인물이라 해야 할 것이
다.

3

　萬海가 식민지 조선의 역사적 현실을 발견하게 되는 계기 역시 공허
한 관념 속에서가 아니라 실천적 투쟁 속에서 주어졌다. 그것이 곧 해
인사 주지였던 친일파 승려 李晦光 일당의 음모를 분쇄하는 운동이었
다. 이 李晦光이란 자는 庚戌國恥를 당하던 1910년 8월 圓宗의 大宗正
자격으로 일본에 건너가 그해 10월 6일 불교확장이라는 미명하에 일본
曹洞宗과 聯合盟約을 체결하고 돌아왔다. 6개 조항으로 되어 있는 이
조약은 한 마디로 우리 불교를 일본 불교에 예속시키는 내용으로서 日
常의 조선 식민지 지배를 종교의 분야에까지 확대한 것에 지나지 않았
다. 萬海는 李晦光 일파의 책동에 분개하여 이듬해(1911년) 1월 15일
朴漢永・陳震應・金鍾來・張錦峰 등과 함께 순천 松廣寺에서 승려대회
를 개최하고 李晦光을 宗門亂賊으로 규탄했다. 여기서 仙岩寺의 金擎雲
장로가 臨濟宗의 임시관장으로 추대되고 萬海는 그 서리를 맡아보게 되
었다. 이들은 동래 梵魚寺에서 거듭 승려대회를 열고 일본 불교와의 연
합획책을 규탄하여, 마침내 李晦光 일파의 친일흉계를 분쇄하고 말았
다. 그후 萬海는 「朝鮮佛敎維新論」(1913)과 「佛敎大典」(1914)을 간행한
다음 영남과 호남 지방의 여러 사찰들을 두루 순례하며 가는 곳마다 대
강연회를 열어 열변을 토했다. 그후 강원도 오세암에서 안거하던 중
1917년 12월 2일 밤 10시경 坐禪을 하다가 바람에 물건이 떨어져 깨어
지는 소리를 듣고 문득 깨달았다고 한다. 이때 그가 무엇을 깨달았는지
그리고 도대체 어떤 깨달음이라고 하는 것이 그처럼 돌연히 찾아올 수
있는 것인지 어쩐지 하는 것은 필자와 같은 俗人으로서 감히 추측할 길
조차 없으나, 다만 분명히 말할 수 있는 것은 이 무렵 李晦光 일파의

친일음모와 투쟁하는 과정 속에서 비로소 그가 우리 이 땅을 옭아 매고
있는 일본 제국주의의 실체를 똑똑히 보게 되었다는 점이다. 그것은 바
로 조선 불교의 현실을 민족적 현실의 필연적인 일부로서 발견하고, 제
국주의 일본과 식민지 조선 사이의 불평등이 불교적 평등의 실현에 근
본적인 장애임을 인식한 것이었다. 어쨌든 전투적 抗日鬪士로서의 萬海
가 확립되는 것은 1917년 이후라고 생각된다. 不惑의 나이가 가까와진
이 무렵에 이르러 마침내 그는 지금 우리가 흠모하여 뒤따르고자 하는
승려와 독립투사와 시인으로서의, 그리고 사상가와 실천가로서의 일체
화된 자기를 완성했다.

1919년의 거족적인 3.1독립운동에 있어 萬海가 적극적 주동적으로
참여했었다는 것은 이미 너무나 잘 알려진 사실이다. 독립선언의 준비
과정에서 그는 崔麟과 더불어 가장 핵심적인 역할을 맡았고, 六堂이 집
필한 선언서에 공약삼장을 붙였으며, 거사 당일에도 이른바 민족대표들
이 모인 자리에서 『오늘 우리가 모인 것은 조선의 독립을 선언하기 위
함이니, 진실로 기쁘고 영광스럽다. 우리는 민족대표로서 이와 같은 선
언을 하게 되어 그 책임이 중하므로 앞으로 공동협심하여 독립의 완성
에 노력하지 않으면 안된다』고 연설을 하였고, 재판을 받는 동안에도
가장 의연한 태도를 지켜 ① 변호사를 대지 말고 ② 私食을 취하지 말
며 ③ 保釋을 요구하지 말자는 주의로 만 3년 동안의 옥고를 치렀다.
그의 정연한 논리와 고결한 식견은 담당했던 일본인 검사로 하여금 당
신의 이론은 정당하나 本國政府의 방침이 변치 않으므로 어쩔 수 없다』
고 실토하게 하였다는 일화가 전해지고 있다. 이러한 그의 독립사상이
집약절으로 표현된 것은 「朝鮮獨立理由書」혹은 「朝鮮獨立의 書」로 알
려진 논문이다. 이 글은 1910년 7월 10일 일본인 검사의 심문에 대한
답변으로 작성된 것인 바, 萬海는 이 글의 全文을 작은 글씨로 휴지에
적은 다음 여러 겹으로 접어서 종이노끈을 만들어 형무소로부터 차출하
는 의복 갈피에 삽입, 간수의 눈을 피해 세상으로 내보냈다고 한다.

이「朝鮮獨立理由書」는「朝鮮佛教維新論」에서 확립된 萬海思想이 민

족적 현실의 인식을 통해 더욱 심화된 모습을 기록하고 있다. 萬海는
우선 인류역사가 몽매와 쟁탈을 버리고 문명과 평화를 향해 나아간다고
설명하고, 이러한 進步史觀에 입각하여 제국주의 및 그 수단으로서의
군국주의가 판치는 세계사의 현단계를 분석한다. 그리고 그는 『군국주
의, 즉 침략주의는 인류의 행복을 희생시키는 가장 흉악한 마술』이라고
규정하고 이러한 침략주의자들의 위장된 평화선전을 다음과 같이 폭로
하였다.

　이른바 강대국, 즉 침략국은 군함과 총포만 많으면 스스로의 야심
과 욕망을 충족시키기 위하여 도의를 무시하고 정의를 짓밟는 쟁탈을
자행한다. 그러면서도 그 이유를 설명할 때는 세계 또는 어떤 지역의
평화를 위한다거나 쟁탈의 목적물 즉 침략을 받는 자의 행복을 위한
다거나 하는 기만적인 헛소리로써 정의의 天使國을 자처한다. 예를
들면 일본이 폭력으로 조선을 합병하고 2천만 민중을 노예로 취급하
면서도, 겉으로는 조선을 병합함이 동양평화를 위함이요 조선민족의
안녕과 행복을 위한다고 하는 것이 그것이다.

萬海는 인류문명이 진보를 향해 나아가며 결코 뒷걸음치지 않는다는
확고한 신념을 바탕으로 『어찌 이같은 군국주의가 무궁한 생명을 유지
할 수 있겠는가. 이론보다 사실이 그렇다』고 말한다. 제국주의 및 그
수단으로서의 야만적인 군국주의가 인류역사의 낡은 遺物로 되어 가는
증거로 그는 1차대전에서 독일이 패망한 사실을 들고 있다. 막강한 군
사력을 휘두르던 독일의 카이젤이 하루아침에 멸망하게 되었음은 무슨
까닭이냐. 그것은 연합국의 무력이 강했기 때문이 아니다. 연합국측도
독일의 군국주의를 타파한다고 큰소리쳤으나 그 수단과 방법은 역시 군
국주의의 유물인 군함과 총포 등의 살인도구였으니 연합국 또한 準軍國
主義인 셈이다. 그러면 독일의 카이젤이 패망한 것은 무슨 까닭인가.
그것은 전쟁의 쓰라림을 느끼고 군국주의의 잘못을 통감한 독일 인민들

이 전쟁을 스스로 파기하고 군국주의의 칼을 분질러 그 자살을 도모케
함으로써 共和革命의 성공을 얻고 평화적인 새 운명을 개척한 것이다.
그러므로 이 전쟁의 결과는 카이젤의 패배가 아니라 군국주의의 패배요
연합국의 승리가 아니라 독일 인민의 승리이다. 萬海는 당시의 세계 대
세를 이렇게 분석한 다음 『현재로부터 미래의 대세는 침략주의의 멸망,
自存的 평화주의의 승리』가 되지 않을 수 없을 것이라고 말한다. 따라
서 萬海가 보기에 조선의 독립은 제국주의와 침략주의가 멸망해 가는
세계사의 대세에 비추어 필연적인 것이다. 한편, 나라의 독립은 모든
물질문명이 완전히 구비된 뒤라야 되는 것이 아니라 독립할 만한 自存
의 기운과 정신적 준비만 있으면 충분한 것이며, 또한 다른 누가 독립
을 시켜주는 것이 아니라 스스로 독립국가라고 선언함으로써 족한 것이
다. 『일본인은 말끝마다 조선에는 물질문명이 부족하다고 하지만, 조선
인을 어리석게 하고 야비케 하려는 虐政과 劣等敎育을 폐지하지 않으면
문명의 실현을 보기 어려울 것이다』이렇게 萬海는 日帝가 한편으로는
조선 사람이 독립국가를 이룰 만한 실력과 준비가 없다고 비웃으면서,
다른 한편 그러한 실력과 준비를 갖추지 못하도록 온갖 수탈과 탄압을
자행하고 있다고 지적하여 일제 침략정책의 본질을 갈파하였다. 당시
우리 나라의 역사적 현실을 인식함에 있어서 萬海의 가장 탁월했던 점
은 근본적 모순이 총독부의 가혹한 武斷政治에 있는 것이 아니라 일제
의 식민주의 자체에 있음을 옳게 보았던 데에 있다. 이 점을 제대로 인
식하지 못했던 까닭에 소위 독립지사들 중의 상당수는 일본제국주의의
아량에 의지하여 <內政獨立>이니 <參政權>이니 <自治>니 하는 것
을 얻어 보려고 했던 것이고, 3.1 독립선언에 참가했던 소위 민족대표
들 중에서도 <독립선언> 대신에 <독립청원>으로 하자는 주장이 나
왔던 것이다. 萬海는 이런 종류의 모든 투항주의에 반대하여 일체의 식
민지 체제를 철폐하는 것만이 유일한 해결책이라고 다음과 같이 주장하
였다.

조선인은 이같이 학정 아래 노예가 되고 소와 말이 되면서도 10년
동안 조그마한 반발도 일으키지 않고 그저 순종할 뿐이었다. 이는 주
위의 압력으로 반항이 불가능했기 때문이기도 하겠으나, 그보다는 총
독정치를 중요시하여 반항을 일으키려는 생각이 없었기 때문이었다.
왜냐하면 총독정치 이상으로 합병이란 근본문제가 있었던 까닭이다.
다시 말하면 언제라도 합방을 깨뜨리고 獨立自存을 꾀하려는 것이 2
천만 민족의 머리에 박힌 불멸의 정신이었다. 그러므로 총독정치가
아무리 극악해도 여기에 보복을 가할 이유가 없고 아무리 완전한 정
치를 한다 해도 감사의 뜻을 나타낼 까닭이 없어, 결국 총독정치는
지엽적 문제로 취급했던 까닭이다.

萬海는 일본 제국주의에 대한 이러한 인식을 토대로 하여 『조선의 독
립은 산위에서 굴러내리는 둥근 돌과 같이 목적지에 이르지 않으면 그
기세가 멎지 않을 것』이라는 확고한 낙관적 견해를 표명하였고, 3.1독
립운동을 거치는 동안 그러한 낙관주의의 궁극적 근거를 민중의 무한한
힘에서 찾게 되었던 것이다.

4

1922년 3월 감옥에서 나온 萬海는 그해 6월경 학생회 주최로 기독교
청년회관에서 <鐵窓哲學>이라는 연제로, 10월경에는 동경 학생회 주최
로 천도교회관에서 <六波羅蜜>이라는 연제로 강연을 했으며, 이듬해
4월에는 民立大學 설립운동을 지원하는 <自助>라는 강연으로 청중들
에게 감동을 주었다. 1924년에는 佛敎靑年會 총재에 취임하였고, 한편
으로 장편소설에 손대어 「죽음」이란 작품을 탈고 하였다. 그러다가 그
는 1926년 시집 「님의 沈默」을 간행하여 문단에 일대 충격을 주게 되었
다. 후일에도 萬海는 「黑風」(1935, 朝鮮日報), 「後悔」(1936, 朝鮮中央
日報), 「薄命」(1938, 朝鮮日報) 등의 장편소설들을 발표했고 상당수의

漢詩와 時調들을 남겼으나, 그의 문학사적 위치는「님의 沈默」단 한권
으로 결정적인 중요성을 갖게 되었다. 이 시집을 중심으로 萬海의 문학
사적 위치를 검토해 보기로 하자.

萬海는 우리 근대사에 있어서 거물인 그만큼 또한 우리 문학사에 있
어서 거물이다. 지금까지 출판된 文學史들은 대체로 그를 소홀하게 취
급했거나 기껏해야 예외적인 중요성만을 인정하는 데 그치기 일쑤였다.
이것은 당시의 그의 文壇的 위치와 정확하게 대응하는 현상이기도 하
다. 그러나 萬海가 소위 문단이라고 하는 것의 권외에 있었던 사실, 낭
만주의니 상징주의니 하는 수입된 문예사조를 업고 다니지 않았던 사
실, 대단치도 않은 흔한 同人誌의 구성원이 되지 않았던 사실 때문에
그의 문학사적 위치가 낮게 평가되어서 안된다는 것은 두말할 필요도
없는 일이다. 도리어 그는 당시의 문단이 빠져있던 反 역사성과 非사회
성——식민지 시절에 식민지적 현상의 일부로 형성되어 아직도 완강하
게 남아 있는 성질——에서 동떨어짐으로 말미암아 문단적 테두리 안에
서는 결코 가능하지 못했던 문학적 깊이와 폭을 달성하고 있는 것이다.

萬海가 우리 나라 최초의 근대시인이요 3.1운동 세대가 낳은 최대의
문학자임은 이미 지적된 바 있다. (白樂晴,「市民文學論」) 지금까지 문
학사가들은 일반적으로 六堂의「海에게서 少年에게」(1908)를 과거의 唱
歌調의 詩에 결별을 이룩한 최초의 문학적 시도로 보는 데 의견이 일치
했고, 宋耀翰의「불놀이」(1919)를『독자들이 여기서 비로소 近代詩다운
詩를 대하게 되었다』고 말한 金東仁의 과대망상증적 주장대로 받아들여
왔다. 이 두 작품을 新詩와 自由詩의 최초의 획기적 업적으로 평가하는
것은 아직도 여전히 우리 나라의 문학사적 관례로 되어 있는 것 같다.
그러나, 식민지적인 문학의식에 입각하여 문학다운 문학이 문단에서만
이루어질 수 있고 신문의 문예란과 몇 개 안되는 잡지와 끼리끼리 돌려
읽는 동인지들, 요컨대 식민지 통치기구가 소위 文化政治의 미명하에
허용해 준 그 한줌 안되는 소위 문단이란 것에 문학을 가두고 그 문단
을 민족적 현실로부터 떼어 놓을 때에만 <최초의 자유시>라느니 <최

초의 근대소설>이라느니 하는 호언장담이 가능할 것이다. 과연 그렇게 한다면 六堂이나 春園 이전에 문단이 없었고 따라서 문학이 없었다고 말할 수조차 있을 것이다. 『조선인에게는 詩도 없고 小說도 없고 劇도 없고, 즉 文藝라 할 만한 文藝가 없고, 즉 조선인에게는 정신적 생활이 없었다』는 春園의 발언은 바로 그러한 문학관을 솔직하게 대변한 것이라 할 수도 있다. 두말할 것 없이 이것은 참된 한국적 전통과 참된 민족적 생명력과 참된 우리 문학을 외면하고 부인하는 발언이요, 또 그렇게 되기를 목표로 삼는 식민주의자들에게 내면적으로 동조하는 발언이 아닐 수 없다. 이런 허무맹랑한 소리가 염치없이 횡행하고 그것이 정교한 형태로 거듭 되풀이되는 이 문단이라고 하는 데에 끼지 못한 것이 萬海를 과소평가하는 연유가 되었다면 도리어 민족시인으로서의 萬海의 영광이 아니면 안된다. 실제 작품발표에 있어서도 萬海는「創造」(1919)의 동인들보다 앞섰다고 한다. 그는 자신이 발행하던 잡지「惟心」(1918. 9, 통권 3호 발간)에「님의 沈默」의 것들과 유사한 수준의 작품들을 발표했던 것이다. 그러나 물론 萬海가 한국 최초의 근대시인이라는 사실은 이런 단순한 연대적 선후관계에 이유가 있는 것이 아니라, 나라의 주권을 빼앗기고 남의 나라 식민지로 떨어진 민족적 현실을 진실로 뼈아프게 체험하고 그 아픔을 처음으로 근대적인 시형태 속에 구체화했다는 데 이유가 있는 것이다.

우리가 萬海에게서 얻을 수 있는 교훈은 허다하게 많지만, 그중에는 그가 이처럼 소위 문단적 시인이 아니었다는 사실도 포함되어야 할 것이다. 오늘날 우리 문단과 문학에서 찾아볼 수 있는 여러 病理的 현상들이 이미 신문학 초창기에 형성되었다고 한다면, 그것은 바로 문단형성과정의 식민지적 성격에서 유래하는 것이다. 잘 알려진 것처럼 한국의 문단은 六堂과 春園의 이른바 二人時代를 거쳐「創造」「廢墟」「白潮」등의 동인지가 나오고 상징주의·낭만주의·자연주의 등속의 서구적 문예사조가 들어옴으로써 이루어졌다. 초기에는 그래도 『조선인에게는 정신적 생활이 없었다』고 생각하는 따위의 반민족적 獨善이 섞여 있었음에도 불구하고 그 나름의 일정한 문화계몽적 요소를 지니고 있었으나, 1920년대 이후의 소위 문화정치를 거치는 동안 그것마저 희미해지고 말았다. 물론 양심을 가지고 괴로와 한 인물들이 상당수 있었지만, 문단 전체는 나라의 운명과 민족의 생존을 까맣게 잊어버린 식민지 소시민들의 모임으로 전락해 버렸다고 해야 할 것이다. 이러한 상황에서 태어난 萬海文學은 문단적 제한이 바로 식민주의적 제한임을 실증해 주는 하나의 거대한 예라고 볼 수 있을 것이다.

「님의 沈默」은 그러한 문단의 바깥에 서서 민족의 현실과 꿈을 절실하게 노래한 시집으로서 우리 문학사상 비길데 없이 순화된 정서적 통일 속으로 우리를 몰아 넣으며 시집에 실린 88편의 어느 하나 우리를 그냥 지나치게 하지 않는다. 그러나, 우리는 萬海가 詩에만 몰두했던 시인이 아니었음을 새삼 상기하고 넘어가는 것이 좋을 것이다. 물론 순전히 詩的인 입장과 안목에서 보더라도 그의 작품이 탁월한 경지에 이르고 있었음은 이미 여러 면에서 분석된 바 있지만, 어쨌든 萬海가 이론가와 실천가, 이른바 승려와 독립지사와 시인을 겸한 인물이었다는 사실은 그의 시를 이해하는 데 있어서도 지극히 중요한 사항이다. 근대 서구적 분석도구에 의해서만 그의 시를 해부하는 데 몰두한다면 萬海는 그저 메타퍼가 풍부한 시인, 종교적인 명상시인, 혹은 깊이있는 형이상학적 시인으로 끝날 것이다. 그러나 그는 인간이 각개의 전문분야로 조각조각 나누어진 서구적 자본주의 사회의 시인이 아니라 정치와 학문과 도덕과 문학의 합일을 추구한 전통에서 자라난 시인인 것이다. 시집「님의 沈默」은 다른 모든 측면들과 함께 「朝鮮佛教維新論」 및 「朝鮮獨立理由書」에 이어지는 측면에서도 고찰되지 않으면 안된다.

萬海의 시작품들은 단 하나의 초점을 중심으로 회전한다. 모든 생각과 연상과 비유와 이미지들은 그초점에서 출발하여 그 초점으로 되돌아온다. 그것이 바로 <님>이다. 萬海의 <님>을 마치 스무고개 풀듯이 무엇을 가리킨다고 꼬집어 말할 수 없다는 것은 이미 여러 사람들이 지

적한 바 있지만, 그러면 이<님>은 어떤 존재인가. 시인이 님을 발견
하게 되는 계기는 님과의 이별이다.

　　이별은 美의 創造입니다.
　　이별의 美는 아침의 바탕(質) 없는 黃金과 밤의 올(糸) 없는 검은
　　비단과 죽음 없는 영원의 生命과 시들지 않는 하늘의 푸른 꽃에도
　　없읍니다.
　　님이여, 이별이 아니면 나는 눈물에서 죽었다가 웃음에서 다시 살
　　아날 수가 없읍니다. 오오! 이별이여.
　　美는 이별의 創造입니다.　　　　　（「이별은 美의 創造」 전문）

　이별은 님의 존재를 깨닫게 하는 계기요 나는 님과의 이별을 통해서
비로소 님을 발견한다. 님은 이별을 자기존재의 구성요소로서 가지며,
그렇기 때문에 이별이 없는 것은 님이 아니기도 하다. (「最初의 님」 참
조) 물론 이것은 하나의 역설이라 할 수 있다. 그러나 이 역설이야말로
萬海의 문학을 성립시키는 근본적 구조이고 또한 그 활력의 원천이 된
다. 부정을 통해 긍정에 이르고 그것을 다시 부정함으로써 더 큰 긍정
에의 길을 준비하는 불교적 변증법은 단 하나의 주제를 맴도는 그의 시
의 단조로움이 아닌 무한한 力動感을 넣어 주는 것이다.

　　당신의 소리는 「沈默」인가요.
　　당신이 노래를 부르지 아니하는 때에 당신의 노래가락은 역력히 들
　　립니다 그려.
　　당신의 소리는 침묵이어요.
　　　　　　　　　　　　　　　（「反比例」 첫 聯）

　이렇게 萬海는 자기 시대를 님이 사라진 시대로, 자기 현실을 님이
침묵하는 현실로 인식했다. 그러나 그에게 있어서<님>의 침묵은 그

자체가 님의 <소리>이며 님의 不在는 님의 實在에 대한 직접적인 증거로 된다. 눈에 보이는 것만이 존재요 목전에 벌어지는 현상이 곧 역사인 것으로 여기는 자들에게는 님의 침묵이 바로 님의 부재를 뜻하며 따라서 그들에게는 현상에 순응하는 것만이 유일하게 사는 길이다. 그러나, 萬海는 눈에 보이는 현상에 집착하는 것이 거짓과 헛것에 얽매여 그 노예가 되는 길임을 정확하게 꿰뚫어 알았다.

나는 너의 침묵을 잘 안다.
너는 철모르는 아이들에게 종작없는 찬미를 받으면서 시쁜 웃음을 참고 고요히 있는 줄을 나는 잘 안다.
　　　　　　　　　　　　　　　　　　　　(「金剛山」 제3聯)

연애가 자유라면 님도 자유일 것이다. 그러나 너희는 이름좋은 자유에 알뜰한 구속을 받지 않느냐. 너에게도 님이 있느냐. 있다면 님이 아니라 너의 그림자니라.
　　　　　　　　　　　　　　　　　　　　(序文「군말」 중에서)

여기서 우리는 당시의 문단과 문학에 대한 萬海의 더없이 신랄한 비판을 읽을 수 있다. 민족이 자유를 잃은 식민지에 있어서 참으로 자유로운 개인은 있을 수 없으며, 나라가 남의 지배를 받는 시대에 있어서 눈에 보이는 어느 것 하나 한스럽지 않을 수 없다. 자연의 예찬이니 연애의 자유니 예술지상주의니 하고 떠드는 것은 그러므로 철모르는 아이들의 종작없는 짓이요 이름좋은 자유에 기만되는 것이며 자기 그림자에 도취하는 것이다. 그것은 현상에 순응하는 길일 뿐더러 현상의 유지에 조력하는 길이기도 하다. 참된 문학은 언제나 지금 있음의 허구성을 깨뜨리고 장차 있어야 할 참된 존재에로 우리를 부단히 이끌어 간다. 그러나 萬海의 시가 진실로 위대한 까닭은 그것이 단지 님의 침묵을 깨달은 데에만 그치지 않고 그 님이 돌아올 것을 확실히 믿고 굳게 기다릴

줄 아는 지혜와 용기를 보여 준 데에 있다. 이런 점에서 萬海의 시는 무엇보다도 다할 줄 모르는 벅찬 희망의 노래인 것이다.

그러나 이별을 쓸데없는 눈물의 源泉으로 만들고 마는 것은 스스로 사랑을 깨치는 것인 줄 아는 까닭에 걷잡을 수 없는 슬픔의 힘을 옮겨서 새 희망의 정수박이에 들어부었읍니다.
우리는 만날 때에 떠날 것을 염려하는 것과 같이 떠날 때에 다시 만날 것을 믿습니다.
아아, 님은 갔지마는 나는 님을 보내지 아니하였읍니다.
제 곡조를 못 이기는 사랑의 노래는 님의 沈默을 휩싸고 돕니다.
　　　　　　　　　　　　　　　　　　　（「님의 沈默」 후반부）

그러므로 만나지 않는 것도 님이 아니요, 이별이 없는 것도 님이 아닙니다.
님은 만날 때에 웃음을 주고 떠날 때에 눈물을 줍니다.
만날 때의 웃음보다 떠날 때의 눈물이 좋고, 떠날 때의 눈물보다 다시 만나는 웃음이 좋습니다.
아아, 님이여！ 우리의 다시 만나는 웃음은 어느 때에 있읍니까.
　　　　　　　　　　　　　　　　　　　（「最初의 님」 끝 聯）

그러므로 이별은 萬海에게 있어 사랑의 종말이 아니라 더 크고 더 확실한 사랑의 시초를 뜻하게 된다. 그래서 님이 멀어지면 멀어질수록 님에 대한 사랑은 적어지는 것이 아니라 도리어 더욱 많아진다. (「사랑의 測量」 참조) 나는 님에 비하여 티끌처럼 보잘 것 없는 존재이지만, 님도 그러한 내가 있음으로 해서 비로소 있는 존재이다. 님은 절대의 존재이나 그러면서도 나를 통해서 존재한다. 나는 님에게 포함되며 님은 나를 통해서 구체화된다. 님은 내가 잊고자 해서 잊혀지는 것이 아니라 잊으려 할 수록 더욱 잊혀지지 않는 절대적 그리움의 대상이며,

또 내가 님을 기다리는 것은 억지로 기다리고자 해서 기다리는 것이 아니라 저절로 기다려지는 것이다. 왜냐하면 님은 내 존재의 유일한 뜻이요. 내 존재의 가능성을 보장해 주는 절대적 근거이며 또한 그 최고의 경지에 있어서는 바로 나 자신이기도 하기 때문이다.

남들은 님을 생각한다지만
나는 님을 잊고저 하여요.
잊고저 할 수록 생각키기로
행여 잊을까 하고 보았읍니다.

(「나는 잊고저」첫聯)

내가 당신을 기다리고 있는 것은 기다리고자 하는 것이 아니라 기다려지는 것입니다.
말하자면 당신을 기다리는 것은 貞操보다도 사랑입니다.

(「自由貞操」첫聯)

한 민족이 다른 민족의 간섭을 받지 않으려 하는 것은 인류가 공통으로 가진 본성으로서 이같은 본성은 남이 꺾을 수 없는 것이며 또한 스스로 자기 민족의 자존성을 억제하려 하여도 되지 않는 것이다.

(「朝鮮獨立理由書」에서)

그러므로 님은 자기에의 목마른 기다림을 속성으로 가진 존재이며, 마찬가지로 님을 그리워 하고 기다리는 것은 내 존재의 지속을 가능하게 하는 징검다리와 같다. 님을 잊는 것은 곧 나를 잊는 것이요. 님을 거부하는 것은 곧 나의 존재를 거부하는 것으로서, 그것은 죽음으로 가는 길이다. 나는 님의 그림자요, 님의 일부분이며 님은 내 존재의 근원이기 때문에, 님에게 속박되는 것은 <이름좋은 자유>의 희생이 아니라 더 근원적인 자기의 회복이요 더욱 진정한 자유의 실현을 의미한다.

그러므로 萬海에게 있어서 이별은 님으로부터의 타율적인 격리가 아니라 참된 님을 찾으려는 투쟁의 시초를 뜻하며, 따라서 님을 그리워 하고 기다리는 과정은 님을 전취하고 님을 실현시키려는 싸움의 형태를 취하게 된다. 이러한 과정 속에서 큰 슬픔은 큰 기쁨으로 轉化되며 거대한 절망은 거대한 희망으로 轉化되는 것이다. 님은 이별을 통해서 자기를 찾게 하고 不在를 통해서 자기 존재를 증명하며 침묵을 통해서 자기의 소리를 들려 주고 거짓과 헛것의 모습이 곧 진실의 即物的 증거임을 깨닫게 한다. 이야말로 色即是空의 경지라 하겠다. 그리하여 죽음은 님이 사라지고 없는 시대에 님의 到來를 예비하는 최후의 확실한 담보가 되는 것이다.

인간생활의 목적은 참된 자유에 있는 것으로서 자유가 없는 생활에 무슨 취미가 있겠으며 무슨 즐거움이 있겠는가. 자유를 얻기 위해서는 어떤 대가도 아까와 할 것이 없으니 곧 생명을 바쳐도 좋은 것이다.　　　　　　　　　　　　（「朝鮮獨立理由書」에서）

당신은 나의 죽음 속으로 오셔요. 죽음은 당신을 위하여 준비가 언제든지 되어 있읍니다.
만일 당신을 쫓아오는 사람이 있으면 당신은 나의 죽음의 뒤에 서십시오.
죽음은 허무와 만능의 하나입니다. 죽음의 사랑은 무한인 동시에 無窮입니다.
죽음의 앞에는 군함과 砲臺가 티끌이 됩니다.
죽음의 앞에는 강자와 약자가 벗이 됩니다.
그러면 쫓아오는 사람이 당신을 잡을 수는 없읍니다.
오셔요. 당신은 오실 때가 되었읍니다. 어서오셔요.
　　　　　　　　　　　　（「오셔요」끝 聯）

여기서 우리는 마침내 萬海의 기다림이 죽음과 똑같은 무게로써 애끓는 호소가 되고 숨막히는 절규가 되고 있음을 보고 전율한다. 이 시의 경지에 이르러 우리는 문학과 종교가 하나로 되고, 사상과 행동이 하나로 되고, 보살과 중생이 하나로 되고, 강자와 약자가 벗이 되고, 허무와 만능이 하나로 되며, 빼앗은 자와 빼앗기는 자의 자리가 뒤바뀌고, 쫓아오는 자와 쫓기는 자의 관계가 해소되며, 군함과 총포가 한낱 티끌로 화하는 예언적 순간을 체험하게 되는 것이다. 이러한 문학적 표현과 종교적 신앙 가운데에서 萬海는 제국주의와 식민주의 및 그 수단으로서의 군국주의가 하나의 역사적 유물임을 깊이 통찰하고 누구보다 열렬하고 전투적인 평화의 시인이 되었다. 그렇게 함으로써 그는 암담한 식민지적 현실에 있어서 그 현실이 허용하는 한계를 뛰어넘어 그 현실의 질곡을 갈파하고 앞으로 도래할 참된 현실의 질서를 노래하는 최초의 시인이 되었으며, 우리 문학사상 가장 빛나는 예술적 形象의 창조자가 되었다.

5

50대 이후의 萬海는 新幹會의 발기(1927년)에 참가하여 그 京城支會長이 되기도 하고, 光州학생의거(1929년) 때에는 민중대회를 열기도 하였으며, 월간 「佛敎」誌 (1931년)를 인수·간행하면서 불교 관계의 수많은 논설들을 정력적으로 집필하였고, 젊은 불교인들의 秘密結社인 <卍黨>의 실질적인 지도자로서 불교청년운동 및 불교대중화 운동을 영도하였다. 이 무렵 萬海의 서릿발 같은 절개와 칼날 같은 의기를 말해 주는 여러 가지 逸話들이 전해져 온다. 그러나 역사의 핵심적인 추진력은 3.1운동 세대인 萬海의 손에서 떠나 3.1운동에 의해 계발된 새로운 세대에게로 넘어갔다고 보아야 하겠다. 1920년대 이후 노동운동의 성장과 농민의식의 각성이 민족독립의 大命題와 결부되어 광범하고 급격하게 진행되었던 사정은 이를 잘 증명해 주는 바이다. 이 점 「님의 沈默」은

역시 「朝鮮佛敎維新論」이나 「朝鮮獨立理由書」의 구체적 현실대결이 비
견이나 예언의 형태로서밖에 자기를 드러낼 수 없는 시대의 특징적인
산물이라 해야 할 것이다. 비견이나 예언을 사회적 실천과 통일시키기
에는 이미 그를 둘러싼 사회적 여건이나 그의 생리적 연령이 허락지 않
았을 것이며, 또한 그것은 한 단순한 생명체로서의 개인에게 주어진 역
사적 역할의 한계를 넘어서는 것인지도 모른다. 어쨌든 일제 군국주의
가 萬海의 예언대로 滿洲를 집어삼키고 중국으로 기어들고 태평양 전쟁
을 일으키며, 그러는 가운데 3.1독립선언의 동지였던 崔麟이 변절하고
六堂과 春園이 변절하고 그밖에 많은 이름있는 인사들이 하나둘씩 변절
해 가던 그 시기에 그는 참으로 잘 참고 잘 견디어 냈다. 천년도 더 계
속될 것처럼 억세고 악독하던 그 첩첩한 어두움이 걷히기 1년 남짓 앞
두고 마침내 그는 지병인 중풍으로 숨을 거두고 말았으니, 님이 가신
날은 1944년 6월 29일이다. 뒷날 우리 님을 두고 爲堂 鄭寅普 선생이
다음과 같은 시조를 읊었는 바, 누가 있어 감히 님의 침묵을 오늘 이
순간엔들 향기 없다 하며 빛 잃었다 하라.

風蘭花 매운 향기
님에게야 견줄손가.
이 날에 님 계시면
별도 아니 더 빛날까.
佛土가 이 외 없으니
魂하 돌아오소서.

對談・한국의 佛教文化

徐　　景　　洙
金　　哲　　埈

徐： 여기서는 한국역사와 佛教의 관계를 전반적으로 다루려는 것이
아니라 다만 시대마다 그 특징적인 인물이나 사상, 문화에 대하여 이야
기를 진행할까 한다. 우선 三國時代에 있어서 外來思想과 文化가 어떻
게 傳來 受容되었는가 하는 점과 다음엔 외래사상인 불교가 어떻게 전
래되어 우리 固有의 문화에 영향을 끼쳤는가 하는 문제부터 시작했으면
한다.

金： 고구려의 廣開土大王碑를 보면 巨石文化인 선돌로써 碑文은 中
國體가 아닌 韓國體로 쓰여져 있다. 이것은 곧 중국문화를 받아들여 韓
國의 특질에 알맞게 부합시키고 있음을 말해준다. 또한 新羅의 土器文
化를 보아도 고구려의 鐵器文化와 동일한 성격을 띠고 있는데 이러한
사실은 한국의 민족성이나 文化土壤이 무조건 중국문화를 흡수한 것이
아니라 고유의 자기 문화를 바탕으로 하여 중국의 문화를 받아들여 새
로운 문화로 변형시켰음을 말해주는 것이다. 다시 말하면 자기 체질이
직접 외래의 문화와 영합될 때 個性있는 문화가 창조된 것이다.

또한 고유의 토양이 좋건 나쁘건 간에 후세에 까지 지속되어 전통으
로 남게 되면 높은 수준의 문화를 만들 수 있는데 우리의 경우 자기사
회를 운영발전 시키고자했던 모습은 이미 新石器時代부터 있었으며 여
기서도 벌써 외래문화를 융합하려는 자세를 보이고 있다. 이것은 뒤에

275

신라의 圓光法師가 제창한 世俗五戒에서도 나타나고 있다. 世俗五戒를
일부에서는 유교의 영향을 받은 것이라고도 하지만 중국의 五倫과는 전
혀 그 성격자체를 달리하고 있다. 가령 世俗五戒가 첫머리에 事君以忠
을 드는데 대하여 五倫에서는 父子有親을 말한다든가 우리의 朋友有信
과 중국의 夫婦有別 등의 대응관계는 곧 불교와 유교 한국과 중국의 차
이점을 드러내는 것으로 世俗五戒는 新羅의 불교만이 갖는 독특한 성격
이라고 볼 수 있다. 또한 五戒와 五倫과의 비교에서 서로 순서와 의취
가 다름은 곧 그 내용이 다르며 社會의 이데올로기가 다름을 뜻하는 것
이라고 볼 수 있다.

徐: 불교의 전래시기에 있어서도 흔히 고구려 소수림왕 2년(372)을
최초로 보고 있으나 이것은 국가 정책상 公認된 해일 뿐이지, 실제 민
간에 유포된것은 이보다 훨씬 앞섰다고 보아야 옳을 것이다. 즉 중앙아
시아를 통하여 불교가 중국에 전래된 연대가 B.C. 1세기 경이므로 당시
고구려와 중국 대륙의 지리적인 상호관계나 정치 군사적 입장에서 미루
어 볼때 4세기 말보다 일찍 들어왔으리라는 것은 쉽게 추측할 수 있는
일이다. 또한 정책상 책정한 불교공인의 소수림왕 2년보다 앞선 8년
전에 이미 중국의 道林과 고구려의 道人 사이에 서신왕래가 있었음은
이를 입증해주는 좋은 예가 아닐까 한다. 이러한 전래 시기문제는 新羅
에 있어서도 최초의 傳法者라 보는 阿道 이전에 이미 민간층에 불교가
들어와 있었다는 점과 함께 불교가 전래된 初期 古代國家의 문화바탕을
다시 고찰 해야할 필요가 있다고 생각한다.

다음 불교가 三國에 들어왔을 때 불교의 三法印이나 四聖諦, 緣起論,
解脫論 같은 教理는 古代社會에서 보편타당성과 평등사상을 상당히 고
취시켰다고 본다. 특히 개인의 해탈을 주장하는 교리는 個體意識을 고
조하고 동시에 佛法앞에서는 누구나 평등하다는 사상을 심어주었다고
본다. 다만 한국에 전래된 불교가 인도와는 달리 중국에서 많이 변화되
어 토착과정을 거친 불교였다는 사실이 주목되는 점이다. 佛法即國法,

다시 말하면 出世間的佛法이 世間的王法과 同一視되는 토착화상태는 이러한 점의 두드러진 현상이 아닐까. 따라서 古代統一國家形成期에 전래된 불교는 지배층과 피지배층에게 각각 다른 형태로 전달되면서 양면작용을 했다고 생각한다. 즉 지배층을 위하여는 王卽佛의 護國佛敎的 이미지를 형성하여 주었고 한편 자기 신화를 잃어버린 서민층엔 새로운 신화를 제시해 주었다고 본다. 여하간 불교가 지닌 보편성은 통일국가의 형성과정에서 고도로 지향된 새로운 이데올로기로 나타났다고 본다.

金: 고구려나 백제도 그러하였지만 신라의 경우 통일되기까지 지배층과 민중은 함께 참여하는 連結性에 있어서 서로 유리된 현상이 비교적 적었다. 이것은 사회적 모순이 적은 과거 부족국가시대의 전통이 그대로 지속되고 있음을 의미하는데 일반적으로 윤리의식이 강하고, 모랄을 지켜 나갈때 階層사이의 격차도 좁혀진다. 따라서 민중은 죄의식이나 부담감 없이 지배층과 함께 불교를 믿었고 심지어는 노예까지도 佛敎儀式參與가 허용되고 있었다. 이것은 당시 사회의 구성요소에도 起因하겠지만 그보다는 불교자체가 갖는 보편적 성격에 더 큰 원인이 있다고 본다. 불교는 전래후 각 지방에 傳敎될때 그 지방의 전통적 土着神을 배제하지 않고 오히려 그대로 인정하면서 불교라는 거대한 스케일속에 영합시켜 버렸다. 이러한 움직임이 점차로 구체화되면서 한국 특유의 불교를 형성하기에 이르렀다고 생각한다.

徐: 불교가 우리나라에 전래될 때 인도의 불교가 원형 그대로 직접 건너온 것이 아니라 3,4세기 동안 중앙 아시아에서 그 지방의 고유신앙과 융합되어 중앙아시아 特有의 불교를 형성한 후 중국에 전래되고 이렇게 전래된 불교가 중국에서 다시 중국적으로 體質바꿈을 한 후 한국에 전래되었다고 본다. 이외에 또 한편으로는 당시의 지역적 거리관계에서 중국을 거치지 않고 직접 전래되는 방법도 있지 않았을까? 그 例로서 고구려나 백제의 彌勒半伽像을 보면 중국이나 우리나라에서는 볼 수 없는

중앙아시아 특유의 모습이 보인다. 여기서부터 귀족이나 서민층에 크게
아필된 新羅의 彌勒·彌陀信仰도 이 영향을 받지 않았나 생각한다. 미
륵이나 미타신앙에 관련된 經典이 나온 것은 일찍 인도였지만 민간신앙
형태로 굳어진 것은 중앙아시아에서 비롯되었다. 이것이 중국을 거쳐
우리에게 전래된 것이 아니라 직접 한국에 전래된 길도 있었으리라 생
각한다. 이렇게 볼 때 불교뿐만 아니라 古代文化의 유입도 여러면에서
고찰되어야 할 것 같다.

　金：당시 고구려나 부여를 중심으로한 北方세력과 중국 본토 漢族이
대립된 국제정세에 비추어 볼 때 중국 문화나 불교를 액면 그대로 흡수
한 것이 아니라 오히려 반발하는 입장에서 받아드렸기 때문에 불교가 중
국을 거치지 않고 중앙아시아에서 직접 들어올 수도 있었을 것이다. 직
접이건 간접이건 이렇게 들어온 불교문화는 고구려와 백제에 이어 신라
에 와서 비로소 마지막 결정체를 이루었다. 이렇게 형성된 불교가 여러
방면에서 지배층과 밀착되었다가 무너질 때 새로 일어나는 新興 세력은
서민적인 새로운 이념을 들고 나오게 되었다.

　이때 彌勒이나 彌陀신앙같은것도 나올 수 있었으며 사회적인 불안과
혼란이 심해지면 질수록 彌勒 彌陀信仰도 매우 강하게 나타났다고 생각
한다. 또 이와 연유하여 신라가 三國統一을 이룩할 무렵 고구려와 백제
는 고대사회의 모순성에 몹시 허덕일 때였으므로 뒤늦게 출발한 신라
는 그틈을 타서 漁夫之利로 통일의 기틀을 잡을 수 있었다. 그러나 신
라도 例外없이 이러한 진통을 羅末 麗初에 겪어야 했다. 신라의 骨品制
度도 羅末에 北方體制의 반발로 인하여 親族共同體의 세력이 줄어들거
나 분리되었는데 이때 고려로 넘어가는 과도기에서 불교의 이데올로기
나 寺院의 형태와 문화전반의 성격과 구조도 많이 달라지게 된다.

　徐：통일신라 이후의 불교문화를 이해하기 이전에 우선 고대 부족
국가가 통일국가로 변천 발전해 나가는 과정에서 불교가 어떻게 영향을

끼쳤으며 또 문화전반에 걸쳐 어떤 영향을 끼쳤는가 또 어떤 변화를 가져왔는지에 대해 살펴보고 넘어 갔으면 한다. 당시 새로운 불교의 이데올로기를 받아드린 세력은 選民的 엘리트 의식을 가질 수 있었으며 또한 통일국가로 전환되는 초창기의 과정에서 이 엘리트 계층은 마이노리티에 속하게 되었다. 이것이 主權계층과 밀착될때 강력한 선민의식이 조장될 수 있었다고 본다.

金 : 部族國家에 있어서의 世界觀은 대략 두가지로 볼 수 있다. 하나는 지배자들이 강한 選民意識을 가지며, 고구려를 중심으로 한 제부족국가들은 같은 부족이라는 동족관계를 의식하면서 외래문화를 받아들여 자기들대로의 새로운 사회질서를 유지했다. 이것은 弘益人間과도 상통된다고 볼 수 있다. 또한 부족장들은 지배력을 과시하기 위하여 영웅적 위대성의 표현을 영웅숭배의 신화를 낳기도 하였다. 또 불교가 들어와서는 그 신화가 불교신화로 대치되었다. 즉 부족국가가 고대국가로 변형되어 갈때 불교는 지배자측엔 과거와 별차이없는 자기 신화를 유지하게 하였다. 한편 신화를 잃었던 民衆에게 불교는 새로운 문화와 새로운 이데올로기를 제시하였으며 한 時代의 문화권을 이끌어 나가는 원동력의 구실을 하였다. 또한 불교는 教理나 의식만을 가져온 것이 아니라 音樂·美術·工藝·哲學을 전달하였고 중국 문화 뿐 아니라 인도와 중앙아시아 및 구라파 문화까지 소개하여 새로운 사회문화의 형성을 도모하였다. 이렇게 한국 고대문화에 다양성을 가져와 불교는 미술관계에 있어서는 일단 고구려에서 미술·공예·벽화 등으로 종합 정리된 양상을 띤 다음 백제를 거쳐 신라에 와서 整齊美를 완성시켰다. 다시 말하여 불교는 종교성이나 철학을 가져오기도 했지만 또한 문화면에 있어서도 고대예술을 형성하는 중요한 역할을 하였다고 본다.

그러나 문제는 이렇게 外來의 영향을 받을때 受容자세가 더욱 중요하였다고 본다. 예를 들어 신라의 眞平王이 자신을 眞宗이라 하여 부처님의 아버지 이름을 취한 것이나 자기부인에게 摩耶부인의 칭호를 사용케 한 것은 불교왕국을 건설하는 데 있어 자기전통의 자세와 자신의 優位性을 견지하는 위에서 새로운 문화를 받아들이려고 한 일면이라고 볼 수 있다. 이렇게 신라가 과거 부족국가 시대의 전통을 망각하지 아니하면서 불교문화를 흡수했기 때문에 新羅 불교의 整齊美가 이루어질 수 있었다고 본다.

徐 : 부족국가에서 고대국가로 넘어오는 과정에 있어서 불교가 새 이데올로기를 제시하면서 왕권과 민중에 양면작용을 하였으며 또 불교가 이념만이 아니라 예술문화도 가져와 새로운 예술창조의 바탕을 마련하였다는 점과 이 불교문화를 받아들임에 있어 단순한 모방이 아니라 우리 고유의 것과 外來의 것을 잘 조화시켜 고구려 문화를 창조하고 백제를 거쳐 신라에 와서 완성되었다는 것이 金敎授님의 要旨이다.

다음 신라말 여러가지 사회불안이 조성되어 아노미 현상이 빚어지는데 이때 불교가 과연 종교로서 역할을 다하고 있었는지——당시 일부에선 彌勒 彌陀 신앙이 강하게 유행되고 있었는데 불교가 이와같은 미륵 미타적 他力신앙에만 그쳐서야 되겠는가. 더우기 고려로 넘어오면서 불교는 貴族的地位에서 상당한 寺院農土를 소유하여 부패현상까지 빚었고 자체반성을 해야할 계제가 여러차례 있었음에도 불구하고 지배층과 밀착되어 종교 본래의 구실을 못한 채 비판받는 현상을 초래하게 되었다고 본다. 구라파 중세기의 교회가 國家와 대립되어 항시 자기 반성을 하면서 교권을 지켜 나갔듯이 불교도 왕권이 자기 이익만을 추구하는 부패현상을 반성하고 그것을 견제하고 비판하며 항상 민중의 편에 서서 잘못된 사회의 부조리를 지적해야 하는데 신라말 고려초의 불교는 종교와 정치의 혼미된 관계에 서서 본래의 종교적 사명의식이 희박해진 것 같다.

金 : 이 문제는 불교가 갖는 敎理自體에 모순성이 있는것이 아니라 당시의 복잡한 사회현상에 요인이 있다고 보지만 또한 불교도 본래의 구실을 다하지 못한 데에 기인한 것이 아닌가 한다. 新羅下代에 들어오면서 반발하는 북방호족들의 세력이 강하게 나타나는데 이때 불교는 중앙

의 귀족세력과 결합하여 사원경제운영에만 급급하였으며 그 피폐도 심
하였다. 이것은 후에 寺院에서 자랐던 崔承老가 儒教의 大家가 되어 佛
教를 공박할 때 불교의 교리나 내용 그 자체를 공박한 것이 아니라 寺院
경제가 극도로 비대함으로 정치와 불교를 분리시키려고 노력한 데서도
엿볼 수 있다. 또한 사회 제도의 모순성도 있었다. 신라가 경주 중심의
지나친 토착세력에만 의존하여 骨品制度 위주의 政治・文化만을 고집하
였지 그보다 넓은 세계를 생각하지 못했기 때문에 그에 대한 반발이 각
지방에서 일어나 慶州本位가 아닌 새로운 체제를 형성하려는 혼란기에
接하게 되었다. 이때 불교는 이 문제를 해결하지 못하였다고 본다.

　　徐： 다음 新羅불교에 있어서 빼놓을 수 없는 것이 藝術文化와 함께
원효의 사상인데 먼저 이미 8세기경에 위대한 작품을 창조한 신라예술
의 바탕이랄까 소재가 어떠했는지. 불교가 제시한 보편사상이 신라의
하늘에 久遠의 이미지를 심을 소지를 충분히 주었다고 보며 또 개인의
해탈을 강조하는 사상은 창조적 작품에 자신을 投影하여 승화하는 길을
제시해 주었다고 보는것이 어떨지.

　　金： 古代文化의 특징은 과학적인 데 있다. 고대 사회를 유지해 나가
려면 高度의 과학기술이 있어야 했다. 이것은 여러갈래의 부족과 종족
계통을 통제하고 파악하는 데 중요한 기능으로 작용하였으며 지리나 人
口 등의 통계는 아주 정확하고 세밀하였다. 이러한 고대사회의 기술은
사원건축이나 配置圖, 藝術조각에도 그대로 적용되었다. 특히 신라미술
의 경우 美가 즉흥적인 것이 아니라 치밀한 과학적 구성에 의해 이루어
졌으며 석굴암 본존불이나 多寶・釋迦塔 등의 위대한 예술품도 과학적
정확성의 소산이라 생각한다. 다시 말해 이같은 結晶體는 古代로부터 내
려온 美的 전통이 과학과 연결된 合一體라 볼 수 있다. 한편으로는 사
원에 대한 貴族들의 경제적 지원과 塔돌이 등 儀式을 중심으로 신앙
세계의 옛 전통 두가지가 안팎으로 결합하여 새로운 新羅文化를 형성하

였다고도 볼 수 있다. 이러한 신라 미술이 下代에 내려오면 양식이 달라지면서 과학적이 못 되고 제멋대로 건축되고 고려에 와서는 귀족생활과 연계된 工藝品 등 多量生産으로 변질되어 간다.

원효는 여러측면에서 위대한 사상가이지만, 특히 당시의 잡다한 여러 종파와 학파를 종합정리하여 새로운 體系를 세운 것은 원효만이 할 수 있었던 것이다. 즉 원효는 불교를 現象的으로만 이해한 것이 아니라 本原的인 역사적 생성과정에서 이해하려 했기 때문에 瑜伽派와 中觀派를 종합정리할 수 있었다고 본다. 원효는 신라에 들어온 小乘 大乘系의 복잡다단성에 대해서 一佛乘의 체계를 세우지 않으면 정리할 수 없다는 불교의 巨觀的 이해방법을 체계화하였다. 물론 원효 이전에도 고구려의 王高得같은 이가 불교의 전체를 이해하려는 작업을 한 적이 있었지만 원효에 이르러 비로소 哲學을 하는 자세가 확립되었고 또 철학의 양상은 달라졌어도 <생각한다>는 철학의 기본자세는 변하지 않고 그대로 남겨질 수 있었다.

徐 : 원효는 불교의 보편사상을 거시적 안목에서 파악하였다고 본다. 다시 말하면 부처님의 가르침을 가장 포괄적이고도 신축성있게 정리 집약하여 後學들이나 一般人에게 전달하려고 애썼다. 따라서 원효는 敎派와 宗派를 묶어 새로운 것을 전달하려는 중계자의 역할을 맡았고 그러기 위해서 먼저 자기의 철학을 정리하려는 필연적인 작업을 앞세웠다. 원효는 자칫 귀족적으로 달리기 쉬운 불교를 서민의 입장으로 끌어내려 그 속에서 민중불교의 확립에 주력하였다. 그러한 동기랄까, 신분적 관계가 있었다고 보는지.

金 : 文武王이 죽을때 그의 아들인 神文王에게 百濟遺民인 熊州人 景一을 國師로 봉하라 유언하였지만 신문왕은 그 명칭을 바꾸어 國老로 봉한 적이 있었다. 이것은 당시 慶州本位인 신분 즉 骨品觀念과 지역관이 노골적으로 강하게 드러난 一例였다. 이러한 사회적 맹점과 결함을

깊이 인식했기 때문에 大衆속으로 들어가게된 동기가 원효에게서는 싹트지 않았나 생각한다. 즉 그의 世界觀은 신라라는 지역위주가 아닌 불교자체의 보편성과 본바닥을 들여다 보는 데 있었다.

徐: 다시말해서 원효는 불교까지도 넘어서서 宗敎本源의 無限을 지향하는 자세에서 진리를 파악한 것이 아닐까.

金: 원효의 위대성은 儒敎의 東文選에서도 論과 疏를 수록하여 그 일면을 엿보게 하고 있다.

徐: 新羅의 불교는 여기서 일단 그치고 고려로 넘어갔으면 한다. 아까도 잠간 언급한 바 있지만 종교에 정치나 경제가 개입되면 부패되기 마련이며 따라서 불교와 정치를 분리시키려는 崔承老의 주장은 아주 타당하고 예리한 안목이라고 본다. 王建이 고려를 세워 訓要十條를 지으면서 불교에 國敎의 대우를 하였고 이와함께 寺院은 귀족에 못지 않은 호화로운 資源을 가져 高利貸金까지 하는 부패를 초래하였다. 신라에서 사원건축의 성행으로 인한 경제적 폐단을 알고있던 王建의 종교정책은 어떠어떠하였으며 그 진의는 어디에 있었을까.

金: 당면과제는 불교가 改革의 第1意的인 것은 아니었으며 그보다는 오히려 고대사회의 골품제도를 폐기하고 백성에게 세금을 받는 데 있어서 法度있게 하라는 取民有度를 내세웠다. 왕건이 고려의 정치와 사회체제를 구축할 때 지방의 豪族勢力과 연합하였는데, 이 호족세력은 불교사원과 밀접한 관계를 유지하고 있었다. 그러므로 자연 사원의 지나침을 알면서도 과격한 정책은 피하였다고 본다. 또한 高麗史列傳에 보면 崔凝이 불교사원의 폐단을 간한 것이 있었지만 이때도 당시 민간에서 불교신앙이 성행하고 있어 왕건은 이러한 폐단을 알면서도 정책상 규제할 수 없었다고 본다. 이 문제는 光宗代에 와 비로소 구체적인 대안이 나왔다. 즉 光宗은 골품 제도 대신에 科擧제도를 마련하였으며 國學을 興起하고 王權確立을 위해 폐단이 많은 호족세력을 억제하였다. 思想統一문제에 있어서도 儒生들을 장려하면서도 한편으로 불교사상도 振作하여 고려의 정신적인 본바탕을 정립하려 하였다. 光宗은 전통의 제약을 받으면서도 여러가지 사회제도의 개혁을 단행하는 데 힘을 썼다. 이 원동력을 정신세계의 일체 감속에서 찾으려 했다. 한편 사원의 건축 造塔 등을 자주 하여 一年間 비용이 王建在位時의 전체비용과 비슷한 국고소모로 인하여 일부의 批判도 있었다. 그러나 南學과 北學의 대립 을 해결하고 儒敎의 政治理念인 貞觀政要를 歷代王가운데서 최초로 읽 었고 스스로 法眼宗의 제자가 되어 萬善同歸集과 宗鏡錄을 보았고 天台 宗과 法眼宗의 宗要로서 思想體系를 세우려했던 점은 왕권체제 확립을 위한 그의 의향을 짐작케한다. 또한 光宗은 天台宗의 會三歸一을 자신 의 思想統一觀에 연결시키고자 諦觀과 義通을 중국에 보내 天台德韶의 書信을 받은 後 천태종관계 經書를 가지고 돌아오게 하여 敎宗과 禪宗 의 대립관계를 해결하려 하였다. 이것은 곧 隋揚帝가 死淸寺를 지어 會 三歸一을 세운일이나 高麗太祖가 後三國統一時 이를 인용했던 점과 함께 光宗도 佛敎를 體制의 統一에 연결시켜보고자 계획한 것으로 볼 수 있 다. 그러나 이 결실을 보지 못한 채 光宗이 죽게되자 아들인 景宗이 先 父의 정책을 계승하지 못하였고 따라서 諦觀과 義通도 귀국하지 못한 채 결국 天台宗은 大覺國師에 의해 다시 수입되는 경로를 밟았다.

徐: 高麗史에 있어서 대개 妙淸의 亂을 계기로 하여 事大主義思想이 싹텄다고 하고 또 金富軾의 三國史記 저술에 否定的인 立場으로 저술한 것이 一然의 三國遺事라하는데 당시 高麗의 內部分裂과 어떤 관련성이 있지않나 보는 견해가 있다. 이와 관련하여 고려중엽의 사회정세와 불 교의 입장이 어떠했는지에 대하여 언급하였으면 한다.

金: 귀족에 못지않은 사원경제에 대해서 儒林들은 언제나 반발하는

태도를 취하고 있었지만 사실 儒林의 대표격이라 할 수 있는 金富軾을
비롯해 대부분의 儒生들이 家庭에 內院과 같은 願堂을 가지고 있었다.
따라서 이러한 정치와 생활의 二律性으로 인해 불교를 전면 공격하지는
못하였다. 오히려 이 사원경제는 儒林의 반발보다는 武臣亂이 일어남으
로써 파탄을 이르켰다. 武臣들은 정권을 장악한 후 우선 文臣들이 형성
해놓은 文化에 대한 반성과 함께 이를 시정하기 위해 李奎報·李仁老
등을 내세워 政治·社會的 改革을 단행코자 하였다. 그러나 武臣들의
私兵育成이 야기하는 경제적 피해가 과거 寺院經濟의 피폐를 답습하는
모순된 결과를 빚게되어 큰 난관에 부딪쳤다. 이러한 시기에 몽고가 침
략해 와 武臣들에 의한 새로운 사회체제수립 및 문화정립의 모색은 결국
실패로 돌아가고 말았다. 그러나 비록 실패는 하였지만 한국 固有傳統
의 체질에 불교가 융합되어 이루어 놓았던 융성시기의 정신문화를 찾고
자 노력한 武臣들의 작업은 높이 평가할 만한 것이었다. 이와같이 여러
면에서 사회체제의 미정립이란 진통을 겪으며 高麗가 末葉에 접어들 때
에도 佛敎는 정치적혼돈에 뚜렷한 해결점을 내놓지 못한 상태에 놓여있
었고 유교가 이 문제해결을 담당하는 입장에 서게 되었다. 그러나 불교가
비록 당시의 사회적 불안을 해결하는 방법은 제시하지 못하였어도 文化
的인 측면에서 大藏經刊行등 지대한 업적을 남겨놓았다.

徐: 高麗王朝에 있어서 大藏經刊行은 역시 가장 위대한 업적이며 또
한 이것은 인쇄술의 發達史에도 획기적인 사건으로 거론될 만한 것이라
본다.

金: 大藏經간행은 당시의 모든 문헌을 集大成한 百科辭典의 편찬에
비유할 수 있다. 또 설사 國家的 규모의 사업이라 하더라도 戰亂中 혼
란기에 그렇게 방대하고도 정교한 간행을 완수할 수 있었다는 사실은
곧 우리민족의 우수성을 입증하여 준 것이라 본다.

徐: 여기서 일단 고려불교를 정리하는 의미에서 몇가지 중요한 문제를 검토하고 넘어갔으면 한다. 우선 고려사상에 독특한 영향을 미친 道詵의 風水圖讖說에 대하여 요즈음 재비판되고 있는데 불교적인 면에서도 다시 평가될 필요가 있지 않을까?

金: 道詵에 대해서 얘기하려면 다시 後三國의 豪族活動과 연결시켜야 될 것 같다. 新羅가 中央勢力의 부패로 인하여 地方豪族들이 반발하게 되는데 이때 그들은 자기의 웅거지를 明堂으로 삼고 각기 분열을 合理化하였으며 이것이 가증될수록 일반백성은 시달림에 지쳐 통일된 안정을 고대하였다. 이러한 백성들의 염원이 羅末에 讖說化되어 나타나기 시작하는데 道詵은 이 讖說을 綜合하여 체계있게 정리하였다. 그는 南部의 慶州中心에서 中部인 松岳으로 백성의 눈을 돌리게 하였고 결과적으로는 후에 王建으로 하여금 後三國을 統一하는데 有利한 입장으로 民心을 쏠리게하였다고 본다. 따라서 이러한 점으로 인하여 高麗가 건국 후 민심을 통일할 수 있는 원동력이 되었기 때문에 고려왕조에서 자주 道詵을 말하게 된다. 즉 道詵의 도참설은 統治者와 백성을 한데 묶어 고려사회의 건강성을 유지시켜 두는 데 크게 공헌하였다고 본다.

徐: 道詵은 당시의 政治 社會風土와 또는 風水地理的 여건을 가장 바르게 직시하여 이를 구체적이고 규모있게 설계시킨 豫言者風의 人物이었다고 볼 수 있다. 즉 한국이라는 지역을 한눈에 들여다보고 매우 질서있게 그 骨格을 배치하여 놓았고 다음 國土의 地脈을 사람의 血脈에 비유하고 다시 密敎와 中國의 讖書를 習合 표출한 道詵의 說은 佛敎를 토착시키고 지도층과 민중을 통합하는 데 밑거름의 역할을 했다. 이 면에서 그의 공헌은 큰 것이었지만, 한편으로는 불교를 讖說과 혼동케 하여 불교의 본질을 외곡되게 나타나게 한 것은 道詵이 범한 과실이라 볼 수 있다. 고려중엽에 와서 妙淸이 다시 圖讖說과 연관하여 西京 천도운동을 벌이게 되는데 이때 묘청이 시도했던 점은 道詵의 그것과 비교하여 성격이나 내용에서 어떻게 달라졌다고 보는가?

金: 高麗社會의 基底엔 불교사상이 깔려있는 만큼 佛教를 표방하지 않은 사상이란 성립할 수 없었는데 나는 道詵과 妙淸이 僧侶였던 것도 이때문이 아니었던가 한다. 두 사람의 비교에 있어 道詵의 도참설이 당시 통일을 염원한 民間讖說의 集大成으로서 開京中心의 統一論이라면 妙淸의 도참설은 이미 문벌화된 開京의 귀족사회의 부패를 떠나서 新興都市인 西京中心의 국토통일론을 지향한 것이라 볼 수 있다. 妙淸이 亂을 일으켰을 때 이미 西京세력은 開京세력에 도전할 수 있을 만큼 성장해 있었으며 妙淸은 이같은 상황을 십분 利用하여 民心을 선동한 것으로 생각된다.

徐: 高麗史에 나타난 非正統의 僧侶랄까 당시 정치사회에 변혁을 시도했던 佛教界의 人物로서 또 한 사람 辛旽을 들 수 있다. 그는 思想界에 준 영향보다도 改革政治에 참여하여 비교적 짧은 기간의 활동으로 많은 영향을 미친 人物이라 할 수 있다.

金: 辛旽은 高麗後期 혼란한 사회를 개혁해 보려는 恭愍王과 新進士類가 舊勢力에 의한 문벌폐단을 막아내고자 등장시켰던 不偏不黨한 人物이었다. 그러나 당시의 佛教界에는 별로 크게 기여한 점이 없었다고 본다. 다만 辛旽으로 인하여 麗末 혼란한 사회가 잠시나마 淨化되었고 붕괴되어가던 왕조가 제모습을 갖출 수 있는 기회가 될 뻔한 것은 높이 평가해야 할 일이다.

徐: 다음 朝鮮王朝初 儒林이 完全히 政權을 장악하고 불교를 박해하기 시작한다. 유교와 불교의 對立도 敎理的 對立이라기보다는 고려의 사회전반에 미친 사원 경제의 피폐에 초점을 두었다고 보며 이것은 三峯鄭道傳의 불교비판에도 불교자체보다는 政治와 경제에 미친 악영향을

지적하고 있는 데서도 엿볼 수 있다. 즉 유교가 비록 지도이념 형성에
있어선 주도권을 잡았지만 불교의 근본사상을 배격할 수는 없었고, 불
교도 신라나 高麗時代와 같이 국가적 理念으로 내세울 입장은 못 되었어
도 민간층에 깊이 信仰的으로 뿌리박혀있어 쉽게 배제당하거나 소멸될
수 없었다. 불교 박해정책은 思想과 文化形成에 있어 아무런 진취성을
가져오지 못했고 도리어 보수적성향과 당파분쟁 그리고 침체와 내분만
을 초래케하는 결과를 빚었을 뿐이다. 그러나 儒林의 핍박을 받으면서
도 불교는 李朝中葉에 와서 西山·四溟을 배출했다. 그런데 이 두 高僧
에게는 宗敎的 순교자보다도 오히려 護國的인 愛國者의 색채가 더욱
농후하다.

金: 高麗中葉 이후 朝鮮에 와서 儒林이 불교를 배격해도 고려조에서
國敎였던 佛敎信仰까지는 배제할 수 없었는데 이것은 곧 信仰이란 언제
든지 서민층, 다시 말하여 基層社會의 고유사상과 영합하여 地下水처럼
끊이지않고 잔존해서 내려오기 때문이다. 儒林이 외형적인 불교배척은
할 수 있어도 그 內面世界까지는 침범할 수 없었다. 그런데 문제는 佛
敎가 기층사회에서부터 면면히 내려온 특유의 에너지를 얼마만큼 광범
위하게 집약하여 나갈 수 있느냐에 있다.

徐: 이제 對談의 진척이 어느정도 終結될 단계에 이른 것 같다. 開化
期에 들어서면 이 나라는 여러가지 면에서 격동기의 현상을 띠게된다.
또 일본과 러시아 중국 등 주변정세가 매우 강한 부채질을 하여 사회적
변혁을 초래케한다. 大院君攝政 이후 壬午軍亂 甲申政變 東學亂 등 여러
變亂이 일어났을 때 역시 불교에서도 開化運動이 일어나 李東仁 같은
權僧도 있었고 鏡虛와 萬海 같은 高僧의 사상은 당시 불교집단 안팎과
독립쟁취에 큰 영향을 미쳤다. 이때의 상황과 특기할 만한 민족사상가에
대해 언급해 주었으면 한다.

金：李朝社會가 막다른 골목에 다다른것은 18세기 말엽인데 이때는 기층사회의 힘이 지극히 약화된 시기였다. 결국 주변 강대국의 시달림을 받으며 일본에 國權을 빼앗겼지만 나라를 잃고난 뒤 잃어버린 주권을 다시 찾아야한다는 구국운동이 일어났다. 3・1운동을 전후하여 祖國光復을 위하여 끝까지 愛國한 분들은 많으나 그가운데 史學界의 申采浩 儒教界의 朴殷植 그리고 佛教界의 韓龍雲같은 이는 대표적인 인물이었다. 萬海의 「朝鮮獨立理由書」는 매우 귀중한 자료가 되고있으며 丹齊와 朴殷植도 史學界에서 재평가되어야 할 중요한 사상을 풍기고 있다. 한마디로 이 3人은 民族의 受難期에 있어 불굴의 정신을 보여준 분들이라 하겠다.

徐：佛教界의 萬海에게 있어 그의 維新論은 불교를 과거에만 치우치는 復古가 아니라 末來指向的인 새로운 자세로 이끌어간 것이라 본다. 이같은 革新的思想은 外勢의 開化思想이 개입되어서 이루어진 것도 있겠지만 불교적 自覺을 바탕으로 하여 시대감각에 민감한 데서 나온 주장도 있다.

韓國文化시리즈第 3 輯

韓國의 佛敎文化

1974년 5월 20일 발행

발행인　　全　信　鎔

인쇄인　　李　學　洙

발행처　　國際文化財團
　　　　　　出　版　部

(非 賣 品)